Domination and the Arts of Resistance

Domination

and the

Arts of

Resistance

Hidden Transcripts

James C. Scott

YALE UNIVERSITY PRESS   NEW HAVEN AND LONDON

For Moorestown Friends' School

Designed by James J. Johnson
Set in Ehrhardt Roman type by
The Composing Room of Michigan, Inc.

The paper in this book meets the guidelines for
permanence and durability of the Committee on
Production Guidelines for Book Longevity of the
Council on Library Resources.

14 15 16 17 18 19 20

Library of Congress Cataloging-in-
Publication Data

Scott, James C.
    Domination and the arts of resistance :
    hidden transcripts / James C. Scott
        p. cm
    Includes bibliographical references.
    ISBN 0-300-04705-3 (cloth)
       978-0-300-05669-3 (pbk.)

    1. Passive resistance.   2. Power (Social
sciences)   3. Dominance (Psychology)
4. Interpersonal relations.   5. Social groups.
I. Title.
HM278.S37   1990
303.6′1—dc20   90-35207
                                          CIP

A catalogue record for this book
is available from the British Library.

When the great lord passes the wise peasant bows deeply and silently farts.
ETHIOPIAN PROVERB

Society is a very mysterious animal with many faces and hidden potentialities,
and . . . it's extremely shortsighted to believe that the face society happens to be
presenting to you at a given moment is its only true face. None of us knows all
the potentialities that slumber in the spirit of the population.
VÁCLAV HAVEL, *May 31, 1990*

Contents

Preface   ix

Acknowledgments   xv

1. Behind the Official Story   1

2. Domination, Acting, and Fantasy   17

3. The Public Transcript as a Respectable Performance   45

4. False Consciousness or Laying It on Thick?   70

5. Making Social Space for a Dissident Subculture   108

6. Voice under Domination: The Arts of Political Disguise   136

7. The Infrapolitics of Subordinate Groups   183

8. A Saturnalia of Power: The First Public Declaration of the Hidden Transcript   202

Bibliography   229

Index   243

Preface

THE IDEA BEHIND THIS BOOK developed as a result of my persistent and rather slow-witted efforts to make sense of class relations in a Malay village. I was hearing divergent accounts of land transactions, wage rates, social reputations, and technological change. By itself, this was not so surprising inasmuch as different villagers had conflicting interests. More troubling was the fact that the same villagers were occasionally contradicting themselves! It was some time before it dawned on me that the contradictions arose especially, but not uniquely, among the poorer and most economically dependent villagers. The dependency was as important as the poverty, since there were several fairly autonomous poor whose expressed opinions were both consistent and independent.

The contradictions, moreover, had a kind of situational logic to them. When I confined the issue to class relations alone—one of many issues—it seemed that the poor sang one tune when they were in the presence of the rich and another tune when they were among the poor. The rich too spoke one way to the poor and another among themselves. These were the grossest distinctions; many finer distinctions were discernible depending on the exact composition of the group talking and, of course, the issue in question. Soon I found myself using this social logic to seek out or create settings in which I could check one discourse against another and, so to speak, triangulate my way into unexplored territory. The method worked well enough for my limited purposes, and the results appeared in *Weapons of the Weak: Everyday Forms of Peasant Resistance* (Yale University Press, 1985), especially pp. 284–89.

Once attuned more closely to how power relations affected discourse *among Malays*, it was not long before I noticed how I measured my own words before those who had power over me in some significant way. And I observed that when I had to choke back responses that would not have been prudent, I often found someone to whom I could *voice* my unspoken thoughts. There seemed to be a nearly physical pressure behind this repressed speech. On those rare occasions on which my anger or indignation had overcome my discretion, I experienced a sense of elation despite the danger of retaliation. Only then did I fully appreciate why I might not be able to take the public conduct of those over whom I had power at face value.

I can claim absolutely no originality for these observations about power relations and discourse. They are part and parcel of the daily folk wisdom of millions who spend most of their waking hours in power-laden situations in which a misplaced gesture or a misspoken word can have terrible consequences. What I have tried to do here is to pursue this idea more systematically, not to say doggedly, to see what it can teach us about power, hegemony, resistance, and subordination.

My working assumption in organizing the book was that the most severe conditions of powerlessness and dependency would be diagnostic. Much of the evidence here, then, is drawn from studies of slavery, serfdom, and caste subordination on the premise that the relationship of discourse to power would be most sharply etched where the divergence between what I call the public transcript and the hidden transcripts was greatest. Where it seemed suggestive I have also brought in evidence from patriarchal domination, colonialism, racism, and even from total institutions such as jails and prisoner of war camps.

This is not a close, textural, contingent, and historically grounded analysis in the way that my study of a small Malay village necessarily was. In its eclectic and schematic way it violates many of the canons of postmodernist work. What it shares with postmodernism is the conviction that there is no social location or analytical position from which the truth value of a text or discourse may be judged. While I do believe that close contextual work is the lifeblood of theory, I also believe there is something useful to be said across cultures and historical epochs when our focus is narrowed by structural similarities.

The analytical strategy pursued here thus begins with the premise that structurally similar forms of domination will bear a family resemblance to one another. These similarities in the cases of slavery, serfdom, and caste subordination are fairly straightforward. Each represents an institutionalized arrangement for appropriating labor, goods, and services from a subordinate population. As a formal matter, subordinate groups in these forms of domination have no political or civil rights, and their status is fixed by birth. Social mobility, in principle if not in practice, is precluded. The ideologies justifying domination of this kind include formal assumptions about inferiority and

superiority which, in turn, find expression in certain rituals or etiquette reg-
ulating public contact between strata. Despite a degree of institutionalization,
relations between the master and slave, the landlord and the serf, the high-
caste Hindu and untouchable are forms of personal rule providing great
latitude for arbitrary and capricious behavior by the superior. An element of
personal terror invariably infuses these relations—a terror that may take the
form of arbitrary beatings, sexual brutality, insults, and public humiliations. A
particular slave, for example, may be lucky enough to escape such treatment
but the sure knowledge that it *could* happen to her pervades the entire relationship. Finally, subordinates in such large-scale structures of domination
nevertheless have a fairly extensive social existence outside the immediate
control of the dominant. It is in such sequestered settings where, in principle,
a shared critique of domination may develop.

The structural kinship just described is analytically central to the kind of
argument I hope to make. I most certainly do not want to claim that slaves,
serfs, untouchables, the colonized, and subjugated races share immutable
characteristics. Essentialist claims of that kind are untenable. What I do wish
to assert, however, is that to the degree structures of domination can be
demonstrated to operate in comparable ways, they will, other things equal,
elicit reactions and patterns of resistance that are also broadly comparable.
Thus, slaves and serfs ordinarily dare not contest the terms of their subordination openly. Behind the scenes, though, they are likely to create and
defend a social space in which offstage dissent to the official transcript of
power relations may be voiced. The specific forms (for example, linguistic
disguises, ritual codes, taverns, fairs, the "hush-arbors" of slave religion) this
social space takes or the specific content of its dissent (for example, hopes of a
returning prophet, ritual aggression via witchcraft, celebration of bandit heroes and resistance martyrs) are as unique as the particular culture and history
of the actors in question require. In the interest of delineating some broad
patterns I deliberately overlook the great particularity of each and every form
of subordination—the differences, say, between Caribbean and North American slavery, between French serfdom in the seventeeth century and in the
mid–eighteenth century, between Russian serfdom and French serfdom, between regions and so on. The ultimate value of the broad patterns I sketch
here could be established only by embedding them firmly in settings that are
historically grounded and culturally specific.

Given the choice of structures explored here, it is apparent that I privilege
the issues of dignity and autonomy, which have typically been seen as secondary to material exploitation. Slavery, serfdom, the caste system, colonialism,
and racism routinely generate the practices and rituals of denigration, insult,

and assaults on the body that seem to occupy such a large part of the hidden transcripts of their victims. Such forms of oppression, as we shall see, deny subordinates the ordinary luxury of negative reciprocity: trading a slap for a slap, an insult for an insult. Even in the case of the contemporary working class it appears that slights to one's dignity and close control of one's work figure as prominently in accounts of exploitation as do narrower concerns of work and compensation.

My broad purpose is to suggest how we might more successfully read, interpret, and understand the often fugitive political conduct of subordinate groups. How do we study power relations when the powerless are often obliged to adopt a strategic pose in the presence of the powerful and when the powerful may have an interest in overdramatizing their reputation and mastery? If we take all of this at face value we risk mistaking what may be a tactic for the whole story. Instead, I try to make out a case for a different study of power that uncovers contradictions, tensions, and immanent possibilities. Every subordinate group creates, out of its ordeal, a "hidden transcript" that represents a critique of power spoken behind the back of the dominant. The powerful, for their part, also develop a hidden transcript representing the practices and claims of their rule that cannot be openly avowed. A comparison of the hidden transcript of the weak with that of the powerful and of *both* hidden transcripts to the public transcript of power relations offers a substantially new way of understanding resistance to domination.

After a rather literary beginning drawing on George Eliot and George Orwell, I try to show how the process of domination generates a hegemonic public conduct and a backstage discourse consisting of what cannot be spoken in the face of power. At the same time, I explore the hegemonic purpose behind displays of domination and consent, asking who the audience is for such performances. This investigation leads in turn to an appreciation of why it is that even close readings of historical and archival evidence tend to favor a hegemonic account of power relations. Short of actual rebellion, powerless groups have, I argue, a self-interest in conspiring to reinforce hegemonic appearances.

The meaning of these appearances can be known only by comparing it with subordinate discourse outside of power-laden situations. Since ideological resistance can grow best when it is shielded from direct surveillance, we are led to examine the social sites where this resistance can germinate.

If the decoding of power relations depended on full access to the more or less clandestine discourse of subordinate groups, students of power—both historical and contemporary—would face an impasse. We are saved from throwing up our hands in frustration by the fact that the hidden transcript is typically expressed openly—albeit in disguised form. I suggest, along these lines, how we might interpret the rumors, gossip, folktales, songs, gestures, jokes, and theater of the powerless as vehicles by which, among other things, they insinuate a critique of power while hiding behind anonymity or behind innocuous understandings of their conduct. These patterns of disguising *ideological* insubordination are somewhat analogous to the patterns by which, in my experience, peasants and slaves have disguised their efforts to thwart material appropriation of their labor, their production, and their property: for example, poaching, foot-dragging, pilfering, dissimulation, flight. Together, these forms of insubordination might suitably be called the infrapolitics of the powerless.

Finally, I believe that the notion of a hidden transcript helps us understand those rare moments of political electricity when, often for the first time in memory, the hidden transcript is spoken directly and publicly in the teeth of power.

Acknowledgments

Too MANY PEOPLE helped me in too many ways with this manuscript. The result was an aggregation of individual acts of exemplary generosity and large-spiritedness that produced, on my part, an intellectual gridlock that lasted for some time. I began to think of this as a kind of perverse mirror-image of Adam Smith's invisible hand. Unsnarling the traffic meant shooting several drivers, burying their vehicles, and resurfacing the road as if they had never existed. Executions and burials were held with all the necessary decorum, and the victims might take comfort in the fact that three of my own children (chapters 2, 3, and 5) were blindfolded, led to the wall, and shot without much ceremony but with much gnashing of teeth. The result, I think, is a reinvigorated intellectual traffic that moves along fairly briskly. Its briskness, I understand, comes at the considerable cost of eliminating intersections that would have permitted travel in different directions to new destinations. The costs can be weighed only against a judgment about whether we have, in the end, gotten to a place worth going to, and it is for the reader to decide that.

Among the tempting destinations left off the itinerary were those that would have integrated my enterprise here more closely with contemporary theoretical work on power, hegemony, and resistance. There is an implicit dialogue between this work and, for example, the work of Jürgen Habermas (particularly his theory of communicative competence), that of Pierre Bourdieu and Michel Foucault where it touches the normalization or naturalization of power, that of Steven Lukes and John Gaventa on the various "faces of power," that of Fredric Jameson on "the political unconscious," and, most recently, that of Susan Stanford Friedman on the "repressed in women's narrative." My argument is carried out in the knowledge of these works. But to have stopped and carried out a full-fledged exchange with any of them would have, I thought, interrupted the logic of my presentation and, more seriously, made the result more forbidding to a less theoretically oriented audience.

I owe the origin of this book to Zakariah Abdullah, a teacher of rare patience and a friend of rare generosity, who taught me most of what I understand about Malay village life.

The members of an informal lunch seminar at Massachusetts Institute of Technology's Science, Technology, and Society Program, where I was an Exxon Fellow in 1984, should be thanked for responding to the first crude version of the idea behind this book. In its various guises the idea was inspected, used, criticized, elaborated, and ridiculed by the undergraduates who have been in my seminar "Powerlessness and Dependency." Their perspectives and papers about slavery, serfdom, concentration camps, prisons, homelessness, old-age homes, and women were more of an education than I had bargained on. I learned to discount their praise and amplify their criticism, since I was giving them grades.

During the summer of 1987, with the intellectual stimulation (not to mention room and board) of the Pacific and Southeast Asian History Department of the Research School of Pacific Studies of the Australian National University, I began pursuing the ideas here in earnest. Tony Reid not only arranged the visit but organized a seminar on which my still preliminary argument was subjected to such an array of well-aimed and high explosive projectiles that I had virtually to begin again. Although I would not have said so at the time, the experience was intellectually bracing, and I want to thank particularly Gyanendra Pandey, Dipesh Chakrabarty, Ranajit Guha, Tony Milner, Clive Kessler, Jamie Mackie, Brian Fegan, Lea Jelinek, Ken Young, and Norman Owen. This was my first encounter with the intellectual energy of the *Subaltern Studies* group that had transformed South Asian historiography in fundamental ways. At the center of this group stands Ranajit Guha, whose original and sweeping work is of fundamental importance. If I had been able to revise my manuscript in more of the ways his discerning eye suggested, it would have been a better book and would have better repaid the friendship he and Mechthild extended. Other friends in Canberra who contributed in one way or another to this book were Tony Johns, Helen Reid, Harjot S. Oberoi, Susan B. C. Devalle, Claire Milner, and Kenny Bradley, who did his best to teach me to shear sheep like a real Aussie.

A year at the Institute for Advanced Study, funded in part also by the American Council of Learned Societies and the National Endowment for the Humanities, represented the oasis that made possible the broad reading and tranquility necessary to begin writing. The minimal routines of the Institute's School of Social Sciences together with the smart neighbors it provides were a nearly ideal combination. Some of those neighbors should be singled out for making my stay rewarding: Clifford Geertz, Albert Hirschman, Joan Scott, Michael Walzer, Valentine Daniel, Elliot Shore, Harry Wolff, Peg Clark, Lucille Allsen, Barbara Hernstein-Smith, Sandy Levinson, and Paul Freedman. Nor can I resist giving public thanks to the "unknown nonbureaucrat" who interceded with the apparatchiks to allow my April Fools' hens to remain in the well-groomed Institute courtyard for a few days.

Bits and pieces of my first draft were imposed on various academic audiences with results that were, at least to me, beneficial if occasionally sobering. Thanks, then, to those who listened and occasionally spilled blood at the University of Washington, Seattle, Vanderbilt University, Johns Hopkins, the University of Minnesota's Center for Comparative Studies in Discourse and Society, the Davis Center at Princeton University, Boston University, University of the South–Sewanee, Washington University, St. Louis, Trenton State University, Trinity College–Connecticut, Cornell University, University of Wisconsin–Madison, St. Lawrence University, University of California–Irvine, Northern Illinois University, University of California–Los Angeles, the University of Copenhagen, the University of Oslo, and Göteberg University.

A few intellectual debts embedded in this book merit special recognition. Barrington Moore's work is a looming presence here even when he is not cited, and much of my argument could be read as a conversation with the more provocative sections of his book *Injustice*. The same could be said for Murray Edelman's work, with which I've been grappling, I've only recently fully realized, for a long time. Even if our answers diverge, Moore and Edelman have asked most of the questions I've set myself to. I also owe a debt to Grant Evans's arresting description of the ceremony in Vientiane appropriated in chapter 3. Daniel Field's *Rebels in the Name of the Tsar* contains the basis of the argument about naive monarchism at the end of chapter 4.

As I wrote earlier, so many people had so many divergent things to say about my argument in its oral or written form that, while they almost certainly improved it, they can hardly have been said to have sped me on my way. Some of them thought I was barking up the wrong tree; others thought I had the right tree but was not going about it right; others wondered why I was barking at all; and still others, thank God, associated themselves with the hunt and worked on improving my bite so it might come up to the level of my bark. I can think of nothing else to do but to list them all more or less indiscriminately so any of them can disavow any affinity with the position I've staked out. They are (deep breath): Edward and Susan Friedman, Jan Gross, Grant Evans, Tony Reid, Don Emmerson, Leonard Doob, Joseph Errington, Joseph LaPalombara, Helen Siu, Susanne Wofford, Deborah Davis, Jean Agnew, Steven

Smith, David Plotke, Bruce Ackerman, George Shulman, Ian Shapiro, Rogers Smith, Jonathan Rieder, Bob Lane, Ed Lindblom, Shelley Burtt, Marc Lendler, Sherry Ortner, Mary Katzenstein, Jack Veugelers, Bob Harms, Ben Kerkvliet, Bill Klausner, Chuck Grench, Joan Scott, Michael Walser, Vivienne Shue, Cheah Boon Keng, Helen Lane, Peter Sahlins, Bruce Lincoln, Richard Leppert, Stuart Hall, Maurice Bloch, Teodor Shanin, Catherine Hall, Denise Riley, Ivan Kats, Louise Scott, Jeffrey Burds, Jim Ferguson, Dan Lev, Michael McCann, Susan Stokes, Ellis Goldberg, Natalie Zemon Davis, Lawrence Stone, Ezra Suleiman, Ben Anderson, Don Scott, David Cohen, Susan Eckstein, John Smail, Georg Elwert, Leslie Anderson, John Bowen, Rodolphe de Koninck, Marie-Andrée Couillard, Jonathan Pool, Judy Swanson, Fritz Gaenslen, Lloyd Moote, Grace Goodell, Andrzej Tymowski, Ron Jepperson, Tom Pangle, Margaret Clark, Phil Eldridge, Viggo Brun, Nancy Abelmann, John Bryant, Melissa Nobles, and Russell Middleton.

A far smaller number of colleagues went through the entire manuscript with a fine-toothed comb and sent me suggestions I could act on as well as searching critiques that occasionally left me at a loss. Their help and criticism have certainly improved the book, and I believe have made me a bit smarter. It may well not have brought the final version up to their expectations. I'll take the rap for that, as if I had any choice. These good colleagues are Murray Edelman, Clifford Geertz, Crawford Young, Jennifer Hochschild, Ramachandra Guha, Michael Adas, Fran Piven, Arlie Russell Hochschild, Lila Abu-Lughod, Aristide Zolberg, and Claire Jean Kim. I assure them that I will never make the mistake of seeking so much advice again—at least as much for my sake as for theirs.

A somewhat different version of chapter 3 has been published under the title "Prestige as the Public Discourse of Domination," in a special issue of *Cultural Critique* on the "Economy of Prestige," edited by Richard Leppert and Bruce Lincoln, no. 12 (Spring, 1989), 145–66.

Kay Mansfield, manager of the Council on Southeast Asian Studies at Yale, did as much as anyone to see this manuscript through to completion. I thank her for her friendship, efficiency, editorial skills, and her efforts. Ruth Muessig, Mary Whitney, and Susan Olmsted were helpful in the final and hectic revisions.

Louise and our children continue to be an impediment to my scholarly productivity. They see no earthly reason why I should want to spend so much time writing books, given the cost in solitude and in opportunities foregone. This book was, like those before it, written in the teeth of their best efforts to bring me to my senses. There is little doubt that without them I could have written more and, who knows, maybe even have gotten smarter. All in all, a very small price to pay for their company.

Domination and the Arts of Resistance

CHAPTER ONE

Behind the Official Story

I tremble to speak the words of freedom before the tyrant.

—CORYPHAEUS, in Euripides, *The Bacchae*

The Labourer and Artisan, notwithstanding they are Servants to their Masters, are quit by doing what they are bid. But the Tyrant sees those that are about him, begging and suing for his Favour; and they must not only do what he commands, but they must think as he would have them [think] and most often, to satisfy him, even anticipate his thoughts. It is not sufficient to obey him, they must also please him, they must harass, torment, nay kill themselves in his Service; and . . . they must leave their own Taste for his, Force their Inclination, and throw off their natural Dispositions. They must carefully observe his Words, his Voice, his Eyes, and even his Nod. They must have neither Eyes, Feet, nor Hands, but what must be ALL upon the watch, to spy out his Will, and discover his Thoughts. Is this to live happily? Does it indeed deserve the Name of Life?

—ESTIENNE DE LA BOETIE, *A Discourse on Voluntary Servitude*

And the intensest hatred is that rooted in fear, which compels to silence and drives vehemence into constructive vindictiveness, an imaginary annihilation of the detested object, something like the hidden rites of vengeance with which the persecuted have a dark vent for their rage.

—GEORGE ELIOT, *Daniel Deronda*

IF THE EXPRESSION "Speak truth to power" still has a utopian ring to it, even in modern democracies, this is surely because it is so rarely practiced. The dissembling of the weak in the face of power is hardly an occasion for surprise. It is ubiquitous. So ubiquitous, in fact, that it makes an appearance in many situations in which the sort of power being exercised stretches the ordinary meaning of *power* almost beyond recognition. Much of what passes as normal social intercourse requires that we routinely exchange pleasantries and smile at others about whom we may harbor an estimate not in keeping with our public performance. Here we may perhaps say that the power of social forms embodying etiquette and politeness requires us often to sacrifice candor for smooth relations with our acquaintances. Our circumspect behavior may also have a strategic dimension: this person to whom we misrepresent ourselves may be able to harm or help us in some way. George Eliot may not have exaggerated in claiming that "there is no action possible without a little acting."

The acting that comes of civility will be of less interest to us in what follows than the acting that has been imposed throughout history on the vast majority of people. I mean the public performance required of those subject to elaborate and systematic forms of social subordination: the worker to the boss, the tenant or sharecropper to the landlord, the serf to the lord, the slave to the master, the untouchable to the Brahmin, a member of a subject race to one of the dominant race. With rare, but significant, exceptions the public performance of the subordinate will, out of prudence, fear, and the desire to curry favor, be shaped to appeal to the expectations of the powerful. I shall use the term *public transcript* as a shorthand way of describing the open interaction between subordinates and those who dominate.[1] The public transcript, where it is not positively misleading, is unlikely to tell the whole story about power relations. It is frequently in the interest of both parties to tacitly conspire in misrepresentation. The oral history of a French tenant farmer, Old Tiennon, covering much of the nineteenth century is filled with accounts of a prudent and misleading deference: "When he [the landlord who had dismissed his father] crossed from Le Craux, going to Meillers, he would stop and speak to me and I forced myself to appear amiable, in spite of the contempt I felt for him."[2]

Old Tiennon prides himself on having learned, unlike his tactless and unlucky father, "the art of dissimulation so necessary in life."[3] The slave narratives that have come to us from the U.S. South also refer again and again to the need to deceive:

> I had endeavored so to conduct myself as not to become obnoxious to the white inhabitants, knowing as I did their power, and their hostility to the colored people. . . . First, I had made no display of the little property or money I possessed, but in every way I wore as much as possible the aspect of slavery. Second, I had never appeared to be even so intelligent as I really was. This all colored at the south, free and slaves, find it particularly necessary for their own comfort and safety to observe.[4]

1. *Public* here refers to action that is openly avowed to the other party in the power relationship, and *transcript* is used almost in its juridical sense (*procès verbal*) of a complete record of what was said. This complete record, however, would also include nonspeech acts such as gestures and expressions.

2. Emile Guillaumin, *The Life of a Simple Man*, ed. Eugen Weber, rev. trans. Margaret Crosland, 83. See also 38, 62, 64, 102, 140, and 153 for other instances.

3. Ibid., 82.

4. Lunsford Lane, *The Narrative of Lunsford Lane, Formerly of Raleigh, North Carolina* (Boston, 1848), quoted in Gilbert Osofsky, ed., *Puttin' on Ole Massa: The Slave Narratives of Henry Bibb, William Wells, and Solomon Northrup*, 9.

As one of the key survival skills of subordinate groups has been impression management in power-laden situations, the performance aspect of their conduct has not escaped the more observant members of the dominant group. Noting that her slaves fell uncharacteristically silent whenever the latest news from the front in the Civil War became a topic of white conversation, Mary Chesnut took their silence as one that hid something: "They go about in their black masks, not a ripple of emotion showing; and yet on all other subjects except the war they are the most excitable of all races. Now Dick might be a very respectable Egyptian Sphinx, so inscrutably silent he is."[5]

Here I will venture a crude and global generalization I will later want to qualify severely: the greater the disparity in power between dominant and subordinate and the more arbitrarily it is exercised, the more the public transcript of subordinates will take on a stereotyped, ritualistic cast. In other words, the more menacing the power, the thicker the mask. We might imagine, in this context, situations ranging all the way from a dialogue among friends of equal status and power on the one hand to the concentration camp on the other, in which the public transcript of the victim bears the mark of mortal fear. Between these extremes are the vast majority of the historical cases of systematic subordination that will concern us.

Cursory though this opening discussion of the public transcript has been, it alerts us to several issues in power relations, each of which hinges on the fact that the public transcript is not the whole story. First, the public transcript is an indifferent guide to the opinion of subordinates. Old Tiennon's tactical smile and greeting mask an attitude of anger and revenge. At the very least, an assessment of power relations read directly off the public transcript between the powerful and the weak may portray a deference and consent that are possibly only a tactic. Second, to the degree that the dominant suspect that the public transcript may be "only" a performance, they will discount its authenticity. It is but a short step from such skepticism to the view, common among many dominant groups, that those beneath them are deceitful, shamming, and lying by nature. Finally, the questionable meaning of the public transcript suggests the key roles played by disguise and surveillance in power relations. Subordinates offer a performance of deference and consent while attempting to discern, to read, the real intentions and mood of the potentially threatening powerholder. As the favorite proverb of Jamaican slaves captures it, "Play fool, to catch wise."[6] The power figure, in turn, produces a performance of mastery

---

5. *A Diary from Dixie,* quoted in Orlando Patterson, *Slavery and Social Death: A Comparative Study,* 208.

6. Ibid., 338.

and command while attempting to peer behind the mask of subordinates to read their real intentions. The dialectic of disguise and surveillance that pervades relations between the weak and the strong will help us, I think, to understand the cultural patterns of domination and subordination.

The theatrical imperatives that normally prevail in situations of domination produce a public transcript in close conformity with how the dominant group would wish to have things appear. The dominant never control the stage absolutely, but their wishes normally prevail. In the short run, it is in the interest of the subordinate to produce a more or less credible performance, speaking the lines and making the gestures he knows are expected of him. The result is that the public transcript is—barring a crisis—systematically skewed in the direction of the libretto, the discourse, represented by the dominant. In ideological terms the public transcript will typically, by its accommodationist tone, provide convincing evidence for the hegemony of dominant values, for the hegemony of dominant discourse. It is in precisely this public domain where the effects of power relations are most manifest, and any analysis based exclusively on the public transcript is likely to conclude that subordinate groups endorse the terms of their subordination and are willing, even enthusiastic, partners in that subordination.

A skeptic might well ask at this point how we can presume to know, on the basis of the public transcript alone, whether this performance is genuine or not. What warrant have we to call it a performance at all, thereby impugning its authenticity? The answer is, surely, that we cannot know how contrived or imposed the performance is unless we can speak, as it were, to the performer offstage, out of this particular power-laden context, or unless the performer suddenly declares openly, on stage, that the performances we have previously observed were just a pose.[7] Without a privileged peek backstage or a rupture in the performance we have no way of calling into question the status of what might be a convincing but feigned performance.

If subordinate discourse in the presence of the dominant is a public transcript, I shall use the term *hidden transcript* to characterize discourse that takes place "offstage," beyond direct observation by powerholders. The hidden transcript is thus derivative in the sense that it consists of those offstage speeches, gestures, and practices that confirm, contradict, or inflect what

7. I bracket, for the moment, the possibility that the offstage retraction or the public rupture may itself be a ruse designed to mislead. It should be clear, however, that there is no satisfactory way to establish definitively some bedrock reality or truth behind any particular set of social acts. I also overlook the possibility that the performer may be able to insinuate an insincerity into the performance itself, thereby undercutting its authenticity for part or all of his audience.

appears in the public transcript.[8] We do not wish to prejudge, by definition, the relation between what is said in the face of power and what is said behind its back. Power relations are not, alas, so straightforward that we can call what is said in power-laden contexts false and what is said offstage true. Nor can we simplistically describe the former as a realm of necessity and the latter as a realm of freedom. What is certainly the case, however, is that the hidden transcript is produced for a different audience and under different constraints of power than the public transcript. By assessing the discrepancy *between* the hidden transcript and the public transcript we may begin to judge the impact of domination on public discourse.

The abstract and general tone of the discussion thus far is best relieved by concrete illustrations of the possibly dramatic disparity between the public and the hidden transcripts. The first is drawn from slavery in the antebellum U.S. South. Mary Livermore, a white governess from New England, recounted the reaction of Aggy, a normally taciturn and deferential black cook, to the beating the master had given her daughter. The daughter had been accused, apparently unjustly, of some minor theft and then beaten while Aggy looked on, powerless to intervene. After the master had finally left the kitchen, Aggy turned to Mary, whom she considered her friend and said,

> Thar's a day a-comin'! Thar's a day a-comin'! . . . I hear the rumblin ob de chariots! I see de flashin ob de guns! White folks blood is a runnin on the ground like a ribber, an de dead's heaped up dat high! . . . Oh Lor! Hasten de day when de blows, an de bruises, and de aches an de pains, shall come to de white folks, an de buzzards shall eat dem as dey's dead in de streets. Oh Lor! roll on de chariots, an gib the black people rest and peace. Oh Lor! Gib me de pleasure ob livin' till dat day, when I shall see white folks shot down like de wolves when dey come hungry out o'de woods.[9]

One can imagine what might have happened to Aggy if she had delivered this speech directly to the master. Apparently her trust in Mary Livermore's friendship and sympathy was such that a statement of her rage could be ventured with comparative safety. Alternatively, perhaps she could no longer choke back her anger. Aggy's hidden transcript is at complete odds with her

---

8. This is not to assert that subordinates have nothing more to talk about among themselves than their relationship to the dominant. Rather it is merely to confine the term to that segment of interaction among subordinates that bears on relations with the powerful.

9. *My Story of the War*, quoted in Albert J. Raboteau, *Slave Religion: The "Invisible Institution" of the Antebellum South*, 313.

public transcript of quiet obedience. What is particularly striking is that this is anything but an inchoate scream of rage; it is a finely drawn and highly visual image of an apocalypse, a day of revenge and triumph, a world turned upside down using the cultural raw materials of the white man's religion. Can we conceive of such an elaborate vision rising spontaneously to her lips without the beliefs and practice of slave Christianity having prepared the way carefully? In this respect our glimpse of Aggy's hidden transcript, if pursued further, would lead us directly to the offstage culture of the slave quarters and slave religion. Whatever such an investigation would tell us, this glimpse itself is sufficient to make any naive interpretation of Aggy's previous and subsequent public acts of deference impossible both for us, and most decidedly for Aggy's master, should he have been eavesdropping behind the kitchen door.

The hidden transcript Aggy revealed in the comparative safety of friendship is occasionally openly declared in the face of power. When, suddenly, subservience evaporates and is replaced by open defiance we encounter one of those rare and dangerous moments in power relations. Mrs. Poyser, a character in George Eliot's *Adam Bede* who finally spoke her mind, provides an illustration of the hidden transcript storming the stage. As tenants of the elderly Squire Donnithorne, Mrs. Poyser and her husband had always resented his rare visits, when he would impose some new, onerous obligation on them and treat them with disdain. He had "a mode of looking at her which, Mrs. Poyser observed, 'allays aggravated her; it was as if you was an insect, and he was going to dab his fingernail on you.' However, she said, 'your servant, sir' and curtsied with an air of perfect deference as she advanced towards him: she was not the woman to misbehave toward her betters, and fly in the face of the catechism, without severe provocation."[10]

This time the squire came to propose an exchange of pasture and grain land between Mr. Poyser and a new tenant that would almost certainly be to the Poysers' disadvantage. When assent was slow in coming, the squire held out the prospect of a longer term farm lease and ended with the observation— a thinly veiled threat of eviction—that the other tenant was well-off and would be happy to lease the Poysers' farm in addition to his own. Mrs. Poyser, "exasperated" at the squire's determination to ignore her earlier objections "as if she had left the room" and at the final threat, exploded. She "burst in with the desperate determination to have her say out this once, though it were to rain notices to quit, and the only shelter were the workhouse."[11] Beginning with a comparison between the condition of the house—frogs on the steps of

---

10. *Adam Bede*, 388–89.
11. Ibid., 393.

the flooded basement, rats and mice coming in through the rotten floorboards to eat the cheeses and menace the children—and the struggle to pay the high rent, Mrs. Poyser let fly her personal accusations as she realized that the squire was fleeing out the door toward his pony and safety:

> You may run away from my words, sir, and you may go spinning underhand ways o' doing us a mischief, for you've got old Harry to your friend, though nobody else is, but I tell you for once as we're not dumb creatures to be abused and made money on by them as ha' got the lash i' their hands, for want o' knowing how t' undo the tackle. An if I'm th' only one as speaks my mind, there's plenty o' the same way o' thinking i' this parish and the next to 't, for your name's no better than a brimstone match in everybody's nose.[12]

Such were Eliot's powers of observation and insight into her rural society that many of the key issues of domination and resistance can be teased from her story of Mrs. Poyser's encounter with the squire. At the height of her peroration, for example, Mrs. Poyser insists that they will not be treated as animals despite his power over them. This, together with her remark about the squire looking on her as an insect and her declaration that he has no friends and is hated by the whole parish, focuses on the issue of self-esteem. While the confrontation may originate in the exploitation of an onerous tenancy, the discourse is one of dignity and reputation. The practices of domination and exploitation typically generate the insults and slights to human dignity that in turn foster a hidden transcript of indignation. Perhaps one vital distinction to draw between forms of domination lies in the kinds of indignities the exercise of power routinely produces.

Notice also how Mrs. Poyser presumes to speak not just for herself but for the whole parish. She represents what she says as the first public declaration of what everyone has been saying behind the squire's back. Judging from how rapidly the story traveled and the unalloyed joy with which it was received and retold, the rest of the community also felt Mrs. Poyser had spoken for them as well. "It was known throughout the two parishes," Eliot writes, "that the Squire's plan had been frustrated because the Poysers had refused to be 'put upon,' and Mrs. Poyser's outbreak was discussed in all the farmhouses with a zest that was only heightened by frequent repetition."[13] The vicarious pleasure of the neighbors had nothing to do with the actual sentiments expressed by Mrs. Poyser—hadn't everyone been saying the same thing about the squire

12. Ibid., 394.
13. Ibid., 398.

among themselves for years? The content, though Mrs. Poyser may have put it with considerable folk elegance, was stale; it was saying it openly (with witnesses) to the squire's face that was remarkable and that made Mrs. Poyser into something of a local hero. The first open statement of a hidden transcript, a declaration that breaches the etiquette of power relations, that breaks an apparently calm surface of silence and consent, carries the force of a symbolic declaration of war. Mrs. Poyser had spoken (a social) truth to power.

Delivered in a moment of anger, Mrs. Poyser's speech was, one might say, spontaneous—but the spontaneity lay in the timing and vehemence of the delivery, not in the content. The content had, in fact, been rehearsed again and again, as we are told: "and though Mrs. Poyser had during the last twelvemonth recited many imaginary speeches, meaning even more than met the ear, which she was quite determined to make to him the next time he appeared within the gates of the Hall Farm, the speeches had always remained imaginary."[14] Who among us has not had a similar experience? Who, having been insulted or suffered an indignity—especially in public—at the hand of someone in power or authority over us, has not rehearsed an imaginary speech he wishes he had given or intends to give at the next opportunity?[15] Such speeches may often remain a personal hidden transcript that may never find expression, even among close friends and peers. But in this case we are dealing with a shared situation of subordination. The tenants of Squire Donnithorne and, in fact, much of the nongentry in two parishes had ample personal reasons to take pleasure in his being publicly humbled and to share vicariously in Mrs. Poyser's courage. Their common class position and their social links thus provided a powerful resolving lens bringing their collective hidden transcript into focus. One might say, without much exaggeration, that they had together, in the course of their social interchange, written Mrs. Poyser's speech for her. Not word for word, of course, but in the sense that Mrs. Poyser's "say" would be her own reworking of the stories, the ridicule, and the complaints that those beneath the Squire all shared. And to "write" that speech for her, the squire's subjects had to have some secure social space, however sequestered, where they could exchange and elaborate their criticism. Her speech was her personal rendition of the hidden transcript of a subordinate group, and, as in the case of Aggy, that speech directs our attention back to the offstage culture of the class within which it originated.

14. Ibid., 388.
15. We are, I think, apt to have the same fantasy when we are bested in argument among equals or insulted by a peer. The difference is simply that asymmetrical power relations do not interfere with the declaration of the hidden transcript in this case.

An individual who is affronted may develop a personal fantasy of revenge and confrontation, but when the insult is but a variant of affronts suffered systematically by a whole race, class, or strata, then the fantasy can become a collective cultural product. Whatever form it assumes—offstage parody, dreams of violent revenge, millennial visions of a world turned upside down— this collective hidden transcript is essential to any dynamic view of power relations.

Mrs. Poyser's explosion was potentially very costly, and it was her daring— some would have said foolhardiness—that won her such notoriety. The word *explosion* is used deliberately here because that is how Mrs. Poyser experienced it:

> "Thee'st done it now," said Mr. Poyser, a little alarmed and uneasy, but not without some triumphant amusement at his wife's outbreak. "Yis, I know I've done it," said Mrs. Poyser, "but I've had my say out, and I shall be the'easier for 't all my life. There's no pleasure in living, if you're to be corked up for iver, and only dribble your mind out by the sly, like a leaky barrel. I shan't repent saying what I think, if I live to be as old as the Squire."[16]

The hydraulic metaphor George Eliot puts in Mrs. Poyser's mouth is the most common way in which the sense of pressure behind the hidden transcript is expressed. Mrs. Poyser suggests that her habits of prudence and deception can no longer contain the anger she has rehearsed for the last year. That the anger will find a passage out is not in doubt; the choice is rather between a safer but less psychologically satisfying process of "dribbl[ing] your mind out by the sly" and the dangerous but gratifying full blast that Mrs. Poyser has ventured. George Eliot has, in effect, taken one position here on the consequences for consciousness of domination. Her claim is that the necessity of "acting a mask" in the presence of power produces, almost by the strain engendered by its inauthenticity, a countervailing pressure that cannot be contained indefinitely. As an epistemological matter, we have no warrant for elevating the truth status of Mrs. Poyser's outburst over that of her prior deference. Both are arguably part of Mrs. Poyser's self. Notice, however, that as Eliot constructs it, Mrs. Poyser feels she has finally spoken her mind. Inasmuch as she and others in comparable situations feel they have finally spoken truthfully to those in power, the concept truth may have a sociological

16. Ibid., 395. For readers unfamiliar with *Adam Bede* who would like to know how things turned out, the squire died providentially some months later, lifting the threat.

reality in the thought and practice of people whose actions interest us. It may have a phenomenological force in the real world despite its untenable epistemological status.

An alternative claim, nearly a logical mirror image of the first, is that those obliged by domination to act a mask will eventually find that their faces have grown to fit that mask. The practice of subordination in this case produces, in time, its own legitimacy, rather like Pascal's injunction to those who were without religious faith but who desired it to get down on their knees five times a day to pray, and the acting would eventually engender its own justification in faith. In the analysis that follows I hope to clarify this debate considerably, inasmuch as it bears so heavily on the issues of domination, resistance, ideology, and hegemony that are at the center of my concern.

If the weak have obvious and compelling reasons to seek refuge behind a mask when in the presence of power, the powerful have their own compelling reasons for adopting a mask in the presence of subordinates. Thus, for the powerful as well there is typically a disparity between the public transcript deployed in the open exercise of power and the hidden transcript expressed safely only offstage. The offstage transcript of elites is, like its counterpart among subordinates, derivative: it consists in those gestures and words that inflect, contradict, or confirm what appears in the public transcript.

Nowhere has the "act of power" been more successfully examined than in George Orwell's essay "Shooting an Elephant," from his days as a subinspector of police in the 1920s in colonial Burma. Orwell had been summoned to deal with an elephant in heat that had broken its tether and was ravaging the bazaar. When Orwell, elephant gun in hand, finally locates the elephant, which has indeed killed a man, it is peacefully grazing in the paddy fields, no longer a threat to anyone. The logical thing would be to observe the elephant for a while to ensure that its heat had passed. What frustrates logic for Orwell is that there are now more than two thousand colonial subjects who have followed and are watching him:

> And suddenly I realized that I should have to shoot the elephant after all. The people expected it of me and I had got to do it; I could feel their two thousand wills pressing me forward, irresistibly. And it was at this moment, as I stood there with the rifle in my hands, that I first grasped the hollowness, the futility of the white man's dominion in the East. Here was I, the white man with his gun, standing in front of the unarmed native crowd—seemingly the leading actor of the piece; but in reality I was only an absurd puppet pushed to and fro by the will of those yellow faces

behind. I perceived in this moment that when the white man turns tyrant it is his own freedom that he destroys. He becomes a sort of hollow posing dummy, the conventionalized figure of a sahib. For it is the condition of his rule that he shall spend his life in trying to impress the "natives", and so in every crisis he has to do what the "natives" expect of him. He wears a mask and his face grows to fit it. . . . A sahib has got to act like a sahib; he has got to appear resolute, to know his own mind and do definite things. To come all that way, rifle in hand, with two thousand people marching at my heels, and then to trail feebly away, having done nothing—no, that was impossible. The crowd would laugh at me. And my whole life, every white man's life in the East, was one long struggle not to be laughed at.[17]

Orwell's use of the theatrical metaphor is pervasive: he speaks of himself as "leading actor of the piece," of hollow dummys, puppets, masks, appearances, and an audience poised to jeer if he doesn't follow the established script. As he experiences it, Orwell is no more free to be himself, to break convention, than a slave would be in the presence of a tyrannical master. If subordination requires a credible performance of humility and deference, so domination seems to require a credible performance of haughtiness and mastery. There are, however, two differences. If a slave transgresses the script he risks a beating, while Orwell risks only ridicule. Another important distinction is that the necessary posing of the dominant derives not from weaknesses but from the ideas behind their rule, the kinds of claims they make to legitimacy. A divine king must act like a god, a warrior king like a brave general; an elected head of a republic must appear to respect the citizenry and their opinions; a judge must seem to venerate the law. Actions by elites that *publicly* contradict the basis of a claim to power are threatening. The cynicism of the taped Oval Office conversations in the Nixon White House was a devastating blow to the public transcript claim to legality and high-mindedness. Similarly, the poorly concealed existence of special shops and hospitals for the party elites in the socialist bloc profoundly undercut the ruling party's public claim to rule on behalf of the working class.[18]

One might usefully compare forms of domination in terms of the kinds of display and public theater they seem to require. Another, perhaps even more revealing way of addressing the same question would be to ask what activities

---

17. *Inside the Whale and Other Essays*, 95–96.

18. Similar inequalities are not nearly so symbolically charged in Western capitalist democracies, which publicly are committed to defend property rights and make no claims to be run for the particular benefit of the working class.

are most sedulously hidden from public view by different forms of domination. Each form of rule will have not only its characteristic stage setting but also its characteristic dirty linen.[19]

Those forms of domination based on a premise or claim to inherent superiority by ruling elites would seem to depend heavily on lavish display, sumptuary laws, regalia, and public acts of deference or tribute by subordinates. The desire to inculcate habits of obedience and hierarchy, as in military organizations, can produce similar patterns. In extreme cases display and performance dominate, as in the case of the Chinese emperor Long Qing, whose public appearances were so minutely choreographed that he became virtually a living icon deployed in rituals that risked nothing to improvisation. Offstage, in the Forbidden City, he might carouse as he wished with princes and aristocrats.[20] This may be something of a limiting case, but the attempt by dominant elites to sequester an offstage social site where they are no longer on display and can let their hair down is ubiquitous, as is the attempt to ritualize contact with subordinates so that the masks remain firmly in place and the risk that something untoward might happen is minimized. Milovan Djilas's early critique of Yugoslavia's new party elite contrasted a meaningful but secret backstage with the empty ritual of public bodies: "At intimate suppers, on hunts, in conversations between two or three men, matters of state of the most vital importance are decided. Meetings of party forums, conferences of the government and assemblies, serve no purpose but to make declarations and put in an appearance."[21] Strictly speaking, of course, the public ritual Djilas denigrates does indeed serve a purpose inasmuch as the theater of unanimity, loyalty, and resolve is intended to impress an audience. Public ritual of this kind is both real and meaningful; Djilas's complaint is rather that it is also a performance designed to conceal an offstage arena of politics that would contradict it. Dominant groups often have much to conceal, and typically they also have the wherewithal to conceal what they wish. The British colonial officials with whom Orwell served in Moulmein had the inevitable club to repair to in the evenings. There, except for the invisible Burmese staff, they were among their own, as they might have put it, and no longer strutting before the audience of colonial subjects. Activities, gestures, remarks, and

19. We all recognize homely versions of this truth. It is, parents sense, unseemly to argue publicly in front of their children, especially over their discipline and conduct. To do so is to undercut the implicit claim that parents know best and are agreed about what is proper. It is also to offer their children a political opportunity to exploit the revealed difference of opinion. Generally, parents prefer to keep the bickering offstage and to present a more or less united front before the children.

20. Ray Huang, *1571: A Year of No Significance.*

21. *The New Class,* 82.

dress that were unseemly to the public role of sahib were safe in this retreat.[22] The seclusion available to elites not only affords them a place to relax from the formal requirements of their role but also minimizes the chance that familiarity will breed contempt or, at least, diminish the impression their ritually managed appearances create. Balzac captures the fear of overexposure, as it now might be termed, among the Parisian magistrates of the mid-nineteenth century,

> Ah what an unfortunate man your true magistrate is! You know, they ought to live outside the community, as pontiffs once did. The world should only see them when they emerged from their cells at fixed times, solemn, ancient, venerable, pronouncing judgment like the high priests of antiquity, combining in themselves the judicial and the sacerdotal powers! We should only be visible on the bench. . . . Nowadays we may be seen amusing ourselves or in difficulties like anybody else. . . . We may be seen in drawing rooms, at home, creatures of passion, and instead of being terrible we are grotesque.[23]

Perhaps the danger that unregulated contact with the public may profane the sacred aura of judges helps explain why, even in secular republics, they retain more of the trappings of traditional authority than any other branch of government.

Now that the basic idea of public and hidden transcripts has been introduced, I will venture a few observations by way of orienting the subsequent discussion. For the study of power relations, this perspective alerts us to the fact that virtually all ordinarily observed relations between dominant and subordinate represent the encounter of the *public* transcript of the dominant with the *public* transcript of the subordinate. It is to observe Squire Donnithorne imposing on Mr. and Mrs. Poyser on all those occasions on which, prior to the explosion, she managed to keep up the pretense of being deferential and agreeable. Social science is, in general then, focused resolutely on the official or formal relations between the powerful and weak. This is the case even for much of the study of conflict, as we shall see, when that conflict has become highly institutionalized. I do not mean to imply that the study of this

22. I suspect that it is for essentially the same reason that the subordinate staff in virtually any hierarchical organization tend to work in open view while the elite work behind closed doors, often with anterooms containing private secretaries.

23. *A Harlot High and Low [Splendeurs et misères des courtisanes]*, trans. Reyner Happenstall, 505. The twentieth-century literary figure who made the masks of domination and subordination the center of much of his work was Jean Genet. See, in particular, his plays *The Blacks* and *The Screens*.

domain of power relations is necessarily false or trivial, only that it hardly exhausts what we might wish to know about power.

Eventually we will want to know how the *hidden* transcripts of various actors are formed, the conditions under which they do or do not find public expression, and what relation they bear to the public transcript.[24] Three characteristics of the hidden transcript, however, merit clarification beforehand. First, the hidden transcript is specific to a given social site and to a particular set of actors. Aggy's oath was almost certainly rehearsed in various forms among the slaves in their quarters or at the clandestine religious services that we know were common. Orwell's peers, like most dominant groups, would risk less from a public indiscretion, but they would have the safety of the Moulmein Club in which to vent their spleen. Each hidden transcript, then, is actually elaborated among a restricted "public" that excludes—that is hidden from—certain specified others. A second and vital aspect of the hidden transcript that has not been sufficiently emphasized is that it does not contain only speech acts but a whole range of practices. Thus, for many peasants, activities such as poaching, pilfering, clandestine tax evasion, and intentionally shabby work for landlords are part and parcel of the hidden transcript. For dominant elites, hidden-transcript practices might include clandestine luxury and privilege, surreptitious use of hired thugs, bribery, and tampering with land titles. These practices, in each case, contravene the public transcript of the party in question and are, if at all possible, kept offstage and unavowed.

Finally, it is clear that the frontier between the public and the hidden transcripts is a zone of constant struggle between dominant and subordinate—not a solid wall. The capacity of dominant groups to prevail—though never totally—in defining and constituting what counts as the public transcript and what as offstage is, as we shall see, no small measure of their power. The unremitting struggle over such boundaries is perhaps the most vital arena for ordinary conflict, for everyday forms of class struggle. Orwell noticed how the Burmese managed to insinuate almost routinely a contempt for the British, while being careful never to venture a more dangerous open defiance:

> Anti-European feeling was very bitter. No one had the guts to raise a riot, but if a European woman went through the bazaars alone somebody would probably spit betel juice over her dress. . . . When a nimble Burman tripped me up on the football field and the referee (another Burman) looked the other way, the crowd yelled with hideous laughter. . . . In the end the sneering yellow faces of the young men that met me everywhere,

24. I overlook, deliberately for the moment, the fact that there are for any actor several public and hidden transcripts, depending upon the audience being addressed.

the insults hooted after me when I was at a safe distance, got badly on my nerves. The young Buddhist priests were the worst of all.[25]

Tactical prudence ensures that subordinate groups rarely blurt out their hidden transcript directly. But, taking advantage of the anonymity of a crowd or of an ambiguous accident, they manage in a thousand artful ways to imply that they are grudging conscripts to the performance.

The analysis of the hidden transcripts of the powerful and of the subordinate offers us, I believe, one path to a social science that uncovers contradictions and possibilities, that looks well beneath the placid surface that the public accommodation to the existing distribution of power, wealth, and status often presents. Behind the "anti-European" acts Orwell noted was undoubtedly a far more elaborate hidden transcript, an entire discourse, linked to Burman culture, religion, and the experience of colonial rule. This discourse was not available—except through spies—to the British. It could be recovered only offstage in the native quarter in Moulmein and only by someone intimately familiar with Burman culture. Nor, òf course, did the Burmans know—except through the tales that servants might tell—what lay behind the more or less official behavior of the British toward them. That hidden transcript could be recovered only in the clubs, homes, and small gatherings of the colonists. The analyst in any situation like this has a strategic advantage over even the most sensitive participants precisely because the hidden transcripts of dominant and subordinate are, in most circumstances, *never in direct contact.* Each participant will be familiar with the public transcript and the hidden transcript of his or her circle, but not with the hidden transcript of the other. For this reason, political analysis can be advanced by research that can compare the hidden transcript of subordinate groups with the hidden transcript of the powerful and both hidden transcripts with the public transcript they share. This last facet of the comparison will reveal the effect of domination on political communication.

Just a few years after Orwell's stint in Moulmein a huge anticolonial rebellion took the English by surprise. It was led by a Buddhist monk claiming the throne and promising a utopia that consisted largely of getting rid of the British and taxes. The rebellion was crushed with a good deal of gratuitous brutality and the surviving "conspirators" sent to the gallows. A portion, at least, of the hidden transcript of the Burmans had suddenly, as it were, leapt onto the stage to declare itself openly. Millennial dreams of revenge and

25. *Inside the Whale,* 91. A shouted insult seems hardly a hidden transcript. What is crucial here is the "safe distance" that makes the insulter anonymous: the message is public but the messenger is hidden.

visions of just kingship, of Buddhist saviors, of a racial settling of scores of which the British had little inkling were being acted on. In the brutality of the repression that followed one could detect an acting out of the admission that Orwell struggled against and that undoubtedly found open expression in the white's only club that "the greatest joy in the world would be to drive a bayonet into a Buddhist priest's guts." Many, perhaps most, hidden transcripts remain just that: hidden from public view and never "enacted." And we are not able to tell easily under what precise circumstances the hidden transcript will storm the stage. But if we wish to move beyond apparent consent and to grasp potential acts, intentions as yet blocked, and possible futures that a shift in the balance of power or a crisis might bring to view, we have little choice but to explore the realm of the hidden transcript.

CHAPTER TWO

Domination, Acting, and Fantasy

Jocasta: What is its nature? What so hard on exiles?
Polyneices: One thing is worst, a man cannot speak out.
Jocasta: But this is slavery, not to speak one's thought.
Polyneices: One must endure the unwisdom of one's masters.

—EURIPIDES, *The Phoenician Women*

Destinations

MY BROAD PURPOSE IS TO SUGGEST how we might more successfully read, interpret, and understand the often fugitive political conduct of subordinate groups. The immodesty of this goal all but ensures that it will not be achieved except in a fragmentary and schematic form. This ambition grew from a prolonged effort to understand the politics of resistance by poor Malay peasants to changes in rice production that systematically worked to their disadvantage.[1] Given the power of landowning elites and officials, the struggle waged by the poor was necessarily circumspect. Rather than openly rebel or publicly protest, they adopted the safer course of anonymous attacks on property, poaching, character assassination, and shunning. They prudently avoided, with few exceptions, any irrevocable acts of public defiance. Anyone who regarded the calm surface of political life in "Sedaka" as evidence of harmony between classes would simply have been looking in the wrong place for political conflict.

For subordinate groups that find themselves in roughly the same boat as the poor of Sedaka, I reasoned, political life might assume analogous forms. That is, their politics too might make use of disguise, deception, and indirection while maintaining an outward impression, in power-laden situations, of willing, even enthusiastic consent.

An argument along these lines requires that we first understand how the public transcript is constructed, how it is maintained, and the purposes it serves. Why are public performances of deference and loyalty so important in power relations? Who is the audience for this symbolic display? What happens

1. James C. Scott, *Weapons of the Weak: Everyday Forms of Peasant Resistance.*

when angry or cheeky subordinates such as Mrs. Poyser spoil the performance?

The public transcript is, to put it crudely, the *self*-portrait of dominant elites as they would have themselves seen. Given the usual power of dominant elites to compel performances from others, the discourse of the public transcript is a decidedly lopsided discussion. While it is unlikely to be merely a skein of lies and misrepresentations, it is, on the other hand, a highly partisan and partial narrative. It is designed to be impressive, to affirm and naturalize the power of dominant elites, and to conceal or euphemize the dirty linen of their rule.

If, however, this flattering self-portrait is to have any rhetorical force among subordinates, it necessarily involves some concessions to their presumed interests. That is, rulers who aspire to hegemony in the Gramscian sense of that term must make out an ideological case that they rule, to some degree, on behalf of their subjects. This claim, in turn, is always highly tendentious but seldom completely without resonance among subordinates.

The distinction between the hidden and the public transcripts, together with the hegemonic aspirations of the public transcript allows us to distinguish at least four varieties of political discourse among subordinate groups. They vary according to how closely they conform to the official discourse and according to who comprises their audience.

The safest and most public form of political discourse is that which takes as its basis the flattering self-image of elites. Owing to the rhetorical concessions that this self-image contains, it offers a surprisingly large arena for political conflict that appeals to these concessions and makes use of the room for interpretation within any ideology. For example, even the ideology of white slave owners in the antebellum U.S. South incorporated certain paternalist flourishes about the care, feeding, housing, and clothing of slaves and their religious instruction. Practices, of course, were something else. Slaves were, however, able to make political use of this small rhetorical space to appeal for garden plots, better food, humane treatment, freedom to travel to religious services, and so forth. Thus, some slave interests could find representation in the prevailing ideology without appearing in the least seditious.

A second and sharply contrasting form of political discourse is that of the hidden transcript itself. Here, offstage, where subordinates may gather outside the intimidating gaze of power, a sharply dissonant political culture is possible. Slaves in the relative safety of their quarters can speak the words of anger, revenge, self-assertion that they must normally choke back when in the presence of the masters and mistresses.

A central argument of this book is that there is a third realm of subordinate group politics that lies strategically between the first two. This is a politics of disguise and anonymity that takes place in public view but is designed to have a double meaning or to shield the identity of the actors. Rumor, gossip, folktales, jokes, songs, rituals, codes, and euphemisms—a good part of the folk culture of subordinate groups—fit this description. As a case in point, consider the Brer Rabbit stories of slaves, and trickster tales more generally. At one level these are nothing but innocent stories about animals; at another level they appear to celebrate the cunning wiles and vengeful spirit of the weak as they triumph over the strong. I argue that a partly sanitized, ambiguous, and coded version of the hidden transcript is always present in the public discourse of subordinate groups. Interpreting these texts which, after all, are designed to be evasive is not a straightforward matter. Ignoring them, however, reduces us to an understanding of historical subordination that rests either on those rare moments of open rebellion or on the hidden transcript itself, which is not just evasive but often altogether inaccessible. The recovery of the nonhegemonic voices and practices of subject peoples requires, I believe, a fundamentally different form of analysis than the analysis of elites, owing to the constraints under which they are produced.

Finally, the most explosive realm of politics is the rupture of the political *cordon sanitaire* between the hidden and the public transcript. When Mrs. Poyser has her "say" (see chapter 1) she obliterates the distinction by making the hitherto hidden transcript public. In her case, the squire fled, but such moments of challenge and open defiance typically provoke either a swift stroke of repression or, if unanswered, often lead to further words and acts of daring. We will examine such moments for the insights they offer into certain forms of charisma and the dynamic of political breakthroughs.

Much of our attention will be devoted to what I have chosen to call the infrapolitics of subordinate groups. By this I mean to designate a wide variety of low-profile forms of resistance that dare not speak in their own name. A grasp of the substance of this infrapolitics, its disguises, its development, and its relationship to the public transcript, can help us clarify several vexed problems in political analysis.

The analysis of infrapolitics offers us a way of addressing the issue of hegemonic incorporation. It would be hard to find a subject on which more ink has been recently spilled—whether in the debates about community power or in the more subtle neo-Marxist formulations of Gramsci and his successors. Exactly what hegemonic incorporation might mean is subject to interpretation but, however one chooses to define it, a crude, one-dimensional answer to the query of whether slaves believe in the justice or inevitability of slavery is out of the question. If we seek instead to assess the ways in which subordinate groups may be socialized into accepting a view of their interests as propagated from above, then we may be able to provide a more complex answer. Evidence from the hidden transcript and from infrapolitics in general allows us, in principle at least, a way of approaching this problem empirically. We are not, in any case, reduced to waiting for open social protest to lift a veil of consent and quiescence. A view of politics focused either on what may be command performances of consent or open rebellion represents a far too narrow concept of political life—especially under conditions of tyranny or near-tyranny in which much of the world lives.

In a similar way, paying close attention to political acts that are disguised or offstage helps us to map a realm of possible dissent. Here, I believe, we will typically find the social and normative basis for practical forms of resistance (for example, what masters called shirking, theft, and flight by slaves) as well as the values that might, if conditions permitted, sustain more dramatic forms of rebellion. The point is that neither everyday forms of resistance nor the occasional insurrection can be understood without reference to the sequestered social sites at which such resistance can be nurtured and given meaning. Done in more detail than can be attempted here, such an analysis would outline a technology and practice of resistance analogous to Michel Foucault's analysis of the technology of domination.[2]

The hidden transcript and disguised forms of public dissent may also help to enlarge our understanding of charismatic acts. Charisma is not a quality—like, say, brown eyes—that someone possesses in any simple way; it is, as we know, a relationship in which engaged observers recognize (and may, in fact, help inspire) a quality they admire. Mrs. Poyser was not a charismatic character in the colloquial use of that term, but she undertook a charismatic act. Understanding that charismatic act, and many others like it, I would argue, depends upon appreciating how her gesture represented a shared hidden transcript that no one had yet had the courage to declare in the teeth of power.

My analysis emphasizes precisely those forms of subordination in which I anticipated finding the greatest divergence between the public transcript and the hidden transcript. Thus much of the evidence I use comes from various forms of tyranny chosen with an eye to how they might vindicate this perspective. Wherever possible, I have drawn material from studies of slavery, serfdom, untouchability, racial domination—including colonialism, and highly stratified peasant societies, which are my particular bailiwick. To a contemporary observer, these forms of domination might seem almost limiting cases;

2. *Discipline and Punish: The Birth of the Prison*, trans. Alan Sheridan.

slavery and serfdom might even be considered antiquarian interests. Stressing such cases, however, has its advantages. As a historical matter, they surely represent a very large share of mankind's melancholy experience. Thanks to a growing attention to social history from below and to the recovery of otherwise mute voices—especially in the case of North American slavery—I have also been able to take advantage of much recently published work.

My strategy amounts to choosing forms of domination that bear a family resemblance to one another so as to lend some cohesion to comparisons across an already dangerously sprawling range of cases. These forms of domination are institutionalized means of extracting labor, goods, and services from a subject population. They embody formal assumptions about superiority and inferiority, often in elaborate ideological form, and a fair degree of ritual and "etiquette" regulates public conduct within them. In principle at least, status in these systems of domination is ascribed by birth, mobility is virtually nil, and subordinate groups are granted few if any political or civil rights. Although they are highly institutionalized, these forms of domination typically contain a strong element of personal rule.[3] Here I have in mind the great latitude for arbitrary and capricious conduct by the master toward his slave, the lord to his serf, the Brahmin to his untouchable. Thus these forms of domination are infused by an element of personal terror that may take the form of arbitrary beatings, sexual violations, and other insults and humiliations. Whether or not they occur to any particular subordinate, the ever-present knowledge that they might seems to color the relationship as a whole. Finally, like most large-scale structures of domination, the subordinate group has a fairly extensive offstage social existence which, in principle, affords it the opportunity to develop a shared critique of power.

This structural family resemblance is an essential analytical underpinning to my argument. I do not intend, in other words, to make "essentialist" assertions about the immutable characteristics of slaves, serfs, untouchables, the colonized, or subjugated races. What I do want to claim, however, is that similar structures of domination, other things equal, tend to provoke responses and forms of resistance that also bear a family resemblance to one

3. My analysis is thus less relevant to forms of *impersonal* domination by say, "scientific techniques," bureaucratic rules, or by market forces of supply and demand. Much of Michel Foucault's work bears on those, for him, quintessentially modern forms of social control. While I believe many apparently impersonal forms of control are mediated by a personal domination that is, and is experienced as, more arbitrary than Foucault would allow, I take his point that there is something qualitatively different about claims to authority based on impersonal, technical, scientific rules.

another.[4] My analysis, therefore, is one that runs roughshod over differences and specific conditions that others would consider essential, in order to sketch the outlines of broad approach. Not only do I ignore the vast differences between each form of subordination, but I also overlook the great particularity of each instance of a given form—for example, between North American and Caribbean slavery, between French and Russian serfdom. If this approach has any merit, that merit would have to be demonstrated in case studies grounding these broad assertions in contexts that were both culturally specific and historically deep.

More than occasionally, I make reference to other forms of subordination that are at some remove from the core of structures mentioned above, but that have some similarities which I think will help advance and illustrate the argument. Evidence from "total institutions" such as prisons, reeducation camps, prisoner-of-war camps—especially where some effort is made at persuasion, even it if takes the form of brainwashing—has seemed helpful for comparative purposes. Similarly, public life in communist states in which the chasm between official ritual and the offstage political culture is often so large can tell us something about how a hidden transcript is elaborated.

The literature on gender-based domination and on working-class culture and ideology has proven insightful at many points. They share enough similarities to the cases I rely most heavily on to be suggestive. At the same time the differences limit the analogies that can be drawn. In the case of women, relations of subordination have typically been both more personal and intimate; joint procreation and family life have meant that imagining an entirely separate existence for the subordinate group requires a more radical step than it has for serfs or slaves. Analogies become more strained in contemporary settings where choice of marriage partner is possible and where women have civil and political rights. For the contemporary working classes in the West who can take or leave a particular job (though they typically *must* work) and who also have some mobility and have gained citizenship rights, many of the same difficulties arise. Both cases illustrate how essential the existence of some choice is in raising the possibility of hegemonic incorporation, and the case of gender highlights the importance of specifying exactly how separate separate spheres are.[5]

Given the choice of structures explored here, it is apparent that I privilege

4. For a similar argument about the structuralist or positional basis of feminist theory, see Lind Alcoff, "Cultural Feminism versus Post-structuralism: The Identity Crisis in Feminist Theory."

5. For an example of separate spheres analyzed in remarkable depth among Bedouin women, see Lila Abu-Lughod, *Veiled Sentiments: Honor and Poetry in a Bedouin Society.*

the issues of dignity and autonomy, which have typically been seen as secondary to material exploitation. Slavery, serfdom, and the caste system routinely generate practices and rituals of denigration, insult, and assaults on the body that seem to occupy a large space in the hidden transcripts of their victims. Such forms of oppression, as we shall see, deny subordinates the ordinary luxury of negative reciprocity: trading a slap for a slap, an insult for an insult. Even in the case of the contemporary working class, it appears that slights to one's dignity and close surveillance and control of one's work loom at least as large in accounts of oppression as do narrower concerns of work and compensation.

Preliminaries

The next two chapters are devoted to an analysis of the public transcript, its symbolic value, its maintenance, its manipulation, and its consequences. Before embarking on that enterprise, however, a few working assumptions must be clarified. The first concerns the epistemological status of the hidden transcript and the nature of the *relative* freedom of the discourse found there. Second, I want to indicate how the distinctions between a public and a hidden transcript accords well with what we know from linguistic practice and from the phenomenology of distinctions between what's said in the face of power and what's said behind its back. Finally, I want to indicate how the hidden transcript receives its normative and emotional resonance from the impulses and assertions that are censored in the presence of power.

Deference and Back(stage) Talk

The younger had always worn a Yoke, but is there any yoked creature without private opinion?
    —GEORGE ELIOT, *Middlemarch*

Any pattern of stratification provides a fairly reliable guide to who gives orders and who receives orders in that society. At the top are those who give orders to virtually all and take none; at the bottom are those who take orders from virtually anyone and give orders to none. Those at each position *defer* to those placed higher. Looked at in this fashion, deference is one of the consequences of a stratification system rather than its creator. We are in danger of making a serious mistake, therefore, whenever we infer anything at all about the beliefs or attitudes of anyone solely on the basis that he or she has engaged in an apparently deferential act. Strictly speaking, we have no basis for any such inference, and the term *deference* is best thought of as "the form of social interaction which occurs in situations involving the exercise of traditional authority."[6] There is little doubt that acts of deference—for example, a bow of greeting or the use of a superior's honorific in addressing him—are intended in some sense to convey the outward impression of conformity with standards sustained by superiors. Beyond this we may not safely go. The act may be performed almost automatically as a ritual or habitual act; it may be the result of calculating its advantages; it may be successful dissembling; it may spring from a conscious desire to honor a respected superior. In addition, since most acts of deference are routinized actions toward the holder of a particular status one might often wish to distinguish the attitude toward the individual from the attitude toward the status in general. One might defer to a particular priest, for example, out of a generalized respect for priests and for the faith they represent, while holding this particular priest in private contempt.

Each and every inference about the attitude behind an act of deference must therefore be based on evidence external to the act itself.[7] And when the acts of deference in question are those of a group that is systematically subject to domination, that evidence is all the more vital inasmuch as public rituals of deference may be highly routinized and shallow. In his comparative study of slavery, Orlando Patterson is at pains to insist that the servile acts of slaves in the presence of their masters are "the outward product of their interaction" and nothing more; we can say next to nothing about group psychology or beliefs on this basis.[8] In any established structure of domination, it is plausible to imagine that subordinate groups are socialized by their parents in the rituals of homage that will keep them from harm. A cruel paradox of slavery, for example, is that it is in the interest of slave mothers, whose overriding wish is to keep their children safe and by their side, to train them in the routines of conformity. Out of love, they undertake to socialize their children to please, or at least not anger, their masters and mistresses. How deep this conformity goes and how much of the backstage resentment and cynicism that may color it underlies the performance is impossible to say on surface evidence alone. Something along similar lines appears to occur in English working-class families. Compared to middle-class families, which emphasize feeling, guilt, and attitude, working-class parents, it is claimed, stress outward conformity

6. Howard Newby, "The Deferential Dialectic," 142. I am much indebted in this brief discussion to Newby's illuminating analysis.

7. The exception, perhaps, is when one can plausibly read in the act of deference itself the insinuation of another attitude altogether—for example, a "Yes, Sir" in a tone of voice or with a sneer that implies contempt. Even here, however, we would want to verify such an impression.

8. *Slavery and Social Death,* 11.

and compliance with far less concern for the motives that lie behind it.[9] The pattern reflects to a great extent the kind of compliance to work life and to the class system that has been expected, and extracted, from their parents. It is as if working-class youngsters are being trained for a life in which there is no necessary connection—perhaps even a contradiction—between their public conformity to the realities of power and their confidential attitudes.

The problem we face in examining a public transcript of deference amounts to this: how can we estimate the impact of power relations on action when the exercise of power is nearly constant? We can only begin to measure the influence of a teacher's presence on a classroom of students once he or she leaves the room—or when they leave the room at recess. Aside from what they say, the typical explosion of chatter and physical exuberance released when school is out, compared with their previous behavior in the classroom, does tell us something retrospectively about the effect of the school and teacher on behavior. The motives behind acts of deference will remain opaque to us until and unless the power that prompts it weakens or else we can speak confidentially, backstage to those whose motives we wish to understand.

It is particularly in this latter realm of relative discursive freedom, outside the earshot of powerholders, where the hidden transcript is to be sought. The disparity between what we find here and what is said in the presence of power is a rough measure of what has been suppressed from power-laden political communication. The hidden transcript is, for this reason, the privileged site for nonhegemonic, contrapuntal, dissident, subversive discourse.

To this point I have used the terms *hidden* and *public transcript* in the singular when, in fact, the plural would be more accurate and would convey the great variety of sites where such transcripts are generated. The accompanying illustration—the crudity and linearity of which we shall later modify—provides an initial sense of this plurality of transcripts in the case of slavery.[10]

As a hypothetical slave finds himself among audiences progressively toward the more secluded (right) side of the continuum, his discourse is rela-

9. Basil Bernstein, *Class, Codes and Control,* vol. 1.

10. A great deal of important information is purposely omitted from this illustration. As depicted, it is entirely static and does not allow for the development and interaction of transcripts over time. It fails to specify the location and circumstances as well as the audience; a slave speaking with a white shopkeeper while making an ordinary transaction is not in the same situation as he would be encountering whites on horseback at night. Finally, it adopts the vantage point of a single individual rather than what might be called the community of discourse. It does, however, serve to orient a discussion of power and discourse—a discussion that might have any number of illustrative cases: serfdom, caste, wage labor, bureaucracy, school.

Hypothetical Discursive Sites, Arranged by Audience, under Slavery

Harsh master/ overseer	Indulgent master or overseer	Whites having no direct authority	Slaves and free blacks	Slaves of same master	Closest slave friends	Immediate family

```
|-------------------------------|    |-----------------------------------|
          Public transcripts                   Hidden transcripts
```

tively freer of intimidation from above. Put in slightly different terms, power over discourse is typically, but not always, less lopsided the more the slave is cloistered within his most intimate circle. This is decidedly not, however, to assert that the slave's actions before a harsh master are necessarily sham and pretense while his conduct with his family and close friends is necessarily genuine and true. The reason we may not leap to this simplifying conclusion is that power relations are ubiquitous. They are surely different at opposite ends of the continuum, but they are never absent.[11]

The difference in power relations toward the hidden transcript segment of the continuum is that they are generated among those who are mutually subject, often as peers, to a larger system of domination. Although the slave may be freer vis-à-vis the master in this setting, it does not follow that relations of domination do not prevail among the slaves. Power relations among subordinates are not necessarily conducted along democratic lines at all. Among the inmates of prisons, who are all subject to a common domination from the institution and its officers, there frequently develops a tyranny as brutal and exploitive as anything the guards can devise. In this domination within domination the subordinate prisoner must measure his words and conduct perhaps more carefully before dominant prisoners than he does before prison officials.

Even if relations among subordinates may be characterized by symmetry and mutuality, the hidden transcript that develops in this case may be experienced as no less tyrannical despite the fact that all have had a hand in shaping it. Consider, for example, the ethos that often prevails among workers which penalizes any laborer who would go out of his way to curry the favor of the bosses. The words used from below to describe such behavior (toady, ass-

11. No real social site can be thought of as a realm of entirely "true" and "free" discourse unless, perhaps, it is the private imagination to which, by definition, we can have no access. Disclosure to anyone else immediately brings power relations into play, and psychoanalysis, which aims at the disclosure of repressed truth in a tolerant, encouraging atmosphere, is, at the same time, a highly asymmetrical power relationship.

kisser, rate-buster, bootlicker) are designed to prevent it. These may be supplemented by glares, shunning, and perhaps even beatings.

The power relations generated among subordinate groups are often the only countervailing power to the determination of behavior from above. Tenant farmers in the Malaysian village I studied had developed a strong norm among themselves condemning anyone who might try to secure or enlarge his acreage by offering the landlord a higher seasonal rent than the current local tenant paid. Fifteen years ago someone apparently defied the norm; since then the family is poorly regarded and has not been spoken to or invited to feasts by any kin or friends of the offended family. In a comparable case no Andalusian farmworkers were said to dare work for less than the minimum wage. If they did, they would be given the cold shoulder, ostracized, or branded "low" or a "creeper."[12] The strength of the sanctions deployed to enforce conformity depends essentially on the cohesiveness of the subordinate group and on how threatening they view the defection. In nineteenth-century rural Ireland when a tenant broke a rent boycott by paying the land agent, he was likely to find his cow "houghed" in the morning: its Achilles tendon severed so that the tenant would have to destroy it himself. All such cases are instances of the more or less coercive pressure that can be generated to monitor and control deviance among a subordinate group.[13] This pressure serves not only to suppress dissent among subordinates but may also place limits on the temptation to compete headlong with one another—at the expense of all—for the favor of the dominant.

As shown in the figure, the dialectical relationship between the public and hidden transcripts is obvious. By definition, the hidden transcript represents discourse—gesture, speech, practices—that is ordinarily excluded from the public transcript of subordinates by the exercise of power. The practice of domination, then, *creates* the hidden transcript. If the domination is particularly severe, it is likely to produce a hidden transcript of corresponding richness. The hidden transcript of subordinate groups, in turn, reacts back on the public transcript by engendering a subculture and by opposing its own variant form of social domination against that of the dominant elite. Both are realms of power and interests.

12. See Juan Martinez-Alier, *Labourers and Landowners in Southern Spain*, 126.

13. Where such domination within domination is pronounced it becomes possible to speak of a hidden transcript within the hidden transcript. Subordinates may be too intimidated by the exercise of domination within the group to say or do anything at odds with what is required. Notice also that when such a situation develops, powerholders among subordinates may well come to have something of a vested interest in the overall pattern of domination that is a precondition of their own power.

The hidden transcript of the dominant is similarly an artifact of the exercise of power. It contains that discourse—gestures, speech, practices—which is excluded from the public transcript by the ideological limits within which domination is cast. It too is a realm of power and interests. Imagining a figure similar to the figure on p. 26 in which we instead took the perspective of the slave master and ranging from audiences of his family and closest friends all the way to his interaction on ceremonial occasions with the slaves assembled, would yield a spectrum of discursive realms of the dominant. Here too, as with a diplomat whose discourse varies enormously depending on whether he is talking informally with his own negotiating team or formally with the chief negotiator of a threatening enemy power, is a realm of masks. The masks may get thicker or thinner, they may be crude or subtle, depending on the nature of the audience and the interests involved, but they are nevertheless performances, as are all social actions.

Power and Acting

> Your presence frightens any common man
> From saying things you would not care to hear
> But in dark corners I have heard them say
> how the whole town is grieving for this girl
> Unjustly doomed if ever woman was
> to die in shame for glorious action done. . . .
>
> This is the undercover speech in town.
>
> —HAEMON TO CREON, *Antigone*

On a daily basis, the impact of power is most readily observed in acts of deference, subordination, and ingratiation. The script and stage directions for subordinate groups are generally far more confining than for the dominant. Putting it in terms of "paying respect" to status, Hochschild observes,

> to have higher status is to have a stronger claim to rewards, including emotional rewards. It is also to have greater access to the means of enforcing claims. The deferential behavior of servants and women—the encouraging smiles, the attentive listening, the appreciative laughter, the comments of affirmation, admiration, or concern—comes to seem normal, even built into personality rather than inherent in the kinds of exchange that low-status people commonly enter into.[14]

A convincing performance may require both the suppression or control of feelings that would spoil the performance and the simulation of emotions that are necessary to the performance. Practical mastery through repetition may make the performance virtually automatic and apparently effortless. In other cases, it is a conscious strain, as when Old Tiennon said that when he met his father's ex-landlord, "I forced myself to be amiable." We often talk in this schizophrenic way as if our tactical self exercises control over our emotional self, which threatens to spoil the performance.[15] The performance, as I shall continually emphasize, comprises not only speech acts but conformity in facial expression and gesture as well as practical obedience to commands that may be distasteful or humiliating.

More of the public life of subordinates than of the dominant is devoted to "command" performances. The change in the posture, demeanor, and apparent activity of an office work force when the supervisor suddenly appears is an obvious case. The supervisor, though she too is constrained, can typically be more relaxed about her manner, less on guard, for it is the supervisor, after all, who sets the tone of the encounter.[16] Power means not *having* to act or, more accurately, the capacity to be more negligent and casual about any single performance. So close was this association between power and acting in the French royal court that the slightest trace of an increase in servility could be taken as evidence of declining status and power: "Let a favorite pay close heed to himself for if he does not keep me waiting as long in his antechamber; if his face is more open, if he frowns less, if he listens to me a little further while showing me out, I shall think he is beginning to fall, and I shall be right."[17] The haughtiness associated with the bearing of power may, in a physical sense, contain more of the unguarded self, while servility virtually by definition requires an attentive watchfulness and attuning of response to the mood and requirements of the powerholder. Less of the unguarded self is ventured

14. Arlie Russell Hochschild, *The Managed Heart: The Commercialization of Human Feeling*, 90–91. This fine, perceptive study of airline flight attendants who are paid, in part, for what Hochschild calls "emotional work" has helped me think through several important issues.

15. The effort to stifle anger necessary for a successful performance and its failure to prevail against a growing rage is the leit-motif of Jean Rhys's fine early novels. Julia, the central character in *After Leaving Mr. McKenzie*, knows how she must please men to live as she prefers, but she can rarely sustain her bad faith performance for long. As Rhys puts it, "She had fits of melancholy when she would lose the self-control necessary to keep up appearances," 27.

16. Thibaut, in an inventory of social psychology findings, agrees: "From the point of view of the individual member of the dyad, the possession of superior power has a number of advantages." "It tends to relieve him of the necessity of paying close attention to his partner's action and being careful in his own actions." John W. Thibaut and Harold Kelley, *The Social Psychology of Groups*, 125.

17. La Bruyère, quoted in Norbert Elias, *Power and Civility*, vol. 2 of *The Civilizing Process*, trans. Edmund Jephcott (originally published in Basel in 1939), 271.

because the possible penalties for a failure or misstep are severe; one must be constantly on one's "best behavior."

The influence that the powerful exercise on public discourse is apparent in the findings of sociolinguists about language use and power. These findings indicate how hierarchies of gender, race, caste, and class are encoded in the domination of talk.

In her study of contemporary language-use differences between women and men, Robin Lakoff emphasizes that the history of male dominance has meant that women increasingly use men's language—imitating the higher status dialect—while the reverse is rarely the case.[18] In a face-to-face encounter the tone, grammar, and dialect of the dominant male is likely to prevail, not to mention that, as in other asymmetrical power relations, the dominant is typically the one who initiates the conversation, controls its direction, and terminates it. The fact of subordination can be read in the use of linguistic forms shaped so as to reflect and anticipate the response of the dominant. Thus Lakoff notes the far more widespread use by women of what linguists call the "tag question formation"—an "isn't it so?" or a rising tone at the end of what would otherwise be a declarative sentence, which indicates a request for reassurance and approval before continuing. Other linguistic marks of subordination include the greater use of hyper-polite forms ("Would you be so kind as to please . . ." in place of a command), of hyper-correct grammar, linguistic hedges ("sort of," "kind of") that weaken a declarative phrase, and a disinclination to tell jokes in public. When the subordination is extreme, as in slavery and racism, it is often observed that stammering is common, a stammering that reflects not a speech defect, since the stammerers can speak fluently in other contexts, but a fear-induced hesitation over producing the correct formula. One can, I think, read in these patterns a consistent risk-averse use of language by the powerless—an attempt to venture as little as possible, to use stock formulas when available, and to avoid taking liberties with language that might give offense. As a high-caste anthropologist conducting interviews among untouchable Chamars in Lucknow discovered, "The triter the inquiry the 'better' the Chamar's response. In less trodden areas, evasive devices—deflection, postponement, containment, cliché, rhetorical questions, and feigned ignorance were deftly employed."[19] Such performances require practice, mastery, and their own kind of improvisation if they are to be exercised successfully, but they are nevertheless all damage-

18. *Language and Women's Place*, 10.

19. R. S. Khare, *The Untouchable as Himself: Ideology, Identity, and Pragmatism among the Lucknow Chamars*, 13.

control maneuvers in the face of power. As Lakoff concludes in the case of women's speech and dress conformity, "Her overattention to appearance and appearances (including perhaps overcorrectness and overgentility of speech and etiquette) is merely the result of being forced to exist only as a reflection in the eyes of others."[20]

Societies with long-established court cultures develop elaborate codes for speech-levels which in extreme cases can nearly constitute a separate language. Here the hyper-correctness of subordinates is institutionalized linguistically. Strong traces of such codes persist in the differences between Saxon and Norman English: the Saxon commoners ate while the Norman conquerors dined. In Malaysia a host of special verbs distinguish quite ordinary actions when the sultan is undertaking them: commoners bathe, the sultan sprinkles himself; commoners walk, the sultan progresses (implying a smooth, gliding motion); commoners sleep, the sultan reclines. Pronouns also change, as they do in most highly stratified societies, depending on the relative status of the speakers. When a commoner is addressing the sultan, he uses the term *hamba*, which translates roughly as "your slave," and he traditionally approached the throne in a posture of abject humility. Every encounter that brings together people of different statuses in such societies is designed to underline and reinforce those differences by rules about language, gesture, tone, and dress.

Terms of address, perhaps because they lend themselves to historical analysis, have been the object of considerable research by sociolinguists. In the past, the polite and the familiar forms of the second person pronoun (*vous* and *tu* in French, respectively) were used asymmetrically in a semantic of power.[21] The dominant class used tu when addressing commoners, servants, peasants and received back the more polite, dignified vous. No one who prudently used the formula could avoid thereby seeming to endorse the distinctions of worth and status inscribed in its use. Inasmuch as there was a determined effort by the revolutionaries in France immediately after 1789 to ban the use of vous, we can take it for granted that this semantic of power was not a matter of popular indifference. To this day, at socialist and communist gatherings, Europeans who are strangers will use the familiar form with one another to express equality and comradeship. In ordinary usage vous is now used *reciprocally* to express not status, but lack of close acquaintance.

20. *Language and Women's Place*, 27.

21. My discussion here is drawn largely from R. Brown and A. Gilman, "The Pronouns of Powers and Solidarity," in *Language and Social Context*, ed. Pier Paolo Giglioli, 252–82, and chap. 5 of Peter Trudgill, *Sociolinguistics: An Introduction to Language and Society.*

A function equivalent to this nonreciprocity of address is the use of *boy* or first names by ruling groups when speaking with inferiors, and the latters' use of *Mister* to address their superiors. Common in systems of stratification by class and by race, this usage has not by any means disappeared in the West, though it is decidedly less universal today than fifty years ago. (It also survives as a kind of curiosity in the French *garçon*, for waiter, although *monsieur* is now increasingly favored.) Afrikaans, significantly, retains today both the asymmetrical use of the second person pronoun and the boy–Mister pattern.

We are in danger of missing much of their significance if we see linguistic deference and gestures of subordination merely as performances extracted by power. The fact is they serve also as a barrier and a veil that the dominant find difficult or impossible to penetrate. A striking example is the usually futile effort by sociolinguists to record "pure," "authentic" versions of lower-class dialect. Since the recorder is almost inevitably someone of higher status and education, a kind of linguistic Heisenberg effect takes place which drives out the more stigmatized forms of the dialect. The only way the semantics of power can be breached is by a highly unethical, surreptitious taping of conversations without the subject's knowledge or permission.[22] From one perspective this fact is merely an example of how power distorts communication. But from another perspective, it also preserves a sequestered site where a more autonomous discourse may develop. How are we to interpret the fact, for example, that lower-caste men in the pluralistic culture of the Punjab are likely to use any of several names, depending upon whom they were speaking to? Confronted with a Hindu, they called themselves Ram Chand, with a Sikh they called themselves Ram Singh, and with a Christian, John Samuel. The frustrated British census takers wrote of the "fickleness" of the lower castes with respect to religion, but it is not hard to recognize the evasive adoption of protective cover.[23] We also learn that black miners in Southern Rhodesia had several names which arose not simply from the confusion of languages but because the confusion could plausibly excuse a delay in responding to a summons or an otherwise unexplained absence.[24] The appearances that power requires are, to be sure, imposed forcefully on subordinate groups. But this does not preclude their active use as a means of resistance and evasion.

22. John R. Rickford, "Carrying the New Wave into Syntax: The Case of Black English BIN," in *Variation in the Form and Use of Language*, ed. Robert W. Fasold, 98–119.

23. Mark Jürgensmeyer, *Religion as Social Vision: The Movement against Untouchability in 20th Century Punjab*, 92.

24. Robin Cohen, "Resistance and Hidden Forms of Consciousness among African Workers," 8–22.

The evasion, it must be noted, however, is purchased at the considerable cost of contributing to the production of a public transcript that *apparently* ratifies the social ideology of the dominant. Subordinates appear deferential, they bow and scrape, they seem amiable, they appear to know their place and to stay in it, thereby indicating that they also know and recognize the place of their superiors.

When the script is rigid and the consequences of a mistake large, subordinate groups may experience their conformity as a species of manipulation. Insofar as the conformity is tactical it is surely manipulative. This attitude again requires a division of the self in which one self observes, perhaps cynically and approvingly, the performance of the other self. Many of the accounts given by untouchables (notice how the term *untouchable* assumes a high-caste perspective) are frank in this respect. Noting that vital goods and services—sugar, kerosene, work, grain, loans—can be procured only by being on the good side of a member of the dominant castes, one observes, "We actually have to encounter, appease, and cajole the caste Hindus in a hundred different ways to secure our share."[25] Thus, conformity is far too lame a word for the active manipulation of rituals of subordination to turn them to good personal advantage; it is an art form in which one can take some pride at having successfully misrepresented oneself. Another untouchable emphasizes the tactical side of concealment: "We must also tactfully disguise and hide, as necessary, our true aims and intentions from our social adversaries. To recommend it is not to encourage falsehood but only to be tactical in order to survive."[26]

Blacks in the South, both before and after emancipation, had to thread their way among dangerous whites in much the same fashion. Thus it was possible for a black man speaking to a white abolitionist audience before the Civil War to explain, "Persons live and die in the midst of Negroes and know comparatively little of their real character. They are one thing before the whites and another before their own color. Deception towards the former is characteristic of them, whether bond or free, throughout the whole U.S."[27]

25. Khare, *The Untouchable as Himself,* 97. Khare and others alert us to the fact that subordinates are, generally, closer observers of the powerful than vice-versa because such observation is a vital safety and survival skill. The slave's or untouchable's "day" depends on an accurate reading of the master's mood; the master's "day" is far more impervious to the mood of his subordinate. For further evidence along these lines, see Judith Rollins, *Between Women: Domestics and their Employers,* and Joan Cocks, *The Oppositional Imagination: Adventures in the Sexual Domain.*

26. Khare, *The Untouchable as Himself,* 130.

27. Quoted in Lawrence Levine, *Black Culture and Black Consciousness,* 101.

The sense of achievement in a successful performance *and* the massive realities of power that make it necessary are each evident in this account of a black sharecropper between the wars:

> I've joked with white people, in a nice way. I've had to play dumb sometimes—I knowed not to go too far and let them know what I knowed, because they taken exception of it too quick. I had to humble down and play shut-mouthed in many cases to get along, I've done it all—they didn't know what it was all about, it's just a plain fact. . . . And I could go to 'em a heap of times for a favor and get it. . . . They'd give you a good name if you was obedient to 'em, acted nice when you met 'em an didn't question 'em 'bout what they said they had against you. You begin to cry about your rights and the mistreatin' of you and they'd murder you.[28]

Nate Shaw reminds us eloquently that the theater of power can, by artful practice, become an actual political resource of subordinates. Thus we get the wrong impression, I think, if we visualize actors perpetually wearing fake smiles and moving with the reluctance of a chain gang. To do so is to see the performance as totally determined from above and to miss the agency of the actor in appropriating the performance for his own ends. What may look from above like the extraction of a required performance can easily look from below like the artful manipulation of deference and flattery to achieve its own ends. The slaves who artfully reinforced their master's stereotyped view of them as shiftless and unproductive may well have thereby lowered the work norms expected of them. By their artful praise at celebrations and holidays, they may have won better food rations and clothing allowances. The performance is often collective, as subordinates collude to create a piece of theater that serves their superior's view of the situation but that is maintained in their own interests.[29] In fact, the stereotypes of the dominant are, from this perspective, a resource as well as an oppression to the subordinate, as Richard Hoggart's observation of the British working-class's use of deference makes plain: "the kind of obvious 'fiddling' of someone from another class which accompanies

28. Theodore Rosengarten, *All God's Dangers: The Life of Nate Shaw,* 545. Nate Shaw did join the Alabama Sharecroppers Union during the depression and used his pistol to defend a neighbor—and union member—whose livestock was being seized by the sheriffs. He was sent to prison for more than a decade, where the mere desire to live out his sentence required constant conformity and self-control. In the violent world of prison, as well, a harmless demeanor may be the most effective means to a successful attack. As Jack Henry Abbot wrote, "You learn to 'smile' him into position. To disarm him with friendliness. So when you are raging inside at anyone you learn to conceal it, to smile or feign cowardice." *In the Belly of the Beast,* 89.

29. See, along these lines, Erving Goffman, *Relations in Public: Microstudies of the Public Order,* 339.

an overreadiness to say 'Sir,' but assumes . . . that it is all a contemptuous game, that one can depend on the middle class distaste for a scene to allow one to cheat easily."[30] Rituals of subordination, then, may be deployed both for purposes of manipulation and concealment. What was often called Uncle Tom behavior, from this angle, may be no more than a label for someone who has mastered the theater arts of subordination. Deference and a smile may be what a poacher habitually deploys before the gentry to avoid suspicion; rather like the normal walk of the fleeing suspect when he encounters a cop on the beat. This achievement is considerable, but we should not forget that it is won on a stage on which the roles have been largely scripted from above and on which the usual performances, no matter how artful, must reinforce the appearances approved by the dominant.

Such performances are seldom, of course, entirely successful. Dominant elites may well not know what lies behind the facade, but it is rare that they merely take what they see and hear at face value. An ancient text from Buddhist India seeks to instruct the master on what the facade conceals:

> O Bhante, our slaves . . . do another thing with their bodies, say another with their speech, and have a third in their mind.
>
> On seeing the master, they rise up, take things from his hands, discarding this and talking that; others show a seat, fan him with a hand fan, wash his feet, thus doing all that needs to be done. But in his absence, they do not even look if oil is being spilled, they do not turn to look even if there were a loss of hundreds or thousands to the master. (This is how they behave differently with the body). . . . Those who in the masters' presence praise him by saying, "our master, our Lord," say all that is unutterable, all that they feel like saying once he is away. (This is how they behave differently in speech.)[31]

The white slave master is always wary of being put on by his slaves; an eighteenth-century Japanese landlord can wonder, "Does anyone lie as much as a peasant?"[32] What is notable here, I believe, is not that the dominant should assume that wily subordinates will try to get around them. To believe this is not to be paranoid; it is merely to perceive reality. They attribute such behavior, however, not to the effect of arbitrary power but rather to the inborn characteristics of the subordinate group itself. In the ersatz science of race at

30. *The Uses of Literacy: Aspects of Working Class Life* (London: Chatto and Windus, 1954), 65.

31. Dev Raj Chanana, *Slavery in Ancient India*, 57, cited in Patterson, *Slavery and Social Death*, 207–08.

32. Tetsuo Najita and Irwin Scheiner, *Japanese Thought in the Tokugawa Period, 1600–1868: Methods and Metaphors*, 40.

the turn of the century the characteristics of subordination became traits of culture, gender, or ethnicity. Accounting for what he termed the negative and superficial quality of women's speech, Schopenhauer explained, "It arises immediately from the want of reason and reflection above alluded to, and is *assisted* by the fact that they, as the weaker, are driven by nature to have recourse not to force but to cunning: hence their instinctive treachery, and their irremediable tendency to lying."[33] Otto Weininger, who wrote a widely read study called *Sex and Character* not long after, made much the same point: "The impulse to lie is much stronger in women, because, unlike that of a man, her memory is not continuous, whilst her life is discrete, unconnected, discontinuous, swayed by the sensations and perceptions of the moment instead of dominating them."[34] Each author gives some evidence here of understanding the structural position of women that might account for the character of their observed speech; but each ultimately explains the difference by gender. In Weininger's case, the argument is extended to cover the "speech-character" of another subordinate group: the Jews. Both groups stood accused of the misuse of language and were "to be identified by the false, manipulative tone of their discourse."[35] The logic of the argument is marvelously perverse. Patterns of speech that are adaptations to inequalities in power are depicted as natural characteristics of the subordinate group, a move that has, in turn, the great advantage of underlining the innate inferiority of its members when it comes to logic, truth, honesty, and reason and thereby justifying their continued domination by their betters.

Control and Fantasy—The Basis of the Hidden Transcript

When vengeance is tabled, it turns into an illusion, a personal religion, a myth which recedes day by day from its cast of characters, who remain the same in the myth of vengeance.

—MILAN KUNDERA, *The Joke*

It is plain enough thus far that the prudent subordinate will ordinarily conform by speech and gesture to what he knows is expected of him—even if that conformity masks a quite different offstage opinion. What is not perhaps

---

33. *Selected Essays of Arthur Schopenhauer*, trans. Ernest Belfort Bax, 341. Quoted in Sander L. Gilman, *Jewish Self-Hatred: Anti-Semitism and the Hidden Language of the Jews*, 243, emphasis added.

34. *Sex and Character*, 146, cited in Gilman, *Jewish Self-Hatred*, 245.

35. Gilman, *Jewish Self-Hatred*, 243–44.

plain enough is that, in any established system of domination, it is not just a question of masking one's feelings and producing the correct speech acts and gestures in their place. Rather it is often a question of controlling what would be a natural impulse to rage, insult, anger, and the violence that such feelings prompt. There is no system of domination that does not produce its own routine harvest of insults and injury to human dignity—the appropriation of labor, public humiliations, whippings, rapes, slaps, leers, contempt, ritual denigration, and so on. Perhaps the worst of these, many slave narratives agree, was not personal suffering but rather the abuse of one's child or spouse while one had little choice but to look on helplessly. This inability to defend oneself or members of one's family (that is, to act as mother, father, husband, or wife) against the abuses of domination is simultaneously an assault on one's physical body and one's personhood or dignity. The cruelest result of human bondage is that it transforms the assertion of personal dignity into a mortal risk. Conformity in the face of domination is thus occasionally—and unforgettably—a question of suppressing a violent rage in the interest of oneself and loved ones.

We may capture the existential dilemma at work here by contrasting it briefly with Hegel's analysis of the duelist. A person challenges another to a duel because he judges that his honor and standing (including often that of his family) have been mortally insulted. He demands an apology or retraction, failing which his honor can be satisfied only by a duel to the death. What the challenge to a duel says, symbolically, is that to accept this insult is to lose standing, without which life is not worth living (the ideal code, seldom rigorously followed, of the warrior aristocrat). Who wins the duel is symbolically irrelevant; it is the challenge that restores honor. If the challenger loses, he paradoxically wins his point by demonstrating that he was willing to wager his physical life in order to preserve his honor, his name. The very logic of the duel makes its status as an ideal apparent; any code that preaches the assertion of standing and honor at the expense of life itself is likely to have many lukewarm adherents in a pinch.

For most bondsmen through history, whether untouchables, slaves, serfs, captives, minorities held in contempt, the trick to survival, not always mastered by any means, has been to swallow one's bile, choke back one's rage, and conquer the impulse to physical violence. It is this systematic *frustration of reciprocal action* in relations of domination which, I believe, helps us understand much of the content of the hidden transcript. At its most elementary level the hidden transcript represents an acting out in fantasy—and occasionally in secretive practice—of the anger and reciprocal aggression denied by the presence of domination.[36] Without the sanctions imposed by power relations, subordinates would be tempted to return a blow with a blow, an insult with an insult, a whipping with a whipping, a humiliation with a humiliation. It is as if the "voice," to use Albert Hirschman's term, they are refused in the public transcript finds its full-throated expression backstage. The frustration, tension, and control necessary in public give way to unbridled retaliation in a safer setting, where the accounts of reciprocity are, symbolically at least, finally balanced.[37]

Later in this analysis I will want to move beyond the elementary, individual, and psychologistic view of the hidden transcript to its cultural determinants, its elaboration, and the forms in which it is expressed. For the moment, however, it is crucial to recognize that there is an important wish-fulfillment component to the hidden transcript.[38]

The greater part of Richard Wright's account, in *Black Boy*, of his youth in Mississippi is infused with his attempt to control his anger when in the presence of whites and, in turn, to give vent to that anger in the safety of black

36. One might, speculatively, imagine a useful parallel analysis of the cultural products of hatred and anger that cannot find direct expression on the one hand, and the cultural products of love that cannot find direct expression on the other. At one extreme, apocalyptic visions of a world upside down and, at the other, a poetry of complete mystical union with the beloved. If we were to proceed in terms of Habermas's analysis of the "ideal speech situation," the hidden transcript would represent the whole reciprocal conversational reply of the subordinate, which, for reasons of domination, cannot be spoken openly. Habermas excludes, by definition, all "strategic" action and dominated discourse from the ideal speech situation and, hence, from the search for rational consensus. What domination achieves, in this context, is the fragmentation of discourse, so that much of what would be a cohesive, integrated discourse is sequestered into the hidden transcript of the subordinate and the hidden transcript of the dominant. See, for example, Thomas McCarthy, *The Critical Theory of Jürgen Habermas*, 273–352.

37. Something very like this equilibrium view of the hidden transcript is invoked by Hochschild in the relatively benign world of flight attendants: "But in the public world of work, it is often part of an individual's job to accept uneven exchanges, to be treated with disrespect or anger by a client, all the *while closeting into fantasy the anger one would like to respond with*. Where the customer is king, unequal exchanges are normal, and from the beginning customer and client assume different rights to feeling and display. The ledger is supposedly evened by a wage." The fantasy in this case involves mostly imagined acts of retaliation to insults of the "what I would like to do if I didn't have to be prudent" kind. Flight attendants thus "pictured" themselves trading insults with abusive passengers, spilling drinks on their laps, putting large doses of a laxative in their coffee, and so forth. Wish fulfillment this most definitely is. *The Managed Heart*, 85–86.

38. Understanding the hidden transcript in this fashion might seem the equivalent of calling it the site of "ressentiment," as Nietzsche used the term. "Ressentiment" arises from the repeated repression of feelings of hatred, envy, and revenge that cannot be acted out. In this respect, at least, the term fits. But for Nietzsche, the psychological dynamics of "ressentiment" depend on these emotions having *literally* no possible outlet—no externalization—so that they come eventually to lie below the level of conscious thought. In our case, it is the social site of the hidden transcript that provides the opportunity for these emotions to take a collective, cultural form and be acted out. As Scheler notes, once an "ill-treated servant can vent his spleen in the ante-

company.[39] His effort at stifling his anger is a daily, conscious effort—one that does not always succeed:

> Each day in the store I watched the brutality with growing hate, yet trying to keep my feelings from registering in my face. When the boss looked at me I would avoid his eyes.[40]

> I feared that if I clashed with whites I would lose control of my emotions and spill out the words that would be my sentence of death.[41]

Among his friends during work breaks, the talk frequently turned to fantasies of retaliation and revenge. The fantasies are explicit and often take the form of rumors about what has happened elsewhere. For example,

> Yeah, if they hava race riot around here, I'm gonna kill all the white folks with poison.

> My momma says, that old white woman where she works talked about slapping her and ma said, "Miz Green, if you slaps me, I'll kill you and go to hell to pay for it."

> They say a white man hit a colored man up north and that colored man hit that white man, knocked him cold, and nobody did a damned thing.[42]

Wright explains that a "latent sense of violence" surrounded all the offstage talk about whites and that such talk was the "touchstone of fraternity" among the black boys who gathered at the crossroads.

Further evidence for the link between the practical need to control anger and its reflection in fantasy may be illustrated by the findings of a remarkable, if deeply flawed, study of the psychological consequences of racial domination on blacks written in the 1940s: Abram Kardiner and Lionel Ovesey's *The Mark of Oppression*.[43] As they understand it, any response to an all-powerful other will be some combination of idealization and hatred. The behavioral

---

chamber, he will remain free from the inner venom of ressentiment" Max Scheler, *Ressentiment*, trans. William W. Holdheim, ed. Lewis A. Coser. See Friedrich Nietzsche, *On The Genealogy of Morals*, trans. Walter Kaufman and F. J. Hollingsdale, particularly First Essay, sections 8, 10, 11, 13; Second Essay, sections 14–16. I was made aware of the relevance of Nietzsche's concept by the fine sociological study of contemporary domestic servants by Judith Rollins, *Between Women*.

39. *Black Boy: A Record of Childhood and Youth.*
40. Ibid., 159.
41. Ibid., 175.
42. Ibid., 67–69.
43. Subtitled *Explorations in the Personality of the American Negro*. This book is in the tradition of the "modal personality" school of cultural studies that Kardiner pioneered.

expression—whether with manipulative intent or not—of idealization would be ingratiation. Idealization might also take the form of emulation—the use of skin-lightening creams, hair straighteners, and other attempts to distance oneself from the oppressors' stereotype of blacks. This last strategy, for all but a very few, is bound to be futile. What is relevant for our purposes, however, is that both ingratiation and emulation (up to a point) readily find an outlet in the public transcript, precisely because they reaffirm the superiority of the dominant group. The equivalent manifestations of hatred—we may call them insolence and rejection—cannot, by definition, however, be expressed openly in the public transcript. They must either be insinuated cleverly into the public transcript to avoid retaliation or else be expressed offstage. The hidden transcript comes, in this way, to be the repository of the assertions whose open expression would be dangerous.

In their summaries of individual profiles, Kardiner and Ovesey emphasize that the major psychological problem for blacks was the control of aggression and its consequences. The aggression they find is not unconsciously repressed so much as consciously suppressed. One of their subjects, G. R., is described as being aware of his anger and capable of expressing it, but only when it is safe to do so. "This means that he is engaged in a constant process of control. He must be ever vigilant and he dare not act or speak on impulse."[44] Putting the issue in terms appropriate to virtually any subordinate group, they conclude,

> The conspicuous feature of rage lies in the fact that it is an emotion that primes the organism for motor expression. Hate is an attenuated form of rage, and is the emotion toward those who inspire fear and rage. The difficult problem for those who are constantly subject to frustration is how to contain this emotion and prevent its motor expression. The chief motive for the latter is to avoid setting into motion retaliatory aggression.[45]

The effort to control open aggression, in the knowledge that it leads almost inevitably to harsh retaliation, was not always successful. Those who did assert themselves defiantly won themselves a place in black folklore—that of the

44. Ibid., 104.
45. Ibid., 304. Kardiner and Ovesey went to some lengths to secure an unbiased picture of the fantasy life of their subjects. Results of Rorschach Tests and Thematic Apperception Tests (TATS), both standard projective tests, were submitted to a panel for blind evaluation. Here, in an imaginative realm with few constraints, the assessment was that "the bulk of their emotional strivings are organized along the lines of aggression. Their inner existences are turbulent with the urge to hit out, hurt, and destroy." The protocols were frequently the mirror image of the control and measured words required in the public transcript of domination. Here one found much of the released violence and revenge that was otherwise suppressed. Ibid., 322.

"baaaad Nigger"—that is one of both admiration and fearful awe. Admiration, for having acted out the hidden transcript and fearful awe, for having often paid for it with their lives. As we shall see later, the more common folk hero of subordinate groups—blacks included—has historically been the trickster figure, who manages to outwit his adversary and escape unscathed.

Some indirect evidence for the effort required to control anger comes from studies of slavery that indicate the circumstances under which the control might momentarily lapse. Gerald Mullin, in his study of slavery in eighteenth-century Virginia, finds repeated evidence that on those occasions when the masters declared a holiday and provided liquor, intoxicated slaves were said to become "aggressive and hostile, insolent, impudent, bold, stubborn."[46] It was as if alcohol loosened slightly the normal inhibitions against aggressive talk, thereby allowing a portion of the hidden transcript to find its way onto the stage.

Whenever a rare event legitimately allowed the black community to vicariously and publicly savor the physical victory of a black man over a white man, that event became an epoch-making one in folk memory. The fight between Jack Johnson and Jim Jeffries (the "White hope") in 1910 and Joe Louis's subsequent career, which was aided by instant radio transmission of the fights, were indelible moments of reversal and revenge for the black community. "When Johnson battered a white man (Jeffries) to his knees, he was the symbolic black man taking out his revenge on all whites for a lifetime of indignities."[47] Lest such moments be seen purely as a safety valve reconciling blacks to their quotidian world of white domination, there were racial fights in every state in the South and in much of the North immediately after the 1910 fight. The proximate causes varied, but it is clear that in the flush of their jubilation, blacks became momentarily bolder in gesture, speech, and carriage, and this was seen by much of the white community as a provocation, a breach of the public transcript. Intoxication comes in many forms.

Fantasy life among dominated groups is also likely to take the form of *schadenfreude:* joy at the misfortunes of others. This represents a wish for negative reciprocity, a settling of scores when the high shall be brought low

---

46. *Flight and Rebellion: Slave Resistance in 18th Century Virginia*, 100. Wright, *Black Boy,* 162, quotes a drunken black man saying the following couplet: "All these white folks dressed so fine / Their ass-holes smell just like mine." For drink and self-assertion among women, see, for example, Mary Field Belenky et al., *Womens' Ways of Knowing: The Development of Self, Voice, and Mind,* esp. 25.

47. Al-Tony Gilmore, *Bad Nigger!: The National Impact of Jack Johnson,* 5. Knowing the likely impact of showing the film, local and state authorities passed ordinances against its being shown in local theaters. Ibid., 76–82.

and the last shall be first. As such, it is a vital element in any millennial religion. Natural events that seem to conform to this wish—as with the Johnson–Jeffries fight—will typically become the focus of symbolic attention. In the case of the black community in the twentieth century, the sinking of the *Titanic* was such an event. The drowning of large numbers of wealthy and powerful whites (the larger losses in steerage were ignored) in their finery aboard a ship that was said to be unsinkable seemed like a stroke of poetic justice to many blacks. It can be said to have "captured the imagination" of blacks in the nearly literal sense of being a prophetic enactment of their hidden transcript. "Official" songs about the loss of the *Titanic* were sung ironically ("It was *saaad* when the great ship went down . . .). Other songs were composed and sung within the black community. A fragment of one serves to indicate the jubilation at the reversals:

> All the millionaires looked around at Shine [a black
> stoker] say, "Now Shine, oh, Shine, save poor me."
> Say, "We'll make you wealthier than one Shine can be."
> Shine say, "you hate my color and you hate my race."
> Say, "Jump overboard and give those sharks a chase."
> And everybody on board realized they had to die.
> But Shine could swim and Shine could float,
> And Shine could throw his ass like a motorboat.
> Say Shine hit the water with a hell of a splash,
> And everybody wondered if that Black sonovabitch could last.
> Say the Devil looked up from hell and grinned
> Say, "He's a black, *swimming motherfucker*. I think he's gon come on
> in."[48]

At a more cosmic level we have the effort by subordinate groups to call down a curse on the heads of their aggressors. The elaborate curse, such as that cited earlier which Aggy invoked against her white master before emancipation, embodies a far more complex symbolic message than the individual dream of a specific revenge against a specific oppressor or the glee at the victory of a black prizefighter. The curse is an open prayer—even if confined to the backstage audience—embodying an intricate and lovingly ornate vision or revenge. From the perspective of magic, the curse, if properly prepared and

---

48. D. C. Dance, ed., *Shuckin' and Jivin': Folklore from Contemporary Black Americans*, 215–16. The reversals here and elsewhere in the song are multiple. Shine, the black stoker from the hot engine room below decks, swims home to new sexual triumphs while the white passengers on the upper decks plunge with the ship to the cold bottom of the sea.

recited, will bring about the wish it expresses. Long after emancipation, in the 1920s, Zora Neale Hurston, black novelist and anthropologist, collected such an elaborate curse from the Deep South. Its length precludes full quotation, but an excerpt will convey its controlled rage:

> O Man God, I beg that this I ask for my enemies shall
>   come to pass
> That the South wind shall scorch their bodies
>   and make them wither and shall not be tempered to
>   them
> That the North wind shall freeze their blood and numb
>   their muscles.
>
> . . .
>
> I pray that death and disease shall be forever with them
>   and that their crops shall not multiply and their
>   cows, their sheep, their hogs and all their living
>   possessions shall die of starvation and thirst.
>
> . . .
>
> I pray that their friends shall betray them and cause
>   them loss of power, of gold and of silver, and that
>   their enemies shall smite them until they beg for
>   mercy, which shall not be given them.
>
> . . .
>
> O Man God, I ask you for all these things because they
>   have dragged me in the dust and destroyed my good
>   name; broken my heart and caused me to curse the
>   day that I was born. So be it.[49]

Considering the curse in its entirety, it would be difficult to imagine a more comprehensive damnation with all the details visualized. The revenge is explicit in the curse itself, which begins and ends with the invocation of the oppressions for which the curse is just retribution.

To understand the more luxuriant fantasies of the hidden transcript, they must be seen not alone but as the reaction to domination in the public tran-

---

49. Quoted by Alice Walker, "Nuclear Exorcism," 20. Alice Walker began a speech at a nuclear disarmament rally with this curse in an effort to explain why many blacks were not much interested in signing nuclear freeze petitions. Their "hope for revenge" made them look on nuclear destruction brought about by a white-ruled world with equanimity if not malevolent pleasure. One has, she implies, no right expecting civic spiritedness from those whose experience of community has mostly been that of victims.

script. The inventiveness and originality of these fantasies lie in the artfulness with which they reverse and negate a particular domination.[50] No one recognized this more fully than W. E. B. Du Bois, who wrote of the double-consciousness of the American black arising from racial domination: "Such a double life with double thoughts, double duties, and double social classes, must give rise to double words and double ideals, and *tempt the mind to pretense or revolt, to hypocrisy or radicalism.*"[51] Occasionally, Du Bois thought of individual blacks as representing one or the other consciousness. Those given to "revolt" or "radicalism" were those who "stood ready to curse God and die," while those given to "pretense" and "hypocrisy" had forgotten that "life is more than meat and the body more than raiment." We can, I think, more usefully think of the former as the hidden transcript and the latter as the public transcript embodied in the same individual; the former being the site of the rage and anger generated by the necessity of preserving a deferential or obsequious public demeanor despite humiliations. If Du Bois associated the radicalism more with the North and the hypocrisy with the South, this was probably because blacks were somewhat freer to speak their mind in the North.

At this point in the argument, a skeptic might wonder if the official, or public, transcript of power relations serves any purpose at all. Who takes it seriously? We have seen that subordinate groups are generally careful to comport themselves in ways that do not breach the etiquette of power relations determined largely from above. Even then, however, they are quite capable of tactically manipulating appearances for their own ends or using a show of servility to wall off a world beyond direct power relations where sharply divergent views may prevail. Dominant elites, for their part, are unlikely to be completely taken in by outward shows of deference. They expect that there is more here than meets the eye (and ear) and that part or all of the performance is in bad faith. They sense that they are being "jockeyed" even if the harness is of their own devising. If, then, this is all a gigantic shell game in which there is no real dupe, why bother with the pretence? The next chapter addresses this question.

---

50. A standard and much commented on traditional woman's fantasy involves an inversion of dependency in which the dominant male, in this case the object of affection, would be imagined as becoming blind or crippled and thus helpless. The woman entertaining such a fantasy imagines both the harm and the devoted care that would demonstrate both power and affection.

51. "On the Faith of the Fathers," in his *The Souls of Black Folk,* 221–22.

CHAPTER THREE

The Public Transcript as a Respectable Performance

The humbling of inferiors is necessary to the maintenance of social order.

—MADAME DE SÉVIGNÉ

He who is master cannot be free.

—J-J. ROUSSEAU

The Value and Cost of the Public Transcript

RELATIONS OF DOMINATION ARE, at the same time, relations of resistance. Once established, domination does not persist of its own momentum. Inasmuch as it involves the use of power to extract work, production, services, taxes against the will of the dominated, it generates considerable friction and can be sustained only by continuous efforts at reinforcement, maintenance, and adjustment. A good part of the maintenance work consists of the symbolization of domination by demonstrations and enactments of power. Every visible, outward use of power—each command, each act of deference, each list and ranking, each ceremonial order, each public punishment, each use of an honorific or a term of derogation—is a symbolic gesture of domination that serves to manifest and reinforce a hierarchical order. The persistence of any pattern of domination is always problematic, and one may well ask what, given the resistances to it, is required to keep it in place—how many beatings, jailings, executions, secret understandings, bribes, warnings, concessions and, not least, how many public demonstrations of grandeur, exemplary punishment, beneficence, spiritual rectitude, and so forth?

I hope in this chapter to identify first, in a rough and ready way, the political work represented by the public transcript. Affirmation, concealment, euphemization and stigmatization, and finally, the appearance of unanimity seem central to the dramaturgy of the sorts of domination analyzed here. Expanding on the notion of unanimity, I then argue that dominant elites attempt to portray social action in the public transcript as, metaphorically, a parade, thus denying, by omission, the possibility of autonomous social action

45

by subordinates. Inferiors who actually assemble at their own initiative are typically described as mobs or rabble. Finally, I return to the question raised at the end of chapter 2: who, precisely, is the audience for these displays?

Some events are planned essentially as discursive affirmations of a particular pattern of domination. The May Day parade in Red Square is a massive display of hierarchy and power, from the order of precedence on the reviewing stand, to the order in the line of march, to the display of armed might of the USSR, creating an impression of power and solidarity designed to awe party members, citizens, and foreign antagonists alike. Most discursive affirmations are, however, not designed as mere displays. A work party of serfs or slaves in the field under the supervision of an overseer on horseback is both a discursive affirmation of power relations and, of course, the process of material production itself.[1] Small "ceremonies," being much more frequent, are perhaps more telling as daily embodiments of domination and subordination. When the peasant removes his cap in the presence of the landlord or official, when the slave owner assembles his slaves to witness a whipping, when seating at a meal is arranged by position or status, when the last piece of meat on the platter is taken by the father of a family, relations of rank and power have been expressed. Elites naturally have the greatest political investment in such affirmations, since each signals a pyramid of precedence of which they form the apex.

The "silent monitor" introduced by Robert Owen into his textile factory at New Lanark was a striking example of an attempt to make relations of power and judgment continually visible.[2] Believed by Owen to be "the most efficient check upon inferior conduct" at the mill, the silent monitor was a small, four-sided piece of wood with each side colored differently—black, blue, yellow, and white—and fitted with hooks so that one or another side could face outward. Each employee—save the owner-manager, presumably—was furnished with a silent monitor that was conspicuously displayed at the work site. The color showing represented his superior's judgment of his performance on the previous day—black/bad, blue/indifferent, yellow/good, and white/ excellent. Appeals from a supervisor's judgment were allowed but rare. Owen or anyone else passing through the factory was thus afforded an instant visual

---

1. In a more contemporary setting, an election, assuming it is not purely ritualistic, may both provide an occasion for an electorate to choose their leaders while, at the same time, serving as a symbolic affirmation of the legitimacy of democratic forms embodying popular sovereignty. When an opposition movement calls for a boycott of what it believes to be a fraudulent or meaningless election, it presumably does this precisely to undercut the value of the election as a symbolic affirmation.

2. This account is drawn from Owen's autobiography, *The Life of Robert Owen*, 110–12.

representation of each worker's performance yesterday and, by the same token, each worker wore around his or her neck, in effect, the management's judgment. To provide the system with historical depth, the colors were coded by number, and each day's judgment was recorded in what Owen calls "books of character," which were maintained for as long as the employee worked in his mill. The parallels between this scheme and the legendary book of St. Peter, in which one's conduct is faultlessly recorded, were not lost on Owen: "The act of setting down the number in the book of character, *never to be blotted out*, might be likened to the supposed recording angel marking the good and bad deeds of poor human nature."[3] The place of God, in this terrestrial plan, is taken by the factory owner, and the role of sin is replaced by judgments according to one's contribution to production and profits. Owen's system simply gave regular, public form to the assessment by the dominant of the work of their subordinates; the public transcript was made visible and pervasive. The hierarchical structure of this great chain of judgment is nearly Orwellian in its capacity to obliterate other relations and criteria of evaluation.

Imagine, for a moment, the symbolic impact the reversal of Owen's scheme might have. That is, imagine a mill in which each superior wore around his neck a daily evaluation of his conduct imposed by his subordinates and that this principle was extended all the way up to Owen himself. To complete the reversal, of course, one would also have to envision a reversal of sanctioning power as well, inasmuch as a string of bad marks in Owen's books of character was not only a public humiliation, but undoubtedly led to demotion, a pay cut, or even dismissal.

Owen's open display of domination and judgment, like other rituals of power, not only pictured a hierarchy with himself at the apex, but also crowded off the public stage any alternative view of production relationships. Some displays, some rituals, however, are more elaborate and closely regulated than others. This seems particularly the case with any venerable institution whose claim to recognition and domination rests in large part on its continuous and faithful link with the past. Royal coronations, national day celebrations, ceremonies for those fallen in war thus seem to be choreographed in a way that is designed to prevent surprises. The same generalization might be hazarded about the far smaller daily ceremonies we call etiquette or politeness. Rules of etiquette represent, after all, a kind of grammar of social intercourse, imposed by the guardians of taste and decorum, which allows its users to safely navigate the shoals of strangers—especially powerful strangers. But even here, as Pierre Bourdieu notes, the performance is infused with power: "The conces-

3. Ibid., 112, emphasis added.

sion of politeness always contains political concessions. . . . the symbolic taxes due from individuals."[4] The political concession involved is most apparent when a failure to observe the rules of politeness is taken as an act of insubordination.

It is tempting to see displays and rituals of power as something of an inexpensive substitute for the use of coercive force or as an attempt to tap an original source of power or legitimacy that has since been attenuated.[5] Effective display may, by conveying the impression of actual power and the will to use it, economize on the actual use of violence.[6] Imagine, for example, a highly stratified agrarian society in which landlords *recently* had the coercive force to reliably discover and punish any tenants or laborers who defied them (for example, through poaching, rent boycotts, petitions, rebellion). So long as they maintained a bold ritual front, brandishing their weapons, celebrating past episodes of repression, maintaining a stern and determined air—and so long as the visible symbolism of their repression remained in place in the form, say, of jails, constabulary, and open threats—they might exert an intimidating influence all out of proportion to the elite's actual, contemporary power. Very small manifestations of landlord force might suffice to sustain the miasma of power for some time. In the absence of any concrete example of landlord weakness, their power might go long unchallenged.

The successful communication of power and authority is freighted with

---

4. *Outline of a Theory of Practice*, trans. Richard Nice, 85.

5. See, for example, J. H. Elliott's account of the spartan ceremonial of the early Spanish monarchy. Elliott observes that where "the supremacy of the king is taken for granted, political imagery can be studiously understated, and there is no need to deck out the ruler with elaborate allegorical trappings." "This form of understatement may represent the ultimate in political sophistication" (151). "Power and Propaganda in the Spain of Philip IV" in *The Rites of Power: Symbolism, Ritual, and Politics since the Middle Ages,* ed. Sean Wilentz, 145–73.

6. An analogy from my personal experience may help illustrate what I have in mind. If sheep are pastured in a field surrounded by a powerful electric fence they will, at first, blunder into it and experience the painful shock. Once conditioned to the fence, the sheep will graze at a respectful distance. Occasionally, after working on the fence, I have forgotten to switch on the power again for days at a time, during which the sheep continue to avoid it. The fence continues to have the same associations for them despite the fact that the invisible power has been cut. How long the fence would continue to exercise its power in the absence of current is not clear; it would presumably depend on the tenacity of memory and on how often sheep still blundered into the fence. Here is where, I believe, the analogy breaks down. With sheep we may only assume a constant desire to get to the pasture beyond the fence—it *is* generally greener on the other side of the fence since they will have grazed everything on their side. With tenants or sharecroppers we may assume both a constant testing through poaching, pilfering, surreptitious gleaning and harvesting, and a cultural capacity for *collective anger and revenge.* The simple human desire to trespass, to do what is forbidden, *because it is forbidden,* may also be germane. The point, however, is simply that the symbols of power, providing that their potency was once experienced, may continue to exert influence after they may have lost most or all of their effective power.

consequences insofar as it contributes to something like a self-fulfilling prophecy. If subordinates believe their superior to be powerful, the impression will help him impose himself and, in turn, contribute to his actual power. Appearances do matter. Adolf Hitler has provided us with the most chilling version of this insight: "One cannot rule by force alone. True, force is decisive, but it is equally important to have this psychological something which the animal trainer also needs to be master of his beast. They must be convinced that we are the victors."[7] Later, I hope to show why we might doubt the ability of many dominant elites to "naturalize" their power in this way. At this point, however, it is worth noting that the audience for such displays is not only subordinates; elites are also consumers of their own performance.

The members of dominant groups, one supposes, learn the knack of acting with authority and self-assurance in the course of socialization. For hereditary ruling groups the training has typically begun at birth; the aristocrat learns how to act like an aristocrat, the Brahmin like a Brahmin, the man like a man. For those whose position is not inherited, on-the-job training is required to make them convincing in their roles as bosses, professors, military officers, colonial officials. The performance of mastery is ostensibly staged for the impression it makes on subordinates, but it stiffens the spines of the rulers as well. As Orwell observes elsewhere in "Shooting an Elephant," acting like a colonial official in front of the natives can become a powerful incentive:

> With the crowd watching me, I was not afraid in the ordinary sense, *as I would have been if I had been alone.* A white man mustn't be frightened in front of the "natives"; and so, in general, he isn't frightened. The sole thought in my mind was that if anything went wrong those two thousand Burmans would see me pursued, caught, trampled on and reduced to a grinning corpse like that Indian up the hill. And if that happened it was quite probable that some of them would laugh. That would never do.[8]

What Orwell does offstage—what his hidden transcript might be—is one thing, but his comportment in front of the natives must embody the ideas by which colonial domination is publicly justified. In this case, it means using his superior firepower publicly to protect the Burman population and doing it in a manner that suggests such mastery is part of the natural endowment of a colonial official. He has so assimilated the code that he appears to fear the possible derision as much as death.

Being on stage in front of subordinates exerts a powerful influence on the

7. Quoted in Gene Sharpe, *The Politics of Nonviolent Action*, part I of *Power and Struggle*, 43.
8. *Inside the Whale*, 96–97.

conduct and speech of the dominant. They have a collective theater to maintain which often becomes part of their self-definition. Above all, they frequently sense that they perform before an extremely critical audience which waits in eager anticipation for any sign that the actors are losing their touch. Sensitive observers of plantation life in the antebellum South noted that the speech and carriage of slaveholders changed the moment a black servant entered the room.[9] The Dutch in eastern Indonesia noticed that the clans of Torajans who held slaves behaved quite differently from clans that had no slaves: "The To Lage and the To Anda'e, who always had to be mindful of keeping their prestige high with regard to their slaves, had in this way achieved a great deal of self-control, through which they made a more civilized impression on the foreigner than did the To Pebato who, not knowing this pressure, behaved more as they are, let themselves go more."[10] Impressive though the front maintained by ruling groups may be, it is designed as much for what it obscures as for the awe it inspires.

Concealment

Chief of Police: He knew I wore a toupée?
The Bishop: (snickering, to the Judge and the General) He's the only one who doesn't know that everyone knows it.

    —GENET, *The Balcony*

In Genet's *The Screens,* set in Algeria, the Arab farm laborers kill their European overseer when his Arab maid discovers that he has used padding on his stomach and buttocks to make an imposing appearance. Once he is reduced to ordinary proportions, they are no longer intimidated. Preposterous though this parable may seem, it does capture an important truth about the dramaturgy of power.

By controlling the public stage, the dominant can create an appearance that approximates what, ideally, they would want subordinates to see. The deception—or propaganda—they devise may add padding to their stature but it will also hide whatever might detract from their grandeur and authority. Thus, for example, the pastoralist Tutsi, who were feudal lords over the agriculturalist Hutu in Rwanda, pretended publicly that they lived entirely on fluids, from their herds—milk products and blood—and never ate meat.[11]

9. Mullin, *Flight and Rebellion,* 63.
10. N. Adriani and Albert C. Kruyt, *De Barée sprekende torajas van Midden-Celebes,* 2: 96; cited in Patterson, *Slavery and Social Death,* 85.
11. Abner Cohen, *Two-Dimensional Man: An Essay on the Anthropology of Power and Symbolism in Complex Society,* chap. 7; see also Luc de Heusch, "Mythe et société féodale: Le culte de Kubandwa dans le Rwanda traditionel," 133–46.

This story, they believed, made them appear more awesome and disciplined in the eyes of the Hutu. In fact, the Tutsi did like meat and ate it surreptitiously when they could. Whenever their Hutu retainers caught them in flagrante delicto they were said to have sworn them to secrecy. One would be astonished if, in their own quarters, the Hutu did not take great delight in ridiculing the dietary hypocrisy of their Tutsi overlords. On the other hand, it is significant that, at that time, the Hutu would not have ventured a public declaration of Tutsi meat-eating, and the public transcript could proceed *as if* the Tutsi lived by fluids alone.

A similar pattern may be seen in public relations between high-caste Hindus and untouchables. Officially, contact between the two is governed by the elaborate rituals of relative purity and pollution. So long as this public reality is sustained, many Brahmins apparently feel free to violate the code privately. Thus, an untouchable procurer delights in maneuvering his high-caste customers into eating with him and using his clothes, and they appear relatively unperturbed, providing this behavior takes place offstage in a sequestered sphere.[12] It seems to matter little, as with the Tutsi, that these violations of official reality are widely known among subordinates. What matters, apparently, is that such behavior not be openly declared or displayed where it would publicly threaten the official story.[13] Only when contradictions are publicly declared do they have to be publicly accounted for.

In extreme cases, certain facts, though widely known, may never be mentioned in public contexts—for example, forced labor camps in the Soviet Union, until Gorbachev's glasnost. Here it is a question of effacing from the public discourse facts that almost all know. What may develop under such circumstances is virtually a dual culture: the official culture filled with bright euphemisms, silences, and platitudes and an unofficial culture that has its own history, its own literature and poetry, its own biting slang, its own music and poetry, its own humor, its own knowledge of shortages, corruption, and inequalities that may, once again, be widely known but that may not be introduced into public discourse.

Occasionally, it has been argued that official power relations are not so much the symbolic, public component of a general domination as a face-

12. James M. Freeman, *Untouchable: An Indian Life History,* 52–53.
13. See, in this connection, the suggestive analysis of power relations in Java by Ina E. Slamet, who writes, "This theatre-like aspect of Javanese life-style is, however, far from being limited to the lower strata of society; it is often still more outspoken with members of the elite, who have to stick to their ideal role in front of their subjects or inferiors (and often before their conscience, too) hiding the less ideal realities of their lives and aims beneath ritual or quasi-ritual appearance and performance" *Cultural Strategies for Survival: The Plight of the Javanese,* 34.

saving strategy that conceals a loss of power. Susan Rogers applies this logic to gender relations in peasant communities in general and to those in the Lorraine region of France in particular.[14] Cultural tradition as well as the law confers authority and prestige on males, who hold virtually all formal positions, while the power of women in the village is "more effective" but, at the same time, covert and informal. The men, she argues, accept this fact so long as there is no public challenge to their authority and so long as they are still given "credit" for running things. To draw the conclusion, however, that the practical informal realities rendered men's power merely cosmetic and vaporous would be to forget that symbolic concessions are "political concessions" as well. That such women's power can be exercised only behind a veil of proprieties that reaffirm men's official rule as powerholders is a tribute—albeit a left-handed one—to the men's continued control of the public transcript.[15] To exercise power in the name of another party is always to run the risk that the formal titleholder will attempt to reclaim its substance as well as its form.[16]

Euphemisms and Stigmas

If the side of the public transcript we have thus far examined served either to magnify the awe in which the dominant elite is held or to keep certain social facts out of public sight altogether, another side serves cosmetically to beautify aspects of power that cannot be denied. For lack of a better word, I will use Bourdieu's term "euphemization" to capture this process.[17]

14. "Female Forms of Power and the Myth of Male Dominance: A Model of Female/Male Interaction in Peasant Society," 727–56. For a more elaborate theoretical elaboration of this position, see Shirley Ardener, ed., *Perceiving Women*, 1–27.

15. This does not for a moment gainsay the fact that the symbols of official male dominance may be used by women as a strategic resource in gaining effective control of affairs. The fact that the "myth" is still a valuable weapon, even as a veil, says something about its continued efficacy.

16. All forms of domination have something to hide from the public gaze of subordinates. But some forms have more to hide. Speculatively, we might imagine that the more august the public image of ruling groups, the more important it would become to closely sequester and guard an offstage sphere where such "postures are relaxed." Those who inherit their right to rule (e.g., caste, estate, race, gender) or who claim a right to rule based on a spiritual claim are likely to fit this stereotype most closely. Those whose claim to authority is based on the superior performance of a verifiable skill—the production manager, the battlefield general, the athletic coach—have less reason for elaborate, staged presentations, either of their power or of the reciprocal deference of subordinates. In this latter case the gap between the public and hidden transcripts of elites is not so great, and, for that reason, its exposure to public view is not so dangerous. See, for example, Randall Collins, *Conflict Sociology: Toward an Explanatory Science*, 118–19, 157.

17. *Outline of a Theory of Practice*, 191. For a brilliant analysis of the social function of euphemisms by powerful groups, see Murray Edelman, "The Political Language of the 'Helping Professions,'" 295–310.

Whenever one encounters euphemism in language it is a nearly infallible sign that one has stumbled on a delicate subject.[18] It is used to obscure something that is negatively valued or would prove to be an embarrassment if declared more forthrightly. Thus we have a host of terms, at least in Anglo-American culture, designed to euphemize that place where urination and defecation take place: john, restroom, comfort station, water closet, lavatory, loo, and so on. The imposition of euphemisms on the public transcript plays a similar role in masking the many nasty facts of domination and giving them a harmless or sanitized aspect. In particular, they are designed to obscure the use of coercion. A mere list of euphemisms that come to mind together with more blunt, noncosmetic alternative terms will amply illustrate their political use:

pacification for armed attack and occupation
calming for confinement by straightjacket
capital punishment for state execution
reeducation camps for prison for political opponents
trade in ebony wood for eighteenth-century traffic in slaves.[19]

The first term in each pair is imposed by the dominant on public discourse either to put a benign face on an activity or fact that would morally offend many. As a result, more graphic, ordinary language descriptions are frowned upon and often driven from the realm of official discourse.

At every occasion on which the official euphemism is allowed to prevail over other, dissonant versions, the dominant monopoly over public knowledge is publicly conceded by subordinates. They may, of course, have little choice in the matter, but so long as the monopoly is not publicly contested, it never has to "explain itself," it has nothing to "answer for." Take, for example, the commonplace of unemployment in capitalist economies. When employers dismiss workers, they are likely to euphemize their action by saying something like, "We had to let them go." In one short phrase they manage to deny their own agency as employers, implying that they had no choice in the matter, and to convey the impression that the workers in question were mercifully re-leased, rather like dogs straining on their leashes. The workers who are now out of work are likely to use more graphic verbs: "They fired me," "They gave me the axe," "They sacked me," and might well make the subject of their sentence, "those bastards . . ." Linguistic forms depend very much on whose

18. I have benefited here from Robin Lakoff's discussion in *Language and Women's Place*, 20 ff.
19. Pierre H. Boulle, "In Defense of Slavery: Eighteenth-Century Opposition to Abolition and the Origins of a Racist Ideology in France," in *History from Below: Studies in Popular Protest and Popular Ideology in Honour of George Rudé*, ed. Frederick Krantz, 230.

ox is being gored. When we hear terms such as *reduction in force, retrenchment, redundancy,* and *letting people go* we can be fairly confident about who is speaking. But, so long as this euphemistic description is left to stand, it remains the public description.

That acts of description should be politically loaded hardly comes as a surprise. The question that remains is the extent to which dominant descriptions monopolize the public transcript. In the Malay village I studied, poor villagers who harvested paddy for their well-off neighbors received, in addition to their wage, a bonus in grain. The bonus had a great deal to do with a shortage of harvest labor at the time, but the gift was *publicly* described by the well-off as *zakat.* Inasmuch as *zakat* is a form of Islamic tithe or gift that enhances the claim of the giver to a reputation for pious generosity, it was in the interest of rich farmers to describe it in this fashion. Behind the backs of wealthy villagers, the harvest laborers considered the bonus an integral part of their wage, as no more than what they were entitled to as compensation for their work. The balance of power in the village, however, was sufficiently skewed against the harvesters that they abstained, out of prudence, from publicly contesting the self-serving definition applied by the rich. By letting it pass, by not contradicting its use, by behaving publicly as if they accepted this description, the poor villagers contributed—one might say wittingly—to the monopoly of public discourse exercised by the village elite.

Euphemisms in the broad sense I am using the term—the self-interested tailoring of descriptions and appearances by dominant powerholders—is not confined to language. It may be seen in gestures, architecture, ritual actions, public ceremonies, any other actions in which the powerful may portray their domination as they wish. Taken together they represent the dominant elite's flattering self-portrait.

In this case as in others, the portrait is not without its political costs since such disguises can become a political resource for subordinates. Ruling groups can be called upon, as we shall see in some detail, to live up to their own idealized presentation of themselves to their subordinates.[20] If they define a wage payment as an act of good-hearted charity, they can be condemned publicly for hard-heartedness when they fail to make "gifts." If the czar is portrayed as powerful and beneficent to his serfs, he can be called upon to waive his serfs' taxes in a time of dearth. If a "people's democracy" claims to

20. So, of course, can individuals be called upon in this sense to put up or shut up. Graham Greene's *The Comedians* focuses precisely on this issue. Its not-quite-a-charlatan antihero is forced to choose between acting bravely in accord with his bragging and admitting finally, before the woman he loves, that he is a fraud. Graham Greene, *The Comedians.*

exist to promote the interest of the working class, it cannot easily explain why it is breaking strikes and jailing proletarians. To be sure, there are situations in which merely announcing a hypocrisy is to take a mortal risk. The point, however, is that the masks domination wears are, under certain conditions, also traps.

Finally, the power to call a cabbage a rose and to make it stick in the public sphere implies the power to do the opposite, to stigmatize activities or persons that seem to call into question official realities. There is a pattern to much of this stigmatization. Rebels or revolutionaries are labeled bandits, criminals, hooligans in a way that attempts to divert attention from their political claims. Religious practices that meet with disapproval might similarly be termed heresy, satanism, or witchcraft. Small traders may be called petty bourgeois bacilli. Foucault has shown with great force how, with the rise of the modern state, this process is increasingly medicalized and made impersonal. Terms like *deviance, delinquency,* and *mental illness* appear to remove much of the personal stigma from the labels but they can succeed, simultaneously, in marginalizing resistance in the name of science.

Unanimity

A fourth function of the public transcript is to create the appearance of unanimity among the ruling groups and the appearance of consent among subordinates. In any highly stratified agrarian society there is usually more than a grain of truth to the former claim. Feudal lords, the gentry, slave masters, and Brahmins, for example, partake in a cultural integration, reinforced by marriage alliances, social networks, and office, which extends at least to the provincial if not the national level. This social integration is likely to be reflected in dialect, ritual practices, cuisine, and entertainment. Popular culture, by contrast, is rather more locally rooted in terms of dialect, religious practices, dress, consumption patterns, and family networks.[21] Beyond the facts of the matter, however, it would seem that most ruling groups take great pains to foster a public image of cohesion and shared belief. Disagreements, informal discussions, off-guard commentary are kept to a minimum and, whenever possible, sequestered out of sight—in teachers' rooms, elite dinner

21. The most persuasive empirical demonstrations of this point I have encountered may be found in McKim Marriott, "Little Communities in an Indigenous Civilization," in *Village India: Studies in the Little Community,* ed. McKim Marriott, and G. William Skinner, *Marketing and Social Structure in Rural China.*

parties, European clubs in the colonies, officers' clubs, mens' clubs and myriads of more informal but protected sites.[22]

The advantages of keeping discord out of sight are obvious enough. If the dominant are at odds with one another in any substantial way, they are, to that degree, weakened, and subordinates may be able to exploit the divisions and renegotiate the terms of subordination. An effective facade of cohesion thus augments the apparent power of elites, thereby presumably affecting the calculations that subordinates might make about the risks of noncompliance or defiance. In the early nineteenth century, Czar Alexander I took care to make certain that the need to discipline members of the nobility was satisfied in a way that did not imply that the czar was on the side of the serfs against their owners. A secret circular was sent to governors directing them to begin an undercover investigation to identify those nobles who had been excessively cruel and inhumane. The czar was aware that any symbolic gains derived from his paternalistic pose would, if made public, be far outweighed by the provocation to defiance that the apparent disunity among elites would set in motion.[23]

It does not follow that public activity between dominant and subordinate is nothing but a kind of tableau of power symbolizing hierarchy. A great deal of communication—especially in contemporary societies—does not materially affect power relations. It is nonetheless true that under nearly any form of domination, those in power make a remarkably assiduous effort to keep disputes that touch on their claim to power out of the public eye. Their control is further enhanced if the impression of unanimity extends beyond themselves to subordinates as well. We might think of such displays as the visual and aural component of a hegemonic ideology—the ceremonial that gives euphemization an air of plausibility. If the sharecropping tenants of a large landowner are restive over higher rents, he would rather see them individually and perhaps make concessions than to have a public confrontation. The importance of *avoiding any public display of insubordination* is not simply derived from a strategy of divide and rule; open insubordination represents a dramatic contradiction of the smooth surface of euphemized power.[24]

22. The striking exceptions to the effort—not always successful—to present a united front are democratic forms of conflict management. Here too, however, only certain forms of disagreement are generally aired before the general electorate, and smoke-filled rooms are used to transact business that would clash with public rhetoric.

23. Peter Kolchin, *Unfree Labor: American Slavery and Russian Serfdom,* 143. The czar's problem was a common one for rulers: how to restrain members of the ruling elite whose conduct threatened revolt from below without, at the same time, actually fostering sedition by revealing a lack of solidarity and common purpose.

24. The exception to this generalization occurs when elites may wish to provoke a confrontation with subordinates because they feel thay have the resources to win in a showdown and thereby realign the terms of subordination in their favor.

The traditional crime of lèse-majesté in this context becomes a serious business indeed. Patterns of domination can, in fact, accommodate a reasonably high level of practical resistance so long as that resistance is not publicly and unambiguously acknowledged. Once it is, however, it requires a public reply if the symbolic status quo is to be restored.

The symbolic restoration of power relations may be seen in the importance accorded to public apologies. Erving Goffman, in his careful analysis of the social microorder, has examined the purposes of public apologies.[25] The subordinate, who has publicly violated the norms of domination, announces by way of a public apology that he dissociates himself from the offense and reaffirms the rule in question. He publicly accepts, in other words, the judgment of his superior that this is an offense and thus, implicitly, the censure or punishment that follows from it. The point has little to do with the sincerity of the retraction and disavowal, since what the apology repairs is the public transcript of apparent compliance. The taxes may be purely symbolic, but they are heavy for those on whom they are imposed. Accounts of slavery in the antebellum South emphasize how much attention was paid to ritual requests for forgiveness by slaves about to be punished for insubordination. Only after "humbling himself" to his master, and before other assembled slaves, was a victim's punishment typically lightened.[26]

In the twentieth century, perhaps the most extensive use of public apologies and confessions—followed typically by execution—was made in the late 1930s in the Stalinist purges and show trials. Doctrinal unanimity was so highly valued it was not enough for the party to crush dissent; the victims had to make a public display of their acceptance of the party's judgment. Those who were unwilling to make an open confession, thereby repairing the symbolic fabric before sentencing, simply disappeared.[27]

From the perspective of a subordinate, of course, an apology may more often represent a comparatively economical means of escaping the most severe consequences of an offense against the dominant order. It may simply be

25. *Relations in Public,* 113 ff.

26. See, for example, Rhys Isaac, "Communication and Control: Authority Metaphors and Power Contests on Colonel Landon Carter's Virginia Plantation, 1752–1778," in *Rites of Power,* ed. Sean Wilentz, 275–302. In Melville's remarkable story "Benito Cereno," the Spanish captain, pretending to be master of a slave-crew, makes an apology the condition for removing shackles: "Say but one word, 'pardon,' and your chains shall be off." Herman Melville, "Benito Cereno," in *Billy Budd and Other Stories,* 183.

27. Milan Kundera writes in *The Joke* about a similar insistence on self-indictment in Czechoslovakia in the mid-1950s. "I had refused to play the role played at hundreds of meetings, hundreds of disciplinary proceedings, and, before long, at hundreds of court cases; the role of the accused who accuses himself and by the very ardor of his self-accusation (his complete identification with the accusers), begs for mercy," 168.

a tactic cynically employed under duress. Once again, however, it is the show of compliance that is important and that is insisted on. Remorse, apologies, asking forgiveness, and generally, making symbolic amends are a more vital element in almost any process of domination than punishment itself. A criminal who expresses remorse at his crime typically earns, in exchange for his petty contribution to the repair of the symbolic order, a reduction in punishment. Similarly, of course, with the "misbehaving" child who says he is sorry and promises never to do it again. What all these actors offer is a *show of discursive affirmation from below*, which is all the more valuable since it contributes to the impression that the symbolic order is willingly accepted by its least advantaged members.

To see why a flow of symbolic taxes is of such vital importance to the moral economy of domination, we have only to consider the symbolic consequences of a boycott of symbolic taxes. If the courts are filled with truculent and defiant criminals, if slaves stubbornly refuse to humble themselves, if children take their punishment sullenly and show no remorse whatever, their behavior amounts to a sign that domination is nothing more than tyranny—nothing more than the successful exercise of power against subordinates too weak to overthrow it but proud enough to defy it symbolically. To be sure, dominant elites would prefer a willing affirmation of their norms; but if this is not available they will extract, whenever they can, at least the simulacrum of a sincere obedience.

Parades vs. Crowds: Authorized and Unauthorized Gatherings

Nothing conveys the public transcript more as the dominant would like it to seem than the formal ceremonies they organize to celebrate and dramatize their rule. Parades, inaugurations, processions, coronations, funerals provide ruling groups with the occasion to make a spectacle of themselves in a manner largely of their own choosing. The examination of the structure of such ceremonies is something of a privileged pathway to the "official mind."

A cursory look, in the manner of Michel Foucault, at the fairly recent tenth anniversary celebration, in December 1985, of the "liberation" of Laos by the Laotian Communist party (Pathet Lao) can tell us something about the self-dramatization of elites.[28] The parade itself was a vastly scaled down and shabbier Vientiane version of the May Day ceremony in Moscow's Red

28. I am much indebted to Grant Evans, University of Hong Kong, for an account of this event, which he attended, and for the acute observations about Laotian agricultural cooperatives that follow.

Square before the Kremlin. Weeks before the celebration steps were taken to ensure a smooth performance; curfews were imposed, banners were hung, buildings were repainted, the parade ground near the important Buddhist shrine of That Luang was recemented, and those having no legal residence or legitimate business in the city were arrested. A modest, "appointed" crowd of cadres and employees was issued placards and told to assemble at 4 A.M. on the appointed morning. As in Red Square, there was a reviewing stand and the dignitaries were arranged in strict order of importance—the Lao secretary general, Kaysone, in the middle, flanked by the visiting heads of state from Vietnam, Le Duan, and Kampuchea, Heng Samrin, then by Prince Souphan-nouvoung and so on in deliberate order through the Lao leadership and envoys from other socialist states.

Marching past, again as in Red Square, were first the military, by service, then the police, the uniformed Lao workers (not the peasantry, mind you, but the fictitious Lao proletariat), minority women militia, motorbike police and military—all of the foregoing, incidentally, wearing white gloves. Next came the obligatory tanks, military hardware, and a flyover by the few airworthy MiG jets of the minuscule Lao air force. Veterans, scouts with red scarves, Lao women dancers, units of the Women's Association, and floats from each ministry brought up the rear. As the obligatory speeches about the glorious history of the party, socialist construction, the tasks ahead, and international socialist solidarity wore on, the equally obligatory crowd leaned more heavily on the poles of their obligatory placards. It is plausible to assume that the entire affair is an attempt to copy, along the banks of the Mekong, what the party chiefs remember from similar "high church" rituals in Hanoi, Moscow, and perhaps even Beijing.

Perhaps the most remarkable thing about this awesome (for Laos at least) display of cohesion and power is that virtually no one comes to see it save those on the reviewing stand and those marching past. The show is all actors and no audience. More accurately, the actors are the audience; this is a ritual that the Laotian party-state organizes for itself. Its purpose, one assumes, is to suggest to the participants that they are a legitimate part of a larger fraternity of communist states with the control, discipline, purpose, and might which that implies. The ceremony serves to link them to Marx and Lenin and to Marxist-Leninist states in much the same way the celebration of any provincial mass links its celebrants to Christ and the apostles and to Rome. These links apparently hold little meaning for the civilian population of Vientiane, who had gathered informally by the thousands a few days earlier in the same place for the most popular Buddhist festival of the year. This self-assembled crowd was frisked before it entered the temple grounds.

Ritualistic activity of this kind, though it is far from being empty ritual, might hardly be worth our notice if this were its only manifestation. The metaphor of the parade, however, appears to permeate other aspects of Laotian official life such as the structure of agricultural production. In a Marxist state worthy of the name it is de rigueur that units of cultivation be collective farms or, failing that, state-sponsored cooperatives. This presents certain obstacles in Laos, where wet rice cultivation has been carried out on quite small household farms and where upland cultivation is mostly of the shifting, slash-and-burn variety. While the backwardness of Lao agriculture and, particularly, of Lao agriculturalists is openly deplored by lower echelon Lao bureaucrats, the latter are under pressure to show progress toward the collectivization of agriculture. Responding to that pressure, they produce agricultural cooperatives for official consumption in much the same way the Potemkin produced charming villages and peasants for Catherine the Great. The actual social organization of cultivation, apparently, remains essentially unchanged, but cooperatives have been created by sleight of hand reinforced by ersatz account books, officeholders, and cooperative activities. What is not clear is how far the sleight of hand reaches. It is reasonable to assume that lower functionaries and villagers are coconspirators in this effort to please their demanding and possibly dangerous superiors. It is harder to determine, however, the extent to which their superiors condone phantom cooperatives—either to please their foreign benefactors or because nothing beyond phantom cooperatives is achievable or both—or actually believe they are functioning units.

We have at the very least, then, two public rituals of domination that are very much at odds with Laotian realities. The parade is the most obvious example. By its very nature a parade of this kind is a living tableau of centralized discipline and control. Its logic assumes, by definition, a unified intelligence at the center which directs all movements of the "body" or, perhaps more appropriate, a Leninist vanguard party which provides the thinking brain for the working class. The leaders stand above and to the side while, at their direction, their subordinates, ranged in order of precedence from most to least, marching in the same direction and in time to the same music, pass by in review. In its entirety, the scene visibly and forcibly conveys unity and discipline under a single purposeful authority, a society that is virtually conjured into existence by the will of its Leninist parade marshall. All is conducted with the high seriousness typical of most state rituals.[29] Any

29. Not all parades are state rituals organized from the top, although all parades imply a hierarchical order. Contrast the Laotian example with the carnival parade in Romans in the late

evidence of the disorder, divisions, indiscipline, and of everyday informality is banished from the public stage.

Ideologically, at least for the Laotian ruling elite, the parade may be convincing. Insofar as an ideology contains, among other things, a vision of how things should be, the parade is an effective idealization of the desired relation between the Central Committee and the society it aspires to direct. It fills, with symbolic display, the considerable chasm between the recalcitrant social and political realities of contemporary Laos and the promise of its new proletarian ideology, just as the phantom cooperatives fill the gap between how the land is actually cultivated and how it should, by the book, be cultivated.

Parades and processions of the kind described are the ultimate in *authorized* gatherings of subordinates. Rather like iron filings aligned by a powerful magnet, subordinates are gathered in an arrangement and for purposes determined by their superiors. The political symbolism of most forms of personal domination carries with it the implicit assumption that subordinates gather only when they are authorized to do so from above. Any *unauthorized* gathering, as we shall see, has therefore been seen as potentially threatening. Even a friend of the New Model Army in the midst of the English Revolution was at pains to distinguish "the people" on their own from "the people" under orders: "The people in gross are but a monster, a rude unwieldy bulk of no use, but here they are gathered together into one excellent life. . . . For an army has in it all government and parts of government, under justice, etc., in highest virtue."[30]

If we consider the official description of feudalism, slavery, serfdom, the caste system, and the ubiquitous patron–client structures of leadership described by anthropologists, they all purport to be based on a network of dyadic (two-person) reciprocities always articulated vertically. Thus feudalism is represented as an exchange of goods and services between individual lords and their vassals, slavery is represented as an individual relationship between master and bondsman implying ownership and paternalism on one side and work and service on the other, and the caste system as a series of contracts

sixteenth century, about which Le Roy Ladurie has written. The parade was a precise gradation of status, historically negotiated, beginning with the representative of the king at the head and the lowliest commoners at the rear. In this case, craftsmen and tradesmen refused to participate on the usual terms. The potential for conflict in municipal ceremonies of this kind was, in general terms, noted by Jean Bodin: "Every procession of all the ranks and all the professions carries the risk of conflicts of priority and the possibility of popular revolts." "Let us not overdo . . . ceremonies of this kind." Quoted in Emmanuel Le Roy Ladurie, *Carnival in Romans*, trans. Mary Feeney, 201.

30. Christopher Hill, "The Poor and the People in Seventeenth-Century England," in *History from Below*, ed. Frederick Krantz, 84.

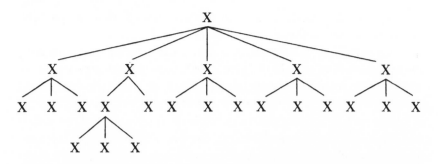

between partners of different castes to exchange ritual and material goods and services. The point of these highly partisan—official transcript—glosses on hierarchy is simply that they assume, contrary to the typical facts of the matter, that there are no horizontal links among subordinates and that, therefore, if they are to be assembled at all it must be by the lord, patron, or master, *who represents the only link joining them.* Without the hierarchy and authority that knits them into a unit, they are mere atoms with no social existence. Like Marx's view of the French peasantry in *The Eighteenth Brumaire,* subordinates are nothing but potatoes in a sack. Thus the social order envisioned by the public transcript of each of these forms of domination is purely hierarchical and resembles the typical diagram of patron-client relations (see accompanying figure). In fact, of course, many horizontal linkages between subordinates, apart from their common subordination, were tacitly acknowledged by ruling groups—for example, village traditions, ethnicity, religious sect, dialect, and other cultural practices. They had, however, no place in the official picture, which acknowledged only social action by subordinates originating with the will of a superordinate. The official rituals like the parade or procession, gatherings to receive instruction or to witness punishment, authorized festivities, and the more banal assemblies for work are precisely the kinds of public collective action foreseen by the official account.[31]

31. Readers who are familiar with Foucault's *Discipline and Punish* will notice the similarities between his analysis of military parades, close-order drill, and the prison and my analysis of the Lao parade. Without the unique eye of Foucault, I could scarcely have taken the perspective I have. As Foucault notes, "Discipline, however, had its own type of ceremony. It was not the triumph but the review, the 'parade,' an ostentatious form of the examination. In it the subjects were presented as 'objects' to the observer of a power that was manifested only by its gaze" (188). The notion of an atomized, subsumed subject whose place is determined by a central authority is Foucault's. My analysis departs from Foucault in that I am largely concerned with structures of *personal* domination, such as serfdom and slavery, rather than with the impersonal, "scientific," disciplinary forms of the modern state that preoccupy him. More important, I am interested in how these idealizations of domination are thwarted by practical forms of resistance. In this connection, see chapters 4–8.

Since no unauthorized *public* gathering of subordinates is imagined or legitimized by the official account, it follows that any such activity is frowned upon. More than that, it is commonly seen as an implicit threat to domination. What possible reason, other than their subordination, could possibly serve to bring them together? The assumption that any such gatherings would lead, unless dispersed, to insubordination was not often mistaken, since the gathering itself was seen as a form of insubordination. One has only to imagine a feudal lord noticing a large number of his serfs advancing, unsummoned, toward his manor, a large number of beggars (masterless men by definition) moving through the countryside, or even a large crowd of factory workers gathered near the plant manager's office to recognize the possibilities. The neutral terms *assembly* and *gathering* I have been using here are, on such occasions, likely to be replaced by charged terms such as *mob* by those who implicitly feel threatened. We might well define *gathering* more broadly to include virtually any act that presupposed an unauthorized coordination of subordinates qua subordinates. In this respect, the petition to the ruler or lord—usually for redress of grievances—no matter how respectfully worded was implicitly a sign of autonomous collective action from below and, hence, troubling. Peasants, rulers seem to have reasoned, should state grievances only when explicitly invited to by their superiors, as in the *cahiers de doléances* before the meeting of the Estates General. In Tokugawa Japan, the presentation of a petition to the ruler for redress of peasant grievances, implying autonomous organization among subordinates, was itself a capital crime; the burial sites of those village heads who paid for such daring with their lives became places of pilgrimage and folk veneration for the peasantry. Petitioning the czar was also an established tradition among Russian serfs. What concerned officials in the Ministry of Internal Affairs most, however, was not the petitioning per se but rather the occasion it provided for seditious assembly. The "unwarranted absence [from the estate] of a whole crowd to present a petition against a *pomeschik*," [gentry landowner] the minister warned, "already constitutes the beginning of disorder and *volnenie* [rebellion]."[32]

One way of minimizing unauthorized gatherings of subordinates was to forbid them. The plantocracies of North America and the West Indies regulated very closely the circumstances in which their slaves could assemble. In the United States, "gatherings of five or more slaves without the presence of a white observer were universally forbidden."[33] No doubt this was a frequently violated regulation, but it is nevertheless indicative that five or more slaves

32. Kolchin, *Unfree Labor,* 299.
33. Raboteau, *Slave Religion,* 53.

together without white supervision were, prima facie, defined as a threat to public order. Authorized gatherings were also suspect and required regulation. The members and clergymen of a black congregation in Savannah in 1782 were whipped for meeting after dark and were freed only on the condition that they worship between sunrise and sunset. Other black clerics, though their sermons were not seditious in any way, could preach only when observed by a white cleric, who would report any deviation from Christianity as it was understood by slaveholders. Holidays, because they lacked the structure of work and because they brought together large numbers of slaves, always bore watching. Thus, one observer of the plantation system could note, "Holidays are days of idleness . . . in which the slaves assemble together in alarming crowds for purposes of dancing, feasting or merriment."[34] Precisely because Sundays, burial rites, holiday dances, and carnivals brought together so many slaves, there was an effort to control them. In the West Indies this meant, among other things, limiting the number of Sunday services a slave might attend.[35] The least dangerous assemblies of slaves were, therefore, small, supervised, work parties during the daylight hours; the most dangerous were large, unauthorized, apart from work, and at night.

Lest we conclude that apprehension about gatherings of subordinates is confined to these systems where unfreedom is legally enforced, we may recall that many of the same apprehensions were experienced by public officials and employers about the working class in the nineteenth century. The locale might be strikingly different, but the logic of "atomization" and surveillance in early nineteenth-century Paris was similar to that of the slaveholding South:

> The interpretation [of the relation between freedom of speech for workers and revolution] was simple. If workers were allowed to congregate together, they would compare injustices, scheme, conspire, and foment revolutionary intrigues. Thus laws like those of 1838 in France came into being which forbade public discussion between work peers, and a system of spies was set up in the city to report on where the little molecules of laborers congregated—in which cafés, at which times.[36]

The working-class café, like the "hush arbors" of the slaves, became the privileged social sites for the hidden transcript even if they were often penetrated by police agents. A good portion of the exhilarating sense of release experienced by the working class in 1848 was due to the newfound ability to speak one's mind, publicly, without fear.

34. Ibid., 66. See 139–44 for the regulation of Christian services.
35. Michael Craton, *Testing the Chains*, 258.
36. Richard Sennett and Jonathan Cobb, *The Fall of Public Man* 214.

The implicit threat the dominant see in autonomous assemblies of their inferiors is not a form of ideologically induced paranoia. There is every reason to believe that such gatherings are, in fact, an incitement to boldness by subordinates. When, for example, the *Ad Dharm,* which preaches solidarity among untouchables in the Punjab, first organized mass meetings in the districts, the effect was electric—for higher castes and for the untouchables themselves. To high-caste observers it was dramatic and provocative evidence that untouchables could assemble without the permission or direction of their social betters.[37] From the description given it is clear that the impact of such mass meetings was in large part visual and symbolic.[38] What was said was less important than the stunning show of force that the mere congregation of untouchables *as untouchables* had on all concerned. If untouchables could show such coordination, discipline, and collective strength, what prevented them from turning these skills to collective struggle against domination? The powerful semiotic of power and purpose here is not lost on subordinate groups. Jean Comaroff, in her sensitive study of the Zion Christian Church among the Tswana people of South Africa, emphasizes the great symbolic importance the huge annual Passover gathering has for the faithful. The fact alone that this church movement, the largest black religious movement in South Africa, can bring together many thousands from all over the country is a demonstration of mass power that is as implicitly threatening to the state as it is sustaining to its black adherents.[39]

Large, autonomous gatherings of subordinates are threatening to domination because of the license they promote among normally disaggregated inferiors. Much later we will want to examine the relationship between an assembly of subordinates and the hidden transcript. Here it is sufficient to note how subordinates might feel emboldened by the act of massing itself. First, there is the visual impact of collective power that a vast assembly of subordinates conveys both to its own number and to its adversaries. Second, such an assembly provides each participant with a measure of anonymity or

37. A small but significant illustration of the provocation that subordinates represent when they decide to collectively discuss their subordination among themselves is provided by Sara Evans in her account of the growth of feminist politics in the New Left in the 1960s. When many women left the main group at a Students for a Democratic Society (SDS) conference to discuss sexism in SDS, making it clear that men were not welcome to join them, the effect was explosive. Both men and women in SDS understood that a watershed had been reached. *Personal Politics: The Roots of Women's Liberation in the Civil Rights Movement and the New Left,* 156–62.

38. Jürgensmeyer, *Religion as Social Vision,* chap. 10.

39. Jean Comaroff, *Body of Power, Spirit of Resistance: The Culture and History of a South African People,* 238–39. Another example of the political impact of unauthorized mass meetings is the annual pilgrimage to the shrine of the Virgin of Czestochowa in Poland and the importance it came to have after the trade union Solidarity was banned.

disguise, thereby lowering the risk of being identified personally for any action or word that comes from the group.[40] Finally, if something is said or done that is the open expression of a shared hidden transcript, the collective exhilaration of finally declaring oneself in the face of power will compound the drama of the moment. There is power in numbers, and it is far more significant than the now long-discredited sociology that treated crowds under the rubric of mere hysteria and mass psychopathology.[41]

Who Is the Audience for the Performance?

My business was to see that they [slaves for sale] were placed in those situations before the arrival of purchasers, and I have often set them to dancing when their cheeks were wet with tears.

—WILLIAM WELLS BROWN, ex-slave

Let us return to the parade, or the dramatization of hierarchy and authority seen more or less from the angle of ruling elites. Elites may give a credible performance of authority, and subordinates, a credible performance of subservience. In the former case a convincing performance is hardly problematic inasmuch as elites are likely to subscribe to the values that underwrite their privileges. In the latter case, however, we cannot assume that the disprivileged are enthusiastic actors in rituals that mark their inferiority. In fact, their participation is perfectly compatible with cynical disbelief. Any combination of fear, expediency, and what Marx aptly called "the dull compulsion of economic relations"—that is, the need to make a living—is quite sufficient to recruit the required cast for a passable performance.

If rituals of subordination are not convincing in the sense of gaining the consent of subordinates to the terms of their subordination, they are, I think, convincing in other ways. They are, for example, a means of demonstrating that, like it or not, a given system of domination is stable, effective, and here to stay. Ritual subservience reliably extracted from inferiors signals quite literally that there is no realistic choice other than compliance. When combined with the exemplary punishment of the occasional act of defiance, the effective display of compliance may achieve a kind of *dramatization* of power relations that is not to be confused with ideological hegemony in the sense of active

40. This is not at all the same as the assertion that an individual in a crowd is leaving moral reasoning behind because he no longer has to assume individual moral responsibility for his acts.
41. Gustav LeBon, *La psychologie des foules*. The revisionist school is led by George Rudé. See his *The Crowd in History: A Survey of Popular Disturbances in France and England, 1730–1848*, and the earlier *The Crowd in the French Revolution*. For a critique that claims Rudé has "bourgeoisified" the crowd too much by obscuring the importance of anger and rage, see R. C. Cobb, *The Police and the People: French Popular Protest, 1789–1820*.

consent. One may curse such domination—in this case preferably offstage—
but one will nevertheless have to accommodate oneself to its hard reality. The
effect of reinforcing power relations in this way may be, behaviorally, nearly
indistinguishable from behavior that arises from willing consent.

Here the distinction between the public transcript of the slave and that of
the master becomes crucial. The slave, after all, knows more or less what
attitude and values lie behind his own bowing and scraping and, if less reliably,
what lies behind the performance of other slaves in his circle. What he cannot
know with anything like the same reliability is the degree of power, self-
confidence, unity, and determination of his master or of masters in general.
The calculations that the slaves make daily in the course of adjusting their
behavior to the realities of power rest, in part, on their estimate of the cohesion
and purposefulness of their masters. So long as subordinate groups cannot
reliably and fully penetrate the hidden transcript of the powerful, they are
obliged to make inferences from the text of power presented to them in the
public transcript. There is every reason, then, for the dominant to police the
public transcript in order to censure any indication of division or weakness
that would appear to improve the odds favoring those ready to stiffen their
resistance to domination or to risk outright defiance. Those renegade members of the dominant elite who ignore the standard script—Brahmins who
publicly defy the regulations of caste purity, plantation owners who spoke
sympathetically of abolition—present a danger far greater than their minuscule numbers might imply. Their public, if petty, dissent breaks the naturalization of power made plausible by a united front.[42]

If much of the purpose of the public transcript of domination is not to gain
the agreement of subordinates but rather to awe and intimidate them into a
durable and expedient compliance, what effect does it have among the dominant themselves? It may well be that insofar as the public transcript represents
an attempt to persuade or indoctrinate anyone, the dominant are the subject of
its attentions. The public transcript as a kind of self-hypnosis within ruling
groups to buck up their courage, improve their cohesion, display their power,
and convince themselves anew of their high moral purpose? The possibility is
not all that farfetched. It is precisely what Orwell was referring to when he
noted how the image of the brave sahib (refracted through the fear of derision)
gave him the pluck to face the elephant (see chapter 1). If autosuggestion

42. This is why a defection among elites has so much more impact on power relations than the
same phenomenon (e.g., rate-busters, prison trusties) among subordinates. Normatively, the elite
renegade cannot be explained in the same terms as the subordinate renegade. It is easier to explain
why a slave might want to be an overseer with all its privileges than to explain why a master would
openly favor emancipation or abolition.

works with individuals it might well characterize one of the purposes of group ritual as well.

Any argument claiming that the ideological efforts of ruling elites are directed at *convincing* subordinates that their subordination is just must confront a good deal of evidence suggesting that it often fails to achieve its purpose. Catholicism, for example, is the logical candidate for the hegemonic ideology of feudalism. But it is abundantly clear that the folk Catholicism of the European peasants, far from serving ruling interests, was practiced and interpreted in ways that often defended peasant property rights, contested large differences in wealth, and even provided something of a millennial ideology with revolutionary import. Rather than being a "general anesthesia," folk Catholicism was a provocation—one that, together with its adherents in the lower clergy, provided the ideological underpinning for countless rebellions against seigneurial authority. For this reason, among others, Abercrombie and his colleagues have persuasively argued that the ideological effect of Catholicism was rather to help unify the feudal ruling class, define its purpose, and create a family mortality that would hold property together.[43] This perspective on religious ideology is very much in keeping with Max Weber's analysis of doctrinal religion generally:

> This universal phenomenon [the belief by the privileged that their good fortune is just] is rooted in certain psychological patterns. When a man who is happy compares his position with that of one who is unhappy, he is not content with the fact of his happiness, but desires something more, namely *the right to his happiness*, the consciousness that he has earned his good fortune, in contrast to the unfortunate one who must equally have earned his misfortune. . . . What the privileged classes require of religion, if anything at all, is this psychological reassurance of legitimacy.[44]

If Weber's assessment is a plausible interpretation of elite religious doctrine it might be applicable to more secular doctrines as well that purport to explain fundamental inequalities in status and condition.[45]

The importance of the dominant ideology and its manifestations for the elite would surely help explain political ceremony that is not even intended for

43. Nicholas Abercrombie, Stephen Hill, and Bryan S. Turner, *The Dominant Ideology Thesis*, chap. 3.

44. *The Sociology of Religion*, 107.

45. Abercrombie would extend this argument forward to characterize both early and contemporary capitalism. There is little evidence, he claims, for the ideological incorporation of the working class and much evidence that bourgeois ideology is, above all, a force for improving the cohesion and self-confidence of the class that has the most direct interest in embracing it: the bourgeoisie. *The Dominant Ideology Thesis*, chaps. 4, 5.

nonelite consumption. If we examine the important rites of monarchy in early modern France it is apparent that, by the time of Louis XIV, a great deal of ceremony was no longer performed before the public at all. No longer did the French monarch make public entries into towns to receive pledges of loyalty and reaffirm the towns' chartered privileges; no longer are there ceremonies in the streets of Paris, in the cathedral, or in the high court. The king could not awe his subjects since they never saw him; his public was only the courtiers and retainers at Versailles itself. Much the same case could be made for the seventeenth-century Spanish court and for the nineteenth-century Russian court.[46]

More elaborate theories of ideological hegemony will be the focus of attention in the next chapter; here I want only to suggest that the self-dramatization of domination may actually exert more rhetorical force among the leading actors themselves than among the far more numerous bit players.

---

46. For France, see Ralph E. Geisey, "Models of Rulership in French Royal Ceremonial," in *Rites of Power,* ed. Wilentz, 41–61; for Spain, Elliott, "Power and Propaganda," ibid., 145–73; for Russia, Richard Wortmann, "Moscow and Petersburg: The Problem of the Political Center in Tsarist Russia, 1881–1914," ibid., 244–71.

CHAPTER FOUR

False Consciousness or Laying It on Thick?

On the one hand, a socio-economic space organized by an immemorial struggle between "the powerful" and "the poor," presented itself as the field of constant victories by the rich and the police, but also as the reign of mendacity (there, no truth is said, except in whispers and among the peasants: "Agora a gente sabe, mas nao pode dizar alto"). In this space the strong always win and words always deceive.

—MICHEL DE CERTEAU, *La Pratique du Quotidien*

THE POWERFUL, as we have seen, have a vital interest in keeping up the appearances appropriate to their form of domination. Subordinates, for their part, ordinarily have good reasons to help sustain those appearances or, at least, not openly to contradict them. Taken together, these two social facts have, I believe, important consequences for the analysis of power relations. In what follows, I examine how the concepts of the public and hidden transcript can help us to a more critical view of the various debates swirling around the troubled terms, *false consciousness* and *hegemony.* A combination of adaptive strategic behavior and the dialogue implicit in most power relations ensures that public action will provide a constant stream of evidence that appears to support an interpretation of ideological hegemony. This interpretation may not be mistaken, but I will argue that it cannot be sustained on the basis of the evidence usually presented and that, in the cases I am examining, there are other good reasons for doubting this interpretation. I conclude with a brief analysis of how forms of domination generate certain rituals of affirmation, certain forms of public conflict, and, finally, certain patterns of profanation and defiance. Throughout, my aim is to clarify the analysis of domination in a way that avoids "naturalizing" existing power relations and that is attentive to what may lie beneath the surface.

The Interpretation of Quiescence

Much of the debate about power and ideology for three decades or more has centered on how to interpret conforming behavior by the less powerful (for example, ordinary citizens, the working class, peasants) when there is no apparent use of coercion (for example, violence, threats) to explain that conformity. Why, in other words, do people seem to knuckle under when they appear to have other options? In North America, the arguments about the reasons for quiescence are to be found in what is known as the community power literature based on local studies demonstrating relatively low levels of political participation despite marked inequalities and a relatively open political system.[1] In continental Europe and England the arguments have been conducted on a larger social terrain and in largely neo-Marxist terms employing Gramsci's concept of hegemony.[2] Here, the attempt is to explain the relative political quiescence of the Western working class despite the continuing provocation of inequities under capitalism and access to the political remedies that might be provided by parliamentary democracy. Why, in other words, does a subordinate class seem to accept or at least to consent to an economic system that is manifestly against its interests when it is not obliged to by the direct application of coercion or the fear of its application? Each of these debates, I should add, begins with several assumptions, any one of which might plausibly be contested. Each assumes that the subordinate group is, in fact, relatively quiescent, that it is relatively disadvantaged, and that it is not directly coerced. We will, for the sake of argument, accept all three assumptions.

With the exception of the pluralist position in the community power debate, virtually all other positions explain the anomaly by reference to a dominant or hegemonic ideology. Precisely what this ideology is, how it is created, how it is propagated, and what consequences it has is hotly contested. Most of the disputants, however, agree that while the dominant ideology does not entirely exclude the interests of subordinate groups, it operates to conceal or misrepresent aspects of social relations that, if apprehended directly, would

1. Some of the representative voices in this debate may be found in Robert A. Dahl, *Who Governs? Democracy and Power in an American City;* Nelson W. Polsby, *Community Power and Political Theory;* Jack E. Walker, "A Critique of the Elitist Theory of Democracy"; Peter Bachrach and Morton S. Baratz, *Power and Poverty: Theory and Practice;* Steven Lukes, *Power: A Radical View;* and John Gaventa, *Power and Powerlessness: Quiescence and Rebellion in an Appalachian Valley.*
2. Some of the representative voices in this debate are Antonio Gramsci, *Selections from the Prison Notebooks,* ed. and trans. Quinten Hoare and Geoffrey Nowell Smith; Frank Parkin, *Class, Inequality and the Political Order;* Ralph Miliband, *The State in Capitalist Society;* Nicos Poulantzas, *State, Power, Socialism;* Anthony Giddens, *The Class Structure of Advanced Societies;* Jürgen Habermas, *Legitimation Crisis;* and Louis Althusser, *Reading Capital.* For penetrating critiques of these approaches, see especially Abercrombie et al., *The Dominant Ideology Thesis,* and Paul Willis, *Learning to Labour.*

be damaging to the interests of dominant elites.[3] Since any theory that purports to demonstrate a misrepresentation of social reality must, by definition, claim some superior knowledge of what that social reality is, it must be, in this sense, a theory of false consciousness. Simplifying things greatly, I believe we can discern a thick and a thin version of false consciousness. The thick version claims that a dominant ideology works its magic by persuading subordinate groups to believe actively in the values that explain and justify their own subordination. Evidence against this thick theory of mystification is pervasive enough to convince me that it is generally untenable[4]—particularly so for systems of domination such as serfdom, slavery, and untouchability, in which consent and civil rights hardly figure even at the rhetorical level. The thin theory of false consciousness, on the other hand, maintains only that the dominant ideology achieves compliance by convincing subordinate groups that the social order in which they live is natural and inevitable. The thick theory claims consent; the thin theory settles for resignation. In its most subtle form, the thin theory is eminently plausible and, some would claim, true by definition. I believe, nevertheless, that it is fundamentally wrong and hope to show why in some detail after putting it in as persuasive a form as possible, so that it is no straw man I am criticizing.

Within the community power literature, the debate is essentially between pluralists and antipluralists. For the pluralists, the absence of significant protest or radical opposition in relatively open political systems must be taken as a sign of satisfaction or, at least, insufficient dissatisfaction to warrant the time and trouble of political mobilization. Antipluralists reply that the political arena is less completely open than pluralists believe and that the vulnerability of subordinate groups allows elites to control the political agenda and create effective obstacles to participation. The difficulty with the antipluralist position, as their opponents lost no time pointing out, is that it creates a kind of political Heisenberg principle. That is, if the antipluralists cannot uncover hidden grievances—grievances that the elite is presumed to have effectively banished—then how are we to know whether apparent acquiescence is genuine or repressive? An elite that did its "anti-pluralist work" effectively would thereby have eliminated any trace of the issues they had suppressed.

3. The sort of misrepresentation referred to might, for a liberal democracy, include the effects of official beliefs in equality of economic opportunity, an open, accessible political system, and what Marx called "commodity fetishism." The effect of each belief in turn might be to stigmatize the poor as entirely responsible for their poverty, to mask the inequalities in political influence underwritten by economic power, and to misrepresent low wages or unemployment to workers as an entirely impersonal, natural (i.e., not social) occurrence.

4. See Abercrombie et al., *The Dominant Ideology Thesis*, and Willis, *Learning to Labour.*

In an attempt to sustain the antipluralist position and to clarify how issues are, in fact, banished, John Gaventa proposes a third level of power relations.[5] The first level is the familiar and open exercise of coercion and influence. The second is intimidation and what Gaventa calls "the rule of anticipated reactions." This second effect typically arises from experience of subordination and defeat in that the relatively powerless elect not to challenge elites because they anticipate the sanctions that will be brought against them to ensure their failure. Here there is no change in values or grievances presumably, but rather an estimate of hopeless odds that discourage a challenge.[6] The third level of power relations is more subtle and amounts to a theory of false consciousness that is both thick and thin. Gaventa claims that the power afforded to a dominant elite in the first two dimensions of power "may allow [them] further power to invest in the development of dominant images, legitimations, or beliefs about [their] power through control, for instance, of the media or other socialization institutions."[7] The result, he claims, may well be a culture of defeat and nonparticipation such as he found in the Appalachian coal valley he studied. What is not clear is how much of the "mystification" Gaventa points to is presumed to actually change values and preferences (for example, as his term "legitimations" implies) and how much is a reinforcement of the belief in the power of dominant elites to prevail in any encounter. Nor is it apparent why such ideological investments should be convincing to subordinate groups beyond the inferences they draw from their direct experience. Gaventa, at any rate, supports both a thick theory of false consciousness and a thin theory of naturalization.

When it comes to understanding why the Western working class has apparently made an accommodation with capitalism and unequal property relations despite its political rights to mobilize, one finds, again, both thick and thin accounts of ideological hegemony. The thick version emphasizes the operation of what have been called "ideological state apparatuses," such as schools, the church, the media, and even the institutions of parliamentary democracy, which, it is claimed, exercise a near monopoly over the symbolic means of production just as factory owners might monopolize the material means of production. Their ideological work secures the active consent of subordinate groups to the social arrangements that reproduce their subordination.[8] Put very briefly, this thick version faces two daunting criticisms.

---

5. *Power and Powerlessness*, chap. 1.

6. This is essentially the point of the electric fence analogy in chap. 3.

7. *Power and Powerlessness*, 22. For a "thicker" version of this argument, see Frank Parkin, *Class, Inequality and the Political Order*, 79–91.

8. Not, however, without real concessions as the price of hegemony on the Gramscian view.

First, there is some rather compelling evidence that subordinate classes under feudalism, early capitalism, and late capitalism have not been ideologically incorporated to anything like the extent claimed by the theory.[9] Second, and far more damaging, there is no warrant for supposing that the acceptance of a broad, idealized version of the reigning ideology prevents conflict—even violent conflict—and some evidence that such acceptance may in fact provoke conflict.[10]

The thin theory of hegemony makes far less grandiose claims for the ideological grip of ruling elites. What ideological domination does accomplish, however, according to this version, is to define for subordinate groups what is realistic and what is not realistic and to drive certain aspirations and grievances into the realm of the impossible, of idle dreams. By persuading underclasses that their position, their life-chances, their tribulations are un-alterable and inevitable, such a limited hegemony can produce the behavioral results of consent without necessarily changing people's values. Convinced that nothing can possibly be done to improve their situation and that it will always remain so, it is even conceivable that idle criticisms and hopeless aspirations would be eventually extinguished. One sympathetic and penetrating account of English working-class culture by Richard Hoggart captures the essence of this thin theory of mystification:

> When people feel that they cannot do much about the main elements of their situation, feel it not necessarily with despair or disappointment or resentment but simply as a fact of life, they adopt attitudes toward that situation which allow them to have a liveable life without a constant and pressing sense of the larger situation. The attitudes move the main elements in the situation to the realm of natural laws, the given and now, the almost implacable material from which a living has to be carved. Such attitudes, at their least adorned a fatalism or plain accepting, are generally below the tragic level, they have too much of the conscript's lack of choice about them.[11]

At one level it is simply undeniable that this account is entirely convincing. No one will doubt that the actual situation of subordinate groups throughout their

9. This criticism is best summarized in Abercrombie et al., *The Dominant Ideology Thesis,* passim.

10. Some of this evidence is summarized in my *Weapons of the Weak,* chap. 8, where I rely heavily on Barrington Moore, Jr., *Injustice: The Social Bases of Obedience and Revolt,* and Willis, *Learning to Labour.*

11. *The Uses of Literacy,* 77–78.

history has seemed an unmovable "given," and realistically so.[12] If such a claim is plausible for the contemporary working class with its political rights and its acquaintance with would-be revolutionary movements, not to mention actual revolutions, historically it should be true in a far more overwhelming way for slaves, serfs, peasants, and untouchables. As an illustration, imagine the situation of an untouchable in eighteenth-century rural India. In the collective historical experience of his or her group, there have always been castes; his caste has always been most looked down upon and exploited, and no one has ever escaped his caste—in his lifetime. Small wonder that in such circumstances the caste system and one's status within it should take on the force of natural law. There is also no standard of comparison that can be used to find the caste system wanting, no alternative experience or knowledge to make one's fate less than inevitable.[13]

This apparently compelling, thin version of the false consciousness argument is not incompatible with a degree of distaste for, or even hatred of, the domination experienced. The claim is not that one's fated condition is loved, only that it is here to stay whether one likes it or not. On my reading, this minimal notion of ideological domination has become almost an orthodoxy, one encountered again and again in the literature on such issues. As Pierre Bourdieu puts it, "Every established order tends to produce (to very different degrees and with very different means) *the naturalization of its own arbitrariness.*"[14] Other formulations vary only in particulars. Thus, Anthony Giddens writes of "the naturalization of the present" in which capitalist economic structures come to be taken for granted.[15] Paul Willis echoes both in claiming that "one of the most important general functions of ideology is the way in which it turns uncertain and fragile cultural resolutions and outcomes into a pervasive naturalism."[16] Quite often, however, there is an attempt to take this

12. Hoggart also implicitly asks us to agree that people do not dream much about what they are convinced they cannot have nor do they waste time railing about what they believe they cannot change. These claims are far more contestable, as we shall see later.

13. The doctrine of karma and reincarnation, the ultimate in ideologies of hegemony, promises that a conforming and humble untouchable will be rewarded by rebirth in a higher status. Justice is promised, and in an entirely mechanical fashion; it is just that the justice operates only between lifetimes, not within them.

14. *Outline of a Theory of Practice,* 164.

15. *Central Problems in Social Theory: Action, Structure, and Contradiction in Social Analysis,* 195.

16. *Learning to Labour,* 162. Zygmunt Bauman sees hegemony as a process by which alternatives to the current structure of power and status are excluded: "The dominant culture consists of transforming everything which is not inevitable into the improbable. . . . An overrepressive society is one which effectively eliminates alternatives to itself and thereby relinquishes spectacular, dramatized displays of its power." *Socialism, the Active Utopia,* 123.

more defensible notion of hegemony and, as it were, to fatten it back up to the thick theory of false consciousness. This transmutation is accomplished by arguing—and occasionally simply asserting—that what is conceived as inevitable becomes, by that fact, just. Necessity becomes virtue. As Bourdieu puts it epigrammatically, subordinate groups manage "to refuse what is anyway refused and to love the inevitable."[17]

Barrington Moore raises this same equation into something like a psychological universal, claiming that "what is or appears to human beings unavoidable must also somehow be just."[18] The logic behind this position is not unlike the logic underlying some of the earlier studies of the personality structure of American blacks.[19] It is of the "face-grows-to-fit-the-mask" variety, beginning with the need for the black in a racist society to act a role and to continuously monitor his or her behavior by the standards imposed by the dominant, that is, white, world. It is difficult if not impossible, the logic goes, for an individual constantly to act a role and to hold a view of the self apart from that role. Since, presumably, the individual has no control over the roles imposed by powerful others, whatever personality integration takes place must bring the self into line with the imposed role.[20]

17. *Outline of a Theory of Practice*, 77. In a later work the same point is put somewhat more obscurely and it is difficult to discern whether "consent" means resignation to the inevitable or the embracing of the inevitable. He writes, "Dominated agents . . . tend to attribute to themselves what the distribution attributes to them, refusing what they are refused ('That's not for the likes of us'), adjusting their expectations to their chances, defining themselves as the established order defines them, reproducing in their verdict on themselves the verdict the economy pronounces on them, condemning themselves to what is in any case their lot . . . consenting to be what they have to be, 'modest,' 'humble,' and 'obscure.'" *Distinction: A Social Critique of the Judgement of Taste*, trans. Richard Nice, 471.

18. *Injustice*, 64.

19. For a discussion of such theories, see John D. McCarthy and William L. Yancey, "Uncle Tom and Mr. Charlie: Metaphysical Pathos in the Study of Racism and Personality Disorganization."

20. If we substitute "servility" for "friendliness" in the following quote from Nietzsche, the process being imagined is apparent: "He who *always* wears the mask of a friendly [servile] man must *at last* gain power over friendliness [servility] of disposition, without which the expression itself of friendliness [servility] is not to be gained—and finally friendliness [servility] of disposition gains the ascendency over him—he *is* benevolent [servile]." We will have ample reason, later, to reject this logic, but it is important to recognize the nature of the argument being made. Nietzsche implies that the mask must never be removed and that the transmutation occurs after a long, but unspecified, period. Notice also that the substitution of "servility" for "friendliness" may fundamentally change the logic. We assume that the man who "wears the mask of a friendly man" actually wishes to become genuinely friendly, whereas there is every reason to assume that the man who "wears the mask of servility" wears it because he has no choice and wishes he could discard it. In the case of servility, the principal motive that might remake a face to fit a mask may well be lacking. Quoted in Hochschild, *The Managed Heart*, 35, emphasis added.

A Critique of Hegemony and False Consciousness

A great many objections can be made to the case for hegemony and false consciousness. Taken singly, many of them are crippling; taken together, I believe they are fatal. Our interest, however, lies for the most part in understanding how the process of domination generates the social evidence that apparently confirms notions of hegemony. For this reason, and because lengthy critiques are available elsewhere, this critique will be brief and even schematic.[21]

Perhaps the greatest problem with the concept of hegemony is the implicit assumption that the ideological incorporation of subordinate groups will necessarily diminish social conflict. And yet, we know that any ideology which makes a claim to hegemony must, in effect, make promises to subordinate groups by way of explaining *why* a particular social order is also in their best interests. Once such promises are extended, the way is open to social conflict. How are these promises to be understood, have they been carried out, were they made in good faith, who is to enforce them? Without elaborating, it is reasonably clear that some of the most striking episodes of violent conflict have occurred between a dominant elite and a rank-and-file mass of subordinates seeking objectives that could, in principle, be accommodated within the prevailing social order.[22] The myriad complaints voiced from all over France in the *cahiers de doléances* prior to the Revolution give little evidence of a desire to abolish serfdom or the monarchy. Virtually all the demands envisioned a reformed feudalism with many "abuses" rectified. But the relative modesty of the demands did not prevent—one might even say they helped stimulate— the violent actions of peasants and sansculottes that provided the social basis for the actual revolution. Similarly, what we know of the demands from the factory committees formed spontaneously throughout European Russia in 1917 leaves no doubt that what these workers sought "was to improve working conditions, not to change them" and certainly not to socialize the means of production.[23] And yet, their revolutionary actions on behalf of reformist goals, such as an eight-hour day, an end to piecework, a minimum wage, politeness from management, cooking and toilet facilities, were the driving force behind the Bolshevik revolution. Further examples abound.[24] The point is simply

21. See, for example, Scott, *Weapons of the Weak*, chap. 8, and Abercrombie, et al., *The Dominant Ideology Thesis*, passim.

22. We shall later have reason to ask whether these objectives are not, themselves, partly an artifact of power relations that preclude voicing more ambitious objectives.

23. Moore, *Injustice*, 369–70.

24. Some that come to mind are those of the German working class in the "near-revolution" after World War I and the peasantry of Morelos under Zapata in the Mexican Revolution. To put it

that the subordinate classes to be found at the base of what we historically call revolutionary movements are typically seeking goals well within their understanding of the ruling ideology. "Falsely conscious" subjects are quite capable, it seems, of taking revolutionary action.

Even if we were, for the sake of argument, to grant that ideological hegemony, once achieved, should contribute to the quiescence of subordinate classes, it then becomes highly questionable whether such hegemony has often prevailed. The problem with the hegemonic thesis, at least in its strong forms as proposed by some of Gramsci's successors, is that it is difficult to explain how social change could ever originate from below. If elites control the material basis of production, allowing them to extract practical conformity, and also control the means of symbolic production, thereby ensuring that their power and control are legitimized, one has achieved a self-perpetuating equilibrium that can be disturbed only by an external shock. As Willis observes, "Structuralist theories of reproduction present the dominant ideology (under which culture is subsumed) as impenetrable. Everything fits too neatly. Ideology always pre-exists and preempts any authentic criticism. There are no cracks in the billiard ball smoothness of process."[25] Even in the relatively stable industrial democracies to which theories of hegemony were meant to apply, their strongest formulation simply does not allow for the degree of social conflict and protest that actually occurs.

If social conflict is an inconvenience for theories of hegemony as applied to contemporary societies, it is a massive, intractable contradiction when applied to the histories of peasant societies, of slavery, and of serfdom. Considering only agrarian Europe in the three centuries before the French Revolution, the proponents of hegemony or naturalization are confronted with a host of anomalous facts. What is remarkable about that period, surely, is the frequency with which peasants were seized with a sense of historical possibilities on which they acted and which, it turned out tragically, were not objectively justified. The thousands of rebellions and violent protests from Wat Tyler's Rebellion in the late fourteenth century, through the great Peasants' War in Germany, to the French Revolution are something of a monument to the tenacity of peasant aspirations in the face of what seem, in retrospect, to have been hopeless odds. As Marc Bloch put it, "A social system is characterized not only by its internal structure but also by the reactions it produces. . . . To the historian, whose task is merely to observe and explain the connections

---

another way, what Lenin saw as "trade-union consciousness"—modest objectives pursued in this case with ferocious intensity—is very common in revolutionary situations.

25. *Learning to Labour*, 175.

between phenomena, agrarian revolt is as natural to the seigneurial regime as strikes, let us say, are to large scale capitalism."[26] For slavery in North America, where the odds were even longer against rebels, surely the remarkable thing is that they occurred at all and that for every actual rebellion there were scores of plots that never came to fruition. Given the dispersion of slaves among farms with relatively few hands, the fact that they were less than one-quarter of the population, and an active surveillance, the observer does not have to assume that slaves came to believe the "unavoidable" was just in order to account for the paucity of rebellion.[27]

If there is a social phenomenon to be explained here, it is the reverse of what theories of hegemony and false consciousness purport to account for. How is it that subordinate groups such as these have so often believed and acted as if their situations were not inevitable when a more judicious historical reading would have concluded that it was? It is not the miasma of power and thralldom that requires explanation. We require instead an understanding of a *misreading* by subordinate groups that seems to exaggerate their own power, the possibilities for emancipation, and to underestimate the power arrayed against them. If the elite-dominated public transcript tends to naturalize domination, it would seem that some countervailing influence manages often to denaturalize domination.

With this historical perspective in mind, we may begin to question the logic of the case made for hegemony and naturalization. The attempt to turn a thin theory of naturalization into a fat theory of hegemony seems, in my view, clearly unwarranted. Even granting the fact that subordinate groups of serfs, slaves, or untouchables have historically often had no knowledge of a social order founded on different principles, the inevitability of domination does not necessarily make it just or legitimate in their eyes. Let us instead assume that the inevitability of domination for a slave will have approximately the same status as the inevitability of the weather for the peasant. Concepts of justice and legitimacy are simply irrelevant to something that is inescapably there, like the weather. For that matter, traditional cultivators actually attempt to *de-naturalize* even the weather by personifying it and developing a ritual repertoire designed to influence or control its course.[28] Once again, what we might

26. *French Rural History: An Essay on Its Basic Character*, trans. Janet Sondheimer, 169.

27. In the West Indies, where agricultural units were much larger on average, where slaves composed the vast majority of the population, and where conditions were materially worse as well, judging from the mortality rates, rebellion was far more common.

28. Traditional peasants not only denaturalize the weather. In rebellions it is common to find traditional peoples wearing charms, amulets, or reciting magic formulas they believe will make them invulnerable to the weapons of their enemies. For several examples of colonial rebellions in

assume to be inevitable is brought into the realm of potential human control. When such efforts appear to fail, traditional cultivators, like their scientific, modern counterparts, are prone to curse the weather. They, at least, do not confound inevitability with justice.

The thin theory of naturalization is far more persuasive because it claims nothing beyond the acceptance of inevitability. It is, nevertheless, mistaken in assuming that the absence of actual knowledge of alternative social arrangements produces automatically the naturalization of the present, however hated that present may be. Consider two small feats of imagination that countless numbers of subordinate groups have historically performed. First, while the serf, the slave, and the untouchable may have difficulty imagining other arrangements than serfdom, slavery, and the caste system, they will certainly have no trouble imagining a total reversal of the existing distribution of status and rewards. The millennial theme of a world turned upside down, a world in which the last shall be first and the first last, can be found in nearly every major cultural tradition in which inequities of power, wealth, and status have been pronounced.[29] In one form or another most folk utopias have included the central idea behind this Vietnamese folksong:

> The son of the king becomes king.
> The son of the pagoda caretaker knows only how to sweep with the
>   leaves of the banyan tree.
> When the people rise up,
> The son of the king, defeated, will go sweep the pagoda.[30]

These collective hidden transcripts from the fantasy life of subordinate groups are not merely abstract exercises. They are embedded, as we shall see later, in innumerable ritual practices (for example, carnival in Catholic countries, the Feast of Krishna in India, the Saturnalia in classical Rome, the water festival in Buddhist Southeast Asia), and they have provided the ideological basis of many revolts.

The second historical achievement of popular imagination is to negate the

---

which such denaturalization occurs, see Michael Adas, *Prophets of Rebellion: Millenarian Protest against European Colonial Order.*

29. For a more elaborate argument along these lines, see my "Protest and Profanation: Agrarian Revolt and the Little Tradition," *Theory and Society,* part 1, vol. 4 (1977):1–38; part 2, vol. 4 (1977):211–46. The subject of inversions and reversals in art and social thought is examined in Barbara A. Babcock, ed., *The Reversible World: Symbolic Inversion in Art and Society.* In this collection see, particularly, David Kunzle, "World Upside Down: The Iconography of a European Broadsheet Type," 39–94.

30. Nguyen Hong Giap, *La condition des paysans au Viet-Nam à travers les chansons populaires,* 183.

existing social order. Without ever having set foot outside a stratified society, subordinate groups can, and have, imagined the absence of the distinctions they find so onerous. The famous ditty that comes to us from the English Peasants' Revolt of 1381, "When Adam delved and Eve span, who was then the gentleman," was imagining a world without aristocrats or gentry. In the fifteenth century the Taborites anticipated both a radical equality and the labor theory of value: "Princes, ecclesiastical and secular alike, and counts and knights should only possess as much as common folk, then everyone would have enough. The time will come when princes and lords will work for their daily bread."[31] Lest one confine such leveling beliefs to the Judeo-Christian tradition with its myth of a perfect society before the Fall, note that similar leveling beliefs of religious and secular lineage may be found in most, if not all, highly stratified societies. Most traditional utopian beliefs can, in fact, be understood as a more or less systematic negation of an existing pattern of exploitation and status degradation as it is experienced by subordinate groups. If the peasantry is beset by officials collecting taxes, by lords collecting crops and labor dues, by priests collecting tithes, and by poor crops, their utopia is likely to envision a life without taxes and dues and tithes, perhaps without officials, lords, and priests, and with an abundant, self-yielding nature. Utopian thought of this kind has typically been cast in disguised or allegorical forms in part because its open declaration would be considered revolutionary. What is beyond doubt is that millennial beliefs and expectations have often provided, before the modern era, a most important set of mobilizing ideas behind large-scale rebellions when they did occur.

On the historical evidence, then, little or no basis exists for crediting either a fat theory or a thin theory of hegemony. The obstacles to resistance, which are many, are simply not attributable to the inability of subordinate groups to *imagine* a counterfactual social order. They do imagine both the reversal and negation of their domination, and, most important, they have acted on these values in desperation and on those rare occasions when the circumstances allowed. Given their position at the bottom of the heap, it is little wonder they should have a class interest in utopian prophesies, in imagining a radically different social order from the painful one they experience. In concrete terms, the seventeenth-century broadsheet depicting a lord serving an elegant meal to a seated peasant was bound to evoke more pleasure from the peasantry than from their social betters.[32] And having imagined a counterfactual social order, subordinate groups do not appear to have been paralyzed by an elite-fostered

31. Norman Cohn, *The Pursuit of the Millennium*, 245.
32. Kunzle, "World Upside Down," 80–82.

discourse intended to convince them that efforts to change their situation are hopeless. I do not by any means wish to imply that the history of peasants and slaves is a history of one quixotic adventure after another or to ignore the chilling effects a crushed insurrection certainly had. Nevertheless, since slave and peasant uprisings occur frequently enough and fail almost invariably, one can make a persuasive case that whatever misperception of reality prevails was apparently one that was more hopeful than the facts warranted. The penchant of subordinate groups to interpret rumors and ambiguous news as heralding their imminent liberation is striking, and I will examine it more closely in chapter 6.

A Paper-Thin Theory of Hegemony

What, then, is left of the theory of hegemony in this context? Very little, I believe. I do, however, want to suggest the limited and stringent conditions under which subordinate groups may come to accept, even to legitimate, the arrangements that justify their subordination.[33]

Ideological hegemony in cases of *involuntary* subordination is, I believe, likely to occur only if either of two rather stringent conditions are met. The first of these is that there exist a strong probability that a good many subordinates will eventually come to occupy positions of power. The expectation that one will eventually be able to exercise the domination that one endures today is a strong incentive serving to legitimate patterns of domination. It encourages patience and emulation, and, not least, it promises revenge of a kind, even if it must be exercised on someone other than the original target of resentment. If this supposition is correct it would help to explain why so many age-graded systems of domination seem to have such durability. The junior who is

33. We should, of course, set aside from this discussion two kinds of subordination. First, we exclude the voluntary and revocable subordination typified by entering a religious order. The fact that someone who enters such a life makes a voluntary commitment to the principles that underlie the subordination, principles that are usually marked by a solemn oath, but that may be renounced at any time fundamentally changes the nature of domination. Hegemony, if one could call it that, is established by definition since only true believers enter, and when they cease being believers they may leave. Voluntary servitude for a specified time or voluntary enlistment in the military or merchant marine, which it resembles, is less clear-cut. Entry may not be experienced as voluntary if, say, few other economic opportunities exist and one may not escape subordination until the term of enlistment or servitude expires. In principle, however, the greater the freedom of choice in entry and the greater the ease of withdrawal, the more legitimate the subordination. The second form of subordination we exclude is that of infants and children to parents. The asymmetry of power in this situation is extreme—hence the possibility for abuses—but it is typically benign and nurturant rather than exploitative, and it is a biological given.

exploited by elders will eventually get his chance to be an elder; those who do degrading work for others in an institution—providing they can reasonably expect to move up—will eventually have that work done for them; the traditional Chinese daughter-in-law can look forward, if she has a son(!), to becoming a domineering mother-in-law.[34]

Onerous and involuntary subordination can also, perhaps, be made legitimate providing that subordinates are more or less completely atomized and kept under close observation. What is involved is the total abolition of any social realm of relative discursive freedom. In other words, the social conditions under which a hidden transcript might be generated among subordinates are eliminated. The society envisioned is rather like the official story propagated in the public transcript or in Bentham's Panopticon, inasmuch as all social relations are hierarchical and surveillance is perfect. It goes without saying that this ultimate totalitarian fantasy in which there is no life outside relations of domination does not even remotely approximate the situation of any real society as a whole. As Foucault has noted, "Solitude is the primary condition of total submission."[35] Perhaps only in a few penal institutions, thought-reform camps, and psychiatric wards is one afforded a glimpse of what is involved.

The techniques of atomization and surveillance were employed with some success in the prisoner-of-war camps in North Korea and China during the Korean War. For our purposes what is remarkable about these camps was the lengths to which the captors had to go in order to produce the confessions and

34. The promise of being set free in return for a record of service and compliance can also produce a pattern of conformity that looks much like hegemony. This is an excellent example of how the prospects for the future exert a palpable influence on the evaluation of one's present conditions. This effect is vastly magnified if the possibility of emancipation is mediated solely by the will of the dominant. As Orlando Patterson, (*Slavery and Social Death*, 101) has observed in the case of slavery, holding out the promise of eventual manumission upon the death of the master was more effective than any whip in gaining steady compliance. The logic is precisely the same as that of those prison systems that hold out the promise of time off for good behavior. And like the incentive of "good time," the possibility of manumission can never produce hegemony because it is, after all, the slave's desire for emancipation, the prisoner's desire for liberty, that is being manipulated. The very premise of the manipulation is that the subordinate will do almost anything—including comply faithfully for an extended period—if that is the price of liberation. Such a pact or contract is possible only on the assumption that the ideology of domination is not hegemonic.

35. *Discipline and Punish*, 237. Solitude, atomization, and domination are also the themes of some influential interpretations of schizophrenia. Since the experience of victimization and control is an individual one (and not a social one shared by others similarly placed) for the schizophrenic, the boundary between fantasy and action disappears. See, for example, James M. Glass, *Delusion: Internal Dimensions of Political Life*, chap. 3., and Harold F. Searles, *Collected Papers on Schizophrenia and Related Subjects*, chap. 19.

propaganda broadcasts they required.[36] The prisoners were driven to extreme physical exhaustion, denied any contact with the outside world, separated and isolated for weeks at a time during constant interrogation. The interrogator alternated between favors and threats, telling the prisoner that he received no mail because his relatives at home didn't care what became of him. Above all, the captors endeavored to minutely control every action and communication of the captives and to eliminate, with isolation or informers, any possible solidarity or affiliation between them. Draconian conditions did, in fact, produce a small harvest of confessions, and a good many prisoners reported suddenly feeling great affection toward an interrogator who had treated them ruthlessly. What apparently had happened was that the impossibility of validating one's feelings and anger with others in the same situation—of creating an offstage hidden transcript, a different social reality—had allowed the captors to exercise a temporary hegemony.

I want to emphasize exactly how draconian were the conditions that produced this compliance. Captors were not successful when they permitted prisoners to associate with one another; they had to concentrate on destroying any autonomous subordinate group contact. Even then it was often possible for prisoners to communicate secretly under the noses of the authorities. Taking advantage of small linguistic nuances their captors would not notice, they often managed to insert in a publicly read apology or confession before other prisoners an indication that their performance was forced and insincere. The degree of policing and atomization required are in keeping with what we know from social psychology about acts of obedience to authority that offend one's moral judgment. In Stanley Milgram's famous experiments in which volunteers gave what they thought were shocks to subjects who failed to answer questions correctly, several small variations dramatically reduced the rate of compliance.[37] First, if the experimenter (the authority figure) stepped out of the room, the subject would disobey and then lie to the experimenter about the shocks he or she had administered. In another variation of the experimental situation, the subject was provided with one or two peers who refused to administer increasingly severe shocks. With even this modicum of social support, the vast majority of subjects rebelled against the authority of

36. Denise Winn, *The Manipulated Mind: Brainwashing, Conditioning, and Indoctrination*, passim.

37. Stanley Milgram, *Obedience to Authority: An Experimental View*, 116–21. Milgram's experiment showed how easily subjects could be induced to do something against their better judgment and might from one angle be seen as proving the ease of indoctrination. The key fact, however, is that Milgram's subjects were all volunteers rather than unwilling conscripts. As we have seen in chapter 2 this makes all the difference in readiness to be persuaded.

the experimenter. Willing compliance in this context thus evaporates the moment the subject is not under close observation *and* whenever the subject is afforded even a small degree of social support for resistance from peers in the same boat.[38]

It is plausible, then, under certain conditions, to imagine that even an onerous, nonvoluntary subordination can be made to seem just and legitimate. Those conditions, however, are so stringent that they are simply not applicable to any of the large-scale forms of domination that concern us here. Slaves, serfs, peasants, and untouchables have had little realistic prospect of upward mobility or escape from their status. At the same time they have always had something of a life apart in the slave quarters, the village, the household, and in religious and ritual life. It has been neither possible nor desirable to destroy entirely the autonomous social life of subordinate groups that is the indispensable basis for a hidden transcript. The large historical forms of domination not only generate the resentments, appropriations, and humiliations that give, as it were, subordinates something to talk about; they are also unable to prevent the creation of an independent social space in which subordinates can talk in comparative safety.

The Social Production of Hegemonic Appearances

If much of the criticism of theories of hegemony offered above is valid, we would be obliged to find other reasons for compliance and quiescence than the internalization of the dominant ideology by subordinate groups. There are, certainly, a host of factors that might explain why a form of domination persists despite an elite's failure to incorporate ideologically the least advantaged. To mention only a few, subordinate groups might be divided by geography and cultural background, they may judge that the severity of possible

38. Subordinates are never, of course, in precisely the same boat. This raises another question: that of divide and rule. If we imagine, say, that each slave of a given master is treated differently on some uniform scale of harshness or benevolence, then it follows that one half of the slaves in question are treated better than average. This being so, should they not be grateful to be among the privileged and should they therefore not internalize the ideology of slavery? While it is surely true that slaves and other subordinates might strive to please their masters to win such privileges, this does not necessarily imply internalization of hegemonic standards. To assume that it does is to assume that slaves and others are incapable of simultaneously understanding that a form of domination is unjust *and* that they are relatively better off than other slaves. Consider the following statement made by a recently emancipated slave about her ex-mistress: "Well, she was as good as most any old white woman that ever broke bread. She was the best white woman that ever broke bread, but you know, honey, that wasn't much, 'cause they all hated the po' nigger." Quoted in Eugene G. Genovese, *Roll, Jordan, Roll: The World the Slaves Made,* 125.

reprisal makes open resistance foolhardy, their daily struggle for subsistence and the surveillance it entails may all but preclude open opposition, or they may have become cynical from past failures.

What remains to be explained, however, is why theories of hegemony and ideological incorporation have nevertheless retained an enormous intellectual appeal to social scientists and historians. We must remember, in this context, that theories of ideological incorporation have been equally seductive both to mainstream social science and to neo-Marxist followers of Gramsci. In the structural-functional world of Parsonian sociology, subordinate groups came naturally to an acceptance of the normative principles behind the social order without which no society could endure. In the neo-Marxist critique it is also assumed that subordinate groups have internalized the dominant norms but, now, these norms are seen to be a false view of their objective interests. In each instance, ideological incorporation produces social stability; in the former case, the stability is laudable, while in the latter case it is a stability that permits the continuation of class-based exploitation.[39]

The most obvious reason why notions of ideological incorporation should find such resonance in the historical record is simply that domination, as we have seen, produces an official transcript that provides convincing evidence of willing, even enthusiastic complicity. In ordinary circumstances subordinates have a vested interest in avoiding any *explicit* display of insubordination. They also, of course, always have a practical interest in resistance—in minimizing the exactions, labor, and humiliations to which they are subject. The reconciliation of these two objectives that seem at cross-purposes is typically achieved by pursuing precisely those forms of resistance that avoid any open confrontation with the structures of authority being resisted. Thus the peasantry, in the interest of safety and success, has historically preferred to disguise its resistance. If it were a question of control over land, they would prefer squatting to a defiant land invasion; if it were a matter of taxes, they would prefer evasion rather than a tax riot; if it were a question of rights to the product of the land, they would prefer poaching or pilfering to direct appropriation. Only when less dramatic measures failed, when subsistence was threatened, or when there were signs that they could strike with relative safety would the peasantry venture on the path of open, collective defiance. It is for

39. There are also interests involved here. For conservative social theorists the notion of ideological consent from below is obviously comforting. For the Leninist left, on the other hand, it offers a role for the vanguard party and its intelligentsia, who must lift the scales from the eyes of the oppressed. If the working class is capable of generating not only the force of numbers and economic leverage but also the ideas of their own liberation, the role of the Leninist party becomes problematic.

this reason that the official transcript of relations between the dominant and subordinate is filled with formulas of subservience, euphemisms, and uncontested claims to status and legitimacy. On the open stage the serfs or slaves will appear complicitous in creating an appearance of consent and unanimity; the show of discursive affirmations from below will make it seem as if ideological hegemony were secure. The official transcript of power relations *is* a sphere in which power appears naturalized because that is what elites exert their influence to produce and because it ordinarily serves the immediate interests of subordinates to avoid discrediting these appearances.

The "official transcript" as a social fact presents enormous difficulties for the conduct of historical and contemporary research on subordinate groups. Short of actual rebellion, the great bulk of public events, and hence the great bulk of the archives, is consecrated to the official transcript. And on those occasions when subordinate groups do put in an appearance, their presence, motives, and behavior are mediated by the interpretation of dominant elites. When the subordinate group is almost entirely illiterate the problem is compounded. The difficulty is, however, not merely the standard one of records of elite activities kept by elites in ways that reflect their class and status. It is the more profound difficulty presented by earnest efforts of subordinate groups to conceal their activities and opinions, which might expose them to harm. We know relatively little about the rate at which slaves in the United State pilfered their masters' livestock, grain, and larder. If the slaves were successful, the master knew as little about this as possible, although he could certainly know there were losses. We know even less, of course, concerning what slaves said among themselves about this reappropriation of value from the masters. What we do know typically comes to us, significantly, from ex-slaves who had been able to escape this form of subordination—for example, from narratives given by runaways who had made it to the North or to Canada and from accounts collected after emancipation. The goal of slaves and other subordinate groups, as they conduct their ideological and material resistance, is precisely to escape detection; to the extent that they achieve their goal, such activities do not appear in the archives. In this respect, subordinate groups are complicitous in contributing to a sanitized official transcript, for that is one way they cover their tracks. Acts of desperation, revolt, and defiance can offer us something of a window on the hidden transcript, but, short of crises, we are apt to see subordinate groups on their best behavior. Detecting resistance among slaves under "normal" conditions, then, would seem rather like detecting the passage of subatomic particles by cloud chamber. Only the trail of resistance—for example, so much corn missing—would be apparent.

Consider, for example, the difficulties reported by Christopher Hill in his attempts to establish the social and religious antecedents of the radical ideas associated with the Levellers in the English Civil War.[40] It is, of course, perfectly clear that the social gospel of the Levellers was not invented on the spot in 1640, but it is another thing to track down its origins. The religious views associated with the Lollards are the obvious place to look. Examining Lollardy, however, is vastly complicated by the fact that the adherents of such heterodox religious views were considered, and correctly so, dangerous to the established order. As Hill observes, "By definition, those who held them [these views] were anxious to leave no traces."[41] Lollardy was, given the circumstances, a fugitive and underground sect with no means to enforce an orthodoxy on those who believed. It can be glimpsed in reports of illegal preaching, in occasional anticlerical incidents, and in some radically democratic readings of the Scriptures later echoed by the Baptists and Quakers. We do know they preached the refusal of both "hat honor" and the use of honorifics in address, that they believed as early as the fifteenth century in direct confession to God and in the abolition of tithes for all those poorer than the priest, and that, like the Familists, Ranters, and Levellers, they would preach in taverns or in the open air. They thrived best in those areas where surveillance was least—the pastoral, moorland, and forest areas with few squires or clergy. And when they were challenged, they, like the Familists after them, were likely to disavow holding any heterodox views. Hill writes, "This unheroic attitude was related to their dislike of all established churches, whether protestant or Catholic. Their refusal of martyrdom no doubt helped their beliefs to survive but it increases the historians' difficulty in identifying heretical groups with confidence."[42] The last thing the Lollards or Familists wanted, in this period, was to stand up and be counted. In fact, it is significant that the interest in Lollardy derives, in this case, from the public, open explosion of radical heterodoxy that so typified the English Civil War beginning in 1640. Their subterranean history became a matter of some historical importance because the ideas it embodied could, in the political mobilization and power vacuum of the Civil War, finally find open expression. Without such favorable moments to cast a retrospective light on a previously hidden transcript, one imagines that much of the offstage history of subordinate groups is permanently lost or obscured.

A parallel historical argument could be made about the dissimulation deployed by subordinate groups to conceal practices of resistance. Malay

40. "From Lollardy to Levellers," 86–103, in Janos M. Bak and Gerhard Benecke, eds., *Religion and Rural Revolt: Papers Presented to the Fourth Interdisciplinary Workshop on Peasant Studies.*
41. Ibid., 87.
42. Ibid., 93.

paddy farmers, in the region in which I have conducted fieldwork, have resented paying the official Islamic tithe.[43] It is collected inequitably and corruptly, the proceeds are sent to the provincial capital, and not a single poor person in the village has even received any charity back from the religious authorities. Quietly and massively, the Malay peasantry has managed to nearly dismantle the tithe system so that only 15 percent of what is formally due is actually paid. There have been no tithe riots, demonstrations, protests, only a patient and effective nibbling in a multitude of ways: fraudulent declarations of the amount of land farmed, simple failures to declare land, underpayment, and delivery of paddy spoiled by moisture or contaminated with rocks and mud to increase its weight. For complex political reasons, the details of which need not concern us, neither the religious authorities nor the ruling party wishes to call public attention to this silent, effective defiance. To do so would, among other things, expose the tenuousness of government authority in the countryside and perhaps encourage other acts of insubordination.[44] The low profile adopted by the two antagonists amounts to something of a joint con- spiracy to keep the conflict out of the public record. Someone examining the newspapers, speeches, and public documents of the period a few decades hence would find little or no trace of this conflict.

The seductiveness of theories of hegemony and false consciousness thus depends in large part on the strategic appearances that elites and subordinates alike ordinarily insert into the public transcript. For subordinates, the need for protective ingratiation[45] ensures that, once they come under scrutiny from above, the Lollard becomes an orthodox believer, the poacher becomes a peaceful respecter of gentry property, and the tithe evader a peasant ready to meet his obligations. The greater the power exercised over them and the

43. For an extended account comparing this resistance to the resistance of French peasants to the Catholic tithe in the seventeenth and eighteenth centuries, see my "Resistance without Protest and without Organization: Peasant Opposition to the Islamic *Zakat* and the Christian Tithe."

44. This raises a political variant of the philosophical question: If unheard by any living creature, does a tree falling in the forest make a sound? Does "resistance" by subordinates that is purposely overlooked by elites or called by another name, qualify as resistance? Does resistance, in other words, require recognition as resistance by the party being resisted? The issue points to the enormous importance of the power and authority to determine (never entirely unilaterally) what is considered the public transcript and what is not. The ability to choose to overlook or ignore an act of insubordination as if it never happened is a key exercise of power.

45. The term comes from Edward E. Jones, *Ingratiation: A Social Psychological Analysis*, 47. He defines the term as follows: "In protective ingratiation, the goal is not to improve one's outcomes beyond some otherwise expected level, but rather to blunt a potential attack . . . farsightful defensive planning. For the protective ingratiator, the world is peopled with potential antagonists, people who can be unkind, hostile, brutally frank. Ingratiation can serve to transform this world into a safer place by depriving the potential antagonist of any pretext for aggression."

closer the surveillance, the more incentive subordinates have to foster the impression of compliance, agreement, deference. By the same token, we know that compliance extracted under such draconian circumstances is less likely to be a valid guide to offstage opinion. Elites also, as we have seen, may have their own compelling reasons to preserve a public facade of unity, willing compliance, and respect. Unless one can penetrate the official transcript of both subordinates and elites, a reading of the social evidence will almost always represent a confirmation of the status quo in hegemonic terms. Just as subordinates are not much deceived by their own performance there is, of course, no more reason for social scientists and historians to take that performance as, necessarily, one given in good faith.

The Interrogation of Power, or, the Use Value of Hegemony

The only irony allowed to poverty is to drive Justice and Benevolence to unjust denials.
  —BALZAC, *The Country Doctor*

We must, on my reading of the evidence, stand Gramsci's analysis of hegemony upside down in at least one respect. In Gramsci's original formulation, which has guided most subsequent neo-Marxist work on ideology, hegemony works primarily at the level of thought as distinct from the level of action. The anomaly, which the revolutionary party and its intelligentsia will hopefully resolve, is that the working class under capitalism is involved in concrete struggles with revolutionary implications but, because it is in the thrall of hegemonic social thought, is unable to draw revolutionary conclusions from its actions. It is this dominated consciousness that, Gramsci claims, has prevented the working class from drawing the radical consequences inherent in much of its action:

> The active man-in-the-mass has a practical activity, but has no clear theoretical consciousness of his practical activity. . . . His theoretical consciousness can indeed be historically in opposition to his activity. One might almost say that he has two theoretical consciousnesses (or one contradictory consciousness): one which is implicit in his activity and which in reality unites him with all his fellow-workers in the practical transformation of the real world; and one, superficially explicit or verbal, which he has inherited from the past and uncritically absorbed. But this verbal conception is not without consequences . . . the contradictory state

of consciousness does [often] not permit of any action, any decision, or any choice, and produces a condition of moral and political passivity.[46]

We have explored, however, something of the imaginative capacity of subordinate groups to reverse or negate dominant ideologies. So common is this pattern that it is plausible to consider it part and parcel of the religiopolitical equipment of historically disadvantaged groups. Other things equal, it is therefore more accurate to consider subordinate classes *less* constrained at the level of thought and ideology, since they can in secluded settings speak with comparative safety, and *more* constrained at the level of political action and struggle, where the daily exercise of power sharply limits the options available to them. To put it crudely, it would ordinarily be suicide for serfs to set about to murder their lords and abolish the seigneurial regime; it is, however, plausible for them to imagine and talk about such aspirations providing they are discreet about it.

My criticism of Gramsci, a skeptic might object, is applicable only at those times when power relations virtually preclude open forms of resistance and protest. Only under such conditions are the constraints on action so severe as to produce near hegemonic appearances. Surely, the skeptic might continue, at times of open political struggle the mask of compliance and deference may be shed or at least lowered appreciably. Here would certainly be the place to look for evidence of false consciousness. If, however, in the course of active protest, subordinate groups still embrace the bulk of the dominant ideology, then we can reliably infer the effect of a hegemonic ideology.

It is true that protest and open struggle by subordinate groups have rarely taken truly radical ideological turns. This undeniable fact has been used to reclaim a thin version of the theory of hegemony. One persuasive formulation comes from Barrington Moore:

> one main cultural task facing any oppressed group is to undermine or explode the justification of the dominant stratum. Such criticisms may take the form of attempts to demonstrate that the dominant stratum does not perform the tasks that it claims to perform and therefore violates the social contract. Much more frequently they take the form that specified individuals in the dominant stratum fail to live up to the social contract. Such criticism leaves the basic functions of the dominant stratum inviolate. Only the most radical forms of criticism have raised the question

46. *Selections from the Prison Notebooks,* 333.

whether kings, capitalists, priests, generals, bureaucrats, etc., serve any useful social purpose at all.[47]

Moore implicitly asks us to imagine a gradient of radicalism in the interrogation of domination. The least radical step is to criticize some of the dominant stratum for having violated the norms by which they claim to rule; the next most radical step is to accuse the entire stratum of failing to observe the principles of its rule; and the most radical step is to repudiate the very principles by which the dominant stratum justifies its dominance. Criticism of virtually any form of domination might be analyzed in this fashion. It is one thing to claim that *this* king is not as beneficent as his predecessors, another to claim that kings in general don't live up to the beneficence they promise, and still another to repudiate all forms of kingship as inadmissible.

As one among many plausible ways of distinguishing how deeply a particular criticism cuts into a form of domination, this scheme has certain advantages. My quarrel is rather with the use of this criterion to infer the degree of ideological domination that prevails in a particular setting. By itself, the fact that social criticism remains ideologically limited can never, I am convinced, justify the conclusion that the group which makes that criticism is prevented by a hegemonic ideology from consciously formulating a more far-reaching critique. To conclude that slaves, serfs, peasants, untouchables, and other subordinate groups are ethically submissive merely because their protests and claims conform to the proprieties of the dominant class they are challenging would be a serious analytical error.

The fact is that the public representations of claims by subordinate groups, *even in situations of conflict,* nearly always have a strategic or dialogic dimension that influences the form they take. Short of the total declaration of war that one does occasionally find in the midst of a revolutionary crisis, most protests and challenges—even quite violent ones—are made in the realistic expectation that the central features of the form of domination will remain intact. So long as that expectation prevails, it is impossible to know from the public transcript alone how much of the appeal to hegemonic values is prudence and formula and how much is ethical submission.

The potentially strategic element in appeals to the hegemonic values is apparent from almost any setting of inequality; it follows from the domination of language. To take a banal example, imagine someone appealing to his superiors in a capitalist firm for a raise or protesting his failure to receive a raise others have gotten. So long as he anticipates remaining within the

47. *Injustice,* 84.

structure of authority, his case will necessarily be addressed to the institutional interests of his superiors. He may, in fact, want a raise to, say, buy a new car, support a gambling habit, or help fund a fringe political group and feels he is entitled to it for having faithfully covered for his boss's mistakes, and he may say as much to his family and closest friends. None of this, however, will have a legitimate place in the official transcript. He will, therefore, probably emphasize his loyal and effective contribution to the institutional success of the firm in the past and what he can contribute in the future. Strategic action always looks upward, for that is frequently the only way in which it will gain a hearing. The appeal may, of course, be entirely candid, but we cannot judge its candor on the basis of the official transcript alone.

The power of the dominant thus ordinarily elicits—in the public transcript—a continuous stream of performances of deference, respect, reverence, admiration, esteem, and even adoration that serve to further convince ruling elites that their claims are in fact validated by the social evidence they see before their very eyes. Thus the classic claim that "our (serfs, slaves, untouchables) love us" is typically more ingenuous than critics of domination are apt to assume. By a social alchemy that is not, after all, so mysterious, the dross of domination produces the public discursive affirmations that *seem* to transform that domination into the gold of willing, even enthusiastic, consent.

Most acts of power from below, even when they are protests—implicitly or explicitly—will largely observe the "rules" even if their objective is to undermine them. Apart from the homage to the official transcript implied by the invocation of such rules, they may often be seen as habitual and formulaic, implying little in the way of inwardness. The lettres de cachet addressed directly to French kings, and typically complaining about a personal injustice they wish to see righted by the monarch, make liberal use of grandiloquent language in addressing the Crown. The formulas were known, and a notary could be hired to surround the substantive complaint with the appropriate euphemisms stressing the grandeur and beneficence of the Crown and the humility and loyalty of this particular petitioning subject. As Foucault notes, such formulas "cause beggars, poor folks, or simply the mediocre to appear in a strange theatre where they assume poses, declamations, grandiloquences, where they dress up in bits of drapery which are necessary if they want to be paid attention to on the stage of power."[48] The "strange theatre" to which Foucault refers is deployed not merely to gain a hearing but often as a valuable political resource in conflict and even in rebellion. Examples drawn from a

48. Michel Foucault, *Michel Foucault: Power, Truth, Strategy,* ed. Meaghan Morris and Paul Patton. "Working Papers Collection #2," 88.

civilian prison and from patterns of peasant petitioning and revolt should help convey how euphemized power provides the basis for appeals from below.

In his careful description of public strategies used by inmates in a relatively progressive Norwegian prison, Thomas Mathiesen exlores how they manage to advance their interests against those of the treatment staff and administration.[49] It matters little for our purposes whether the prisoners view the institution with cynicism or with legitimacy; their conduct is perfectly compatible with either assumption, so long as their strategic understanding is that they will have to continue to deal with the prison authorities, in one form or another. Deprived of realistic revolutionary options and having few political resources by definition, inmates nevertheless manage to conduct an effective struggle against the institution's authorities, by using hegemonic ideology to good advantage. What the prisoners resent most about daily prison life is their powerlessness before the seemingly capricious and unpredictable distribution of privileges and punishments by administrative personnel. In their dogged attempts to domesticate the power arrayed against them and to render it predictable and manipulatable they pursue a strategy that Mathiesen characterizes as "censoriousness." This consists in stressing the established norms of the rulers of their small kingdom and claiming that these rulers have violated the norms by which they justify their own authority. Prisoners press constantly for the specification of procedures, criteria, and guidelines that will govern the granting of privileges (for example, residence in a minimum security block, good jobs, furloughs). They are partisans of seniority as the major criterion, inasmuch as it would operate automatically and mechanically. The wider society from which they come has established values of law-regarding procedures and mechanical equality for citizens that they deftly employ to make their case. Their behavior in this respect is moralistic; it is the staff who are deviating from legitimate norms, not they. The principle of radical indeterminacy once again prevails. It is virtually impossible to know from the official transcript to what degree the argument of the prisoners is strategic in the sense of being a conscious manipulation of the prevailing norms. The officials of the prison would, in any event, be the last to know.

The treatment and administrative staff have, with limited success, attempted to resist the logic of the inmate's case. Their power quite clearly rests on maximizing their personal discretion in apportioning benefits and discipline; it is virtually their only means of gaining conformity from a population that has already been denied its basic freedoms. Deprived of this discretion, their social control evaporates, and in arguing for some latitude of action they

49. *The Defenses of the Weak: A Sociological Study of a Norwegian Correctional Institution.*

have recourse to the "treatment ideology" of tailoring their conduct to the individual needs of the particular prisoner. For the prisoner, this may simply represent their capacity to punish him for sullenness or sloppy clothes. We have here, then, a useful illustration of how a set of given normative or ideological rules comes to help constitute the exercises of power and conflicts that are easily available within its ambit. The plasticity of any would-be hegemonic ideology which must, by definition, make a claim to serve the real interests of subordinate groups, provides antagonists with political resources in the form of political claims that are legitimized by that ideology.[50] Whether he believes in the rules or not, only a fool would fail to appreciate the possible benefits of deploying such readily available ideological resources.

Use of the ideology of the dominant stratum does not by any means prevent violent clashes of interest; it may in fact be fairly viewed as a common justification for violence. Peasant petitions to the daimyo [feudal barons] in Tokugawa Japan were frequently a prelude to riots and insurrections. Despite capital penalties for petitioning, village leaders did occasionally take this dramatic step and, when they did, their petitions were invariably cast in deferential terms, appealing for the "mercy of the lord" in reducing taxes and invoking a tradition of "benevolent social aid from their superiors."[51] Such wording— even as a prelude to an insurrection—is often taken as a privileged glimpse into the true peasant world view of "benevolent lords and honorable peasants," when, in fact, we are observing a dialogue with power that may have a greater or lesser strategic dimension. One thing, however, is clear. By making appeals that remain within the official discourse of deference, the peasantry may somewhat lessen the mortal risks incurred by the desperate act of petitioning. In the midst of a collective provocation heavy with implicit threat, peasants attempt to cede the symbolic high ground to official values and imply that their quiescence and loyalty will be assured if only the lord abides by their understanding of the hierarchical social contract. Everyone involved knows, certainly, that the petition carries a threat, as virtually all such petitions do, but the document begins by invoking the hierarchical verities that the peasantry professes to accept as given.

The collective insistence, through petitioning, on the "rights" to which subordinate groups feel entitled carries an understood "or else" with the precise consequences of a refusal left to the imagination of the lord. If one can speak of the self-disciplined adherence of an aristocracy to its own code of

50. Over time, of course, the use and manipulation of the ideological rules for novel purposes will transform them in important ways.

51. Najita and Scheiner, *Japanese Thought in the Tokugawa Period,* 41, 43.

values, when that adherence is painful, as noblesse oblige, then one can speak of peasant insistence on elite adherence to its own understanding of the social contract as *paysans obligent*. Such petitions usually refer to the sufferings, the desperation, the tried patience of loyal peasants under taxes, conscription, or whatever, and, as a seventeenth-century French historian correctly observed, "He who speaks of desperation to his sovereign, threatens him."[52] A petition of desperation is therefore likely to amalgamate two contradictory elements: an implicit threat of violence and a deferential tone of address. It is never simple to discern how much of this deference is simply the formula in which elites are addressed—with little significance beyond that—and how much is a more or less self-conscious attempt to gain practical ends by disavowing, publicly, any intention of challenging the basic principles of stratification and authority. We know, for example, from Le Roy Ladurie's reconstruction of the uprising in Romans in 1580, that an insurrectionary atmosphere among the artisans and peasants had taken shape by early 1579. And yet when the Queen Mother Catherine, on a visit to the town, asked Paumier why he was against the king, he is reported to have replied, "*I am the king's servant*, but the people have elected me to save the poor folk afflicted by the tyranny of war, and to pursue *humbly*, the *just remonstrances* contained in their Cahier."[53] Since the moment was not ripe for an open rebellion, it is plausible that Paumier chose to speak prudently. It is also plausible that he used the formulas of respect unreflectively in much the way that standard salutations and closings are employed in contemporary business letters. There is, however, a third alternative, which I wish to explore in detail. It is that subordinate groups have typically learned, in situations short of those rare all-or-nothing struggles, to clothe their resistance and defiance in ritualisms of subordination that serve both to disguise their purposes and to provide them with a ready route of retreat that may soften the consequences of a possible failure. I cannot prove an assertion of this kind, but I believe I can show why it should be seriously entertained.

Naive Monarchism: "Long Live X"

In sketching the case for a not-so-naive interpretation of naive monarchism among the peasantry, I rely heavily on Daniel Field's thoughtful study of the

52. Ladurie, *Carnival in Romans*, 257. The Dauphinois historian quoted here is N. Chorier, *Histoire générale de Dauphiné*, 2:697 (1672).

53. Ibid., 152, emphasis added. At the same time Paumier did not kneel before Catherine while saying this, an omission the enemies of the popular movement found insolent.

phenomenon in Russia.[54] The "myth" of the Czar-Deliverer, who would come to save his people from oppression, was generally believed to have been the great conservative ideological force in Russian history. Until Bloody Sunday in 1905, when the czar was known to have given orders for troops to fire on peaceful demonstrators, Lenin believed it was naive monarchism that had been the major obstacle to peasant rebellion:

> until now [peasants] have been able naively and blindly to believe in the Tsar-*batiushka* [Deliverer], to seek relief from their unbearably hard circumstances from the Tsar-*batiushka* "Himself," and to blame coercion, arbitrariness, plunder, and all other outrages *only* on the officials who deceive the Tsar. Long generations of the oppressed, savage life of the *muzhik*, lived out in neglected backwaters have reinforced this faith. . . . *Peasants could not rise in rebellion, they were only able to petition and to pray.*[55]

Lenin notwithstanding, there is simply no evidence that the myth of the czar promoted political passivity among the peasantry and a fair amount of evidence that, if anything, the myth facilitated peasant resistance.

The myth itself appears to have developed in the seventeenth century during the Time of Troubles and dynastic crises. In one more-or-less standard variant, the Czar-Deliverer desires to free his loyal subjects from serfdom, but wicked courtiers and officials, hoping to prevent this, try to assassinate him. Miraculously, he survives (often saved by a loyal serf) and hides among the people as a pilgrim sharing their sufferings and revealing himself to a faithful few. At length he returns to the capital, is recognized by the people and enthroned, whereupon he rewards the faithful and punishes the wicked. As a just czar he inaugurates a reign of peace and tranquility.[56]

Perhaps the most remarkable feature of the myth was its plasticity in the hands of its peasant adherents. First and foremost, it was an invitation to resist any or all of the czar's supposed agents, who could not have been carrying out the good czar's wishes if they imposed heavy taxes, conscription, rents, military corvée, and so forth. If the czar only knew of the crimes his faithless agents were committing in his name, he would punish them and rectify matters. When petitions failed and oppression continued, it may simply have indicated that an imposter—a false czar—was on the throne. In such cases,

---

54. *Rebels in the Name of the Tsar.*
55. Quoted in ibid., 2, emphasis added.
56. The parallels with the life of Christ can hardly be inadvertent but, as in other cultures, there were in Russia long traditions of the return of a just king. As in Western Europe the anti-Christ and the tyrant were often assimilated to one another.

the peasants who joined the banners of a rebel claiming to be the true czar would be demonstrating their loyalty to the monarchy. Under the reign of Catherine II there were at least twenty-six pretenders. Pugachev, the leader of one of the greatest peasant rebellions in modern European history, owed his success in part to his claim to be Czar Peter III—a claim apparently accepted by many. As a practical matter, the wishes of the benevolent czar were whatever the pressing interests and tribulations of the peasantry projected onto him; and this, of course, was what made the myth so politically incendiary. The myth of the czar could transmute the peasantry's violent resistance to oppression into an act of loyalty to the Crown. Defending themselves before the magistrate, Ukrainian rebels in 1902 claimed that the czar had given them permission to take grain from the gentry and that they had heard there was a *ukase* (decree) from the czar to this effect that had been suppressed. Peasants might resist local authorities, claiming they (the officials) were acting against the will of the czar and then reject messages and messengers to the contrary as fraudulent. They might rebel on behalf of reforms in serfdom, or its abolition, which had been decreed by the czar but concealed from them by cruel officials.

In a form of symbolic jujitsu, an apparently conservative myth counseling passivity becomes a basis for defiance and rebellion that is, in turn, publicly justified by faithful allegiance to the monarch! Once the serfs were convinced that their resistance was serving the czar, the submissive patience and prayer advised by the myth was of no avail to officialdom. As Field concludes, "Naive or not, the peasants professed their faith in the Tsar in forms, *and only in those forms*, that corresponded to their interests. Peasant leaders, finding the myth ready to hand in its folkloric expressions, used it to arouse, galvanize, and unify other peasants. It was a pretext to resistance against heavy odds, and there was no other likely means to that end."[57]

In each of the two cases examined in depth by Field, it was not entirely implausible to believe that local officials were defying the czar's wishes. After the emancipation in 1861, the peasants in Biezdne (Kazan Province) were demoralized to discover that with redemption payments, labor dues, and taxes their burdens were, if anything, heavier than before. When one of their number claimed that the emancipation decree granted them complete freedom from such dues—the term *volia* (freedom) appeared in many contexts in the decree—but that the squires and officials had kept it from being implemented, they leapt at the opportunity, now sanctioned from on high, to refuse payment. Given the fact that they had been formally freed from serfdom, the

57. Ibid., 209.

notion that its full import was being kept from them was not so farfetched. It would not have been the first time nobles and officials had ignored or distorted a decree from the czar. At the same time they drew up a petition to the czar and sent three of their number to Petrograd to deliver it by hand. Whatever they might be charged with, their actions seemed to disavow any temptation to sedition or treason. They avoided questions and, when pressed, "dissimulated."[58]

The second case occurred in Chigirin District, Kiev Province in the Ukraine. It involved a dispute over land allocations—whether they were to be individual or communal—that had continued for more than seven years. A majority was opposed to the allocations imposed earlier and finally, in 1875, refused to make redemption payments and petitioned the czar in the most deferential terms, referring to a more generous *ukase* that had been kept from them. One unique feature of the Chigirin episode is that a populist agitator, hoping to spark an insurrection in these troubled waters, arrived in the area with cash and a bogus imperial charter supposedly from the hand of the czar granting them all their demands. He was attempting to use peasant gullibility and naive monarchism to launch a rebellion. The peasantry treated him as they might any outsider: they relieved him of his money, "they were obsequious and compliant in his presence and otherwise went their own way."[59]

When the imposter was arrested, local villagers, fearful of the consequences for themselves, drafted their own petition to the czar to explain why they might have believed that the czar had decided in their favor. It began, "How could we, simple, backward people, not believe in the kindness of our beloved monarch when the whole world attests to it, when we know of His love and trust for His people, His concern for them . . . ?"[60] Here it is not a question of peasants hilariously slapping their sides or cynically calculating the effect of their phrases. It is, however, a question of understanding at some level the usefulness of naiveté, simplicity, and backwardness in appeals to the czar. If the official view of the peasants as childlike, unenlightened, God-fearing, and basically loyal led to a philosophy of rule that emphasized both strictness and paternal indulgence, this official view was not without its advantages to peasants in a tight spot. By invoking their simplicity and loyalty they

58. Ibid., 79.
59. Ibid., 201.
60. Ibid., 198. Speculatively, the form of the classic petition is a threat embedded in a rhetoric of deference. One imagines it being read by officials who routinely skip the rhetoric of deference in order to get to the operative clause, which may state (though in more decorous terms), "If you don't lower taxes we may make big trouble." But in the dramaturgy of naive monarchism the petition says, in effect, "Alright, we'll pretend to be loyal peasants so long as you pretend to be the beneficent czar, which, in this case, means lowering taxes."

might hope to invoke his generosity and forgiveness as well as that of the judges and police officials they might encounter. And if peasants were notoriously gullible, they could hardly be entirely responsible if they fell prey to clever, seditious propaganda. One can, under the circumstances, scarcely imagine a more effective symbolic rationale for acts of rebellion and insubordination—a rationale that was likely to minimize the consequences of failure in the struggle with gentry and officials over taxes, land, dues, conscription, and grain. A history of the need to dissimulate as well as long practice in the strategic use of hegemonic values are all we need to grasp the use value of naive monarchism.

The usefulness of naive monarchism to the peasantry sprang in part from its value to the czarist bureaucracy. Above all, naive monarchism represented the most comforting interpretation of peasant disorder for those with the most to gain from the existing distribution of property, status, and wealth. If there was discontent, it could be explained by a momentary disturbance of a fundamentally sound and just social order. The serfs/peasants were devoted to the czar and generally met their obligations to the state except when a few agitators or a few rapacious officials or aristocrats provoked them from their allegiance. It sufficed, then, to round up a few agitators or dismiss a few officials and order would be restored. No fundamental changes need be contemplated, and no mass deportations of peasants to Siberia were required. Dealing leniently with the peasants who had expressed their repentance would further confirm the czar's reputation for paternal indulgence, thereby justifying the naive monarchism of the peasantry. And because the peasantry were still naive, backward, and so easily misled—Didn't they admit as much in the petitions?—they needed a strong, authoritarian monarch and his agents to guide and instruct them.

The tacit ideological complicity apparently at work here is a product of the very logic of czarist paternalism. While the peasants could make of naive monarchism an incitement to revolt, they also may well have appreciated the value of the myth of the peasant—the stereotype of the ignorant, dark *narod* could be as handy on occasion as a simple faith in the czar's concern for his people. In this respect, we must not see the myths of the czar and peasant as an ideological creation of the monarchy, then appropriated and reinterpreted by the peasantry. These myths were rather the joint product of a historic struggle rather like a ferocious argument in which the basic terms (simple peasant, benevolent czar) are shared but in which the interpretations follow wildly divergent paths in accordance with vital interests.

The not-so-naive use of naive monarchism by Russian peasants should give us pause about the analysis of those numerous occasions on which a rebellious subordinate group invokes the ritual symbols of a conservative hegemony. Throughout Europe and in Southeast Asia, for example, there are long traditions of the return of a just king or religious savior, despite great differences in cultural and religious lineages.[61] Such traditions have figured prominently in peasant rebellions and may have served much the same ideological function as the myth of the Czar-Deliverer in Russia. The many variations in what have been, in England, called Church and King riots may well, on closer examination, have an important strategic element to them. In France and Italy in the sixteenth and seventeenth centuries it was common for insurgent rioters to cry, "Long Live the Virgin" (Viva Maria) and follow this with particular demands. As Peter Burke has observed, "But it is unlikely that all the rebels were unaware of the strategic value of shouting, 'Viva Maria!' a cry which like 'Vive le Roi!,' made their cause respectable. In that limited sense religious ideas were instruments in the struggle."[62] We might, in this context, think of shouts of "Vive le Roi," when they come first in a series, just before, say, "Down with feudal dues and the salt tax" as having the same performative force as the deferential opening of a petition demanding redress for bitter grievances.[63] It is the accepted form of address, it costs little, it reassures one's antagonist that one is not out utterly to destroy him, it claims loyal intentions, it allows the king to grant the petition while appearing to enhance his prestige, and it offers a welcome defensive posture that may help limit damage if the initiative fails. Such gestures may, in some cultural contexts, become as habitual as the ordinary conversational prefaces to complaints by subordinates who are not yet so alienated as to declare war. I have in mind sentences that might begin with "I don't mean to complain but . . ." or "With all due respect . . ." Any dominant ideology with hegemonic pretensions must, by definition, provide subordinate groups with political weapons that can be of use in the public transcript.

Let us return briefly to the issue of "ethical submission" and hegemony by way of placing the public transcript in its political context. I believe the historical evidence clearly shows that subordinate groups have been capable of revolutionary *thought* that repudiates existing forms of domination. Schwabian artisans and cultivators in the German Peasant War could imagine that

---

61. For a brief discussion of these traditions in Europe, see Peter Burke, *Popular Culture in Early Modern Europe*, chap. 6. For similar traditions in Southeast Asia, see Adas, *Prophets of Rebellion*.

62. "Mediterranean Europe, 1500–1800," in *Religion and Rural Revolt*, ed. Bak and Benecke, 79.

63. This particular shout is reported for sixteenth-century Normandy by David Nicholls, "Religion and Peasant Movements during the French Religious Wars," in ibid., 104–22.

Christ's crucifixion had redeemed all believers from serfdom, bondage, and taxes; untouchables can and have imagined that orthodox Hinduism has hidden the sacred texts proving their equality; slaves can and have imagined a day when they would be free and slave owners punished for their tyranny.

What is rare, then, is not the negation of domination in thought but rather the occasions on which subordinate groups have been able to act openly and fully on that thought. Only under the most extraordinary historical circumstances, when the nearly total collapse of existing structures of domination open unprecedented new vistas of now realistic possibilities, can we expect to witness anything like an unguarded discourse by subordinate groups. In Western history, the German Peasants' War, the English Civil War, the French Revolution, the Russian Revolution, and the Spanish Republic of 1936 offered such brief and privileged moments.[64] Here one glimpses something of the utopias of justice and revenge that are ordinarily marginalized in the hidden transcript.

Under any other circumstances, which is to say, for the great bulk of political life, including most violent conflict, the stakes are less than the conquest of a new world. The conflict will accordingly take a dialogic form in which the language of the dialogue will invariably borrow heavily from the terms of the dominant ideology prevailing in the public transcript. If the official discourse is one of a Christian ruler and pious peasants, the ideological struggle will swirl around the interpretation of these terms.[65] We have seen similarly how, in a dominant discourse of benevolent czar and loyal serf, the ideological struggle will swirl around the interpretation of these terms and need not exclude violent conflict. A dominant ideology of paternalistic lords and faithful retainers does not prevent social conflict but is simply an invitation to a structured argument. We may consider the dominant discourse as a plastic idiom or dialect that is capable of carrying an enormous variety of

64. For a pathbreaking analysis of utopian moments in French history—all recapturing in some sense the initial promise of the Revolution of 1789—see Aristide R. Zolberg, "Moments of Madness."

65. The Filipino revolutionary leader Andreas Bonifacio, for example, issued a manifesto charging the Spanish with having betrayed a pact of brotherhood in which they promised their Filipino younger brothers knowledge, prosperity, and justice: "Do we see them fulfilling their side of the contract which we ourselves fulfilled with sacrifices? We see nothing but treachery as a reward for our favors." Quoted in Reynaldo Clemeña Ileto, "Pasyon and the Interpretation of Change in Tagalog Society," 107. As the Spanish have betrayed the self-proclaimed terms of their domination, the Filipino people are absolved of any obligation to obey. Bonifacio, of course, necessarily implies that if the Spanish had lived up to their Christian professions, the Tagalogs would have remained loyal. Did Bonifacio believe this? We cannot know. What we do know, however, is that he chose to address the Spanish in terms they could understand—in the terms of their own rhetorical discourse, which, on this interpretation, justified armed defense.

meanings, including those that are subversive of their use as intended by the dominant. The appeal to would-be hegemonic values sacrifices very little in the way of flexibility given how malleable the terms are and has the added advantage of appearing to disavow the most threatening goals. For anything less than completely revolutionary ends the terrain of dominant discourse is the only plausible arena of struggle.

Exactly how deep this apparent acceptance of the dominant discourse goes is, again, impossible to judge from the public evidence. If we were to be exceptionally meticulous about the conclusions we could legitimately draw from such appearances, we might say that addressing the dominant elite under less than revolutionary circumstances, and given certain constraining assumptions about the distribution of power, the use of the terms of the dominant ideology in the course of political struggle is both realistic and prudent.

Minding the Public Discourse

You have got to be a model thief if I am to be a model judge. If you are a fake thief, I become a fake judge. Is that clear?

—GENET, *The Balcony*

Any ruling group, in the course of justifying the principles of social inequality on which it bases its claim to power, makes itself vulnerable to a particular line of criticism.[66] Inasmuch as these principles of inequality unavoidably claim that the ruling stratum performs some valuable social function, its members open themselves to attack for the failure to perform these functions honorably or adequately. The basis of the claim to privilege and power creates, as it were, the groundwork for a blistering critique of domination on the terms invoked by the elite. Such a critique from within the ruling discourse is the ideological equivalent of being hoisted on one's own petard. For any particular form of domination one may specify the claims to legitimacy it makes, the discursive affirmations it stages for the public transcript, the aspects of power relations that it will seek to hide (its dirty linen), the acts and gestures that will undermine its claim to legitimacy, the critiques that are possible within its frame of reference, and, finally, the ideas and actions that will represent a repudiation or profanation of the form of domination in its entirety.[67]

66. Moore, *Injustice*, 84.
67. A suggestive analysis along these lines, dealing with conflicts in the jute mills of Bengal earlier in this century, will serve to indicate how valuable such an inquiry might be. Dipesh Chakrabarty shows how the patron–client style of authority exercised by supervisors in the mills required personal discretion, direct relations of both benevolence and brutality, and the display of

The analysis of forms of domination might well begin by specifying the ways in which the structure of claims to power influences the sort of public transcript it requires. It might then examine how such a public transcript may be undermined or repudiated. If, for example, we were studying the relation between warrior aristocrats of feudal Europe and their serfs it would be important to understand how their claim to hereditary authority was based on providing physical protection in return for labor, grain, and military service. This "exchange" might be discursively affirmed in an emphasis on honor, noblesse oblige, bravery, expansive generosity, tournaments and contests of military prowess, the construction of fortifications, the regalia and ceremony of knighthood, sumptuary laws, the assembling of serfs for work or military campaigns, acts of deference and humility of serfs before their lords, exemplary punishment for insubordination, oaths of fealty, and so forth. The feudal "contract" could be *discursively negated* by any conduct that violated these affirmations: for example, cowardice, petty bargaining, stinginess, runaway serfs, failures to physically protect serfs, refusals to be respectful or deferential by serfs, and so forth. A parallel kind of analysis might be applied to relations between the Brahmin (or high-caste superior) and the lower caste. Here the basis for the claim to power is based on sacred hereditary status, superior karma, and on the provision of certain presumably vital ritual services that can be performed only by Brahmins due to their status and knowledge. Discursive affirmations might include all the ritual separations of purity and pollution, diet, dress, refinement of manner, presiding at key rites of birth, marriage, death, observance of taboos on commensuality, other forms of segregation by occupation, residence, drinking wells, temples, and so forth. The discursive negation of these expressions of hierarchy might take the form of refusing to abide by rules about pollution and purity, failure by Brahmins to provide ritual services, insubordination in terms of address or posture by untouchables, and so on. This pattern of analysis might be extended, of course, to any particular historical form of domination in comparable terms; for example, certain forms of priestly rule, specific forms of slavery, various

---

power in the form of dress, retinue, housing, and demeanor. By adopting the parental model as the pattern for the relationship, the supervisor was experienced along a continuum from personal despot to kindly father figure. Unlike relations of industrial discipline derived from a combination of contract, the labor market, the division of labor, and the organization of work, control in the jute mills was phrased in entirely personal, direct, and often violent terms. One result, as Chakrabarty shows, is that the resistance to the supervisors, in turn, tended to take the form of personal vengeance and violence. Insults to the dignity of the worker, used as a form of social control, were repaid in insults to the supervisor when that was possible. The form of resistance mirrored the form of domination. Dipesh Chakrabarty, "On Deifying and Defying Authority: Managers and Workers in the Jute Mills of Bengal circa 1900–1940."

monarchical systems, religious prophets within a specified tradition, modern managerial authority in the firm in Italy or in Japan. Having elaborated the public transcript required by a specific form of domination, one has gone far to specify precisely what a subversive act in this context would look like.

Regardless of the particular form of domination, it is a safe bet that a vital sector of the elite-choreographed public transcript will consist of visual and audible displays of rank, precedence, and honor. Here I have in mind such expressions of domination as terms of address, demeanor, speech levels, codes of eating, dressing, bathing, cultural taste, who speaks first, who gives way to whom. By the same token whenever the public transcript is breached—whether inadvertently or by design—it is also a safe bet that such breaches will disrupt or desacralize the ceremonial reverence.[68] For acts of insubordination of this kind represent a small insurgency within the public transcript.

Just as the official transcript helps define what counts as an insult to the dominant—as lèse-majesté—it also helps to define which of the practices that compose the inevitable dirty work of power must be screened from public view. The very operation of a rationale for inequality creates a potential zone of dirty linen that, if exposed, would contradict the pretensions of legitimate domination. A ruling stratum whose claim to authority rests on the provision of institutionalized justice under law with honest judges will have to go to exceptional lengths to hide its thugs, its hired assassins, its secret police, and its use of intimidation. An elite that bases its power on its self-sacrificing, public-spirited probity will be damaged more by an exposé of corruption in high places than one based on a patronage machine. Every publicly given justification for inequality thus marks out a kind of symbolic Achilles heel where the elite is especially vulnerable.

Attacks that focus on this symbolic Achilles heel may be termed critiques within the hegemony. One reason they are particularly hard to deflect is simply because they begin by adopting the ideological terms of reference of the elite. Although such critiques may be insincere and cynical, they cannot be accused of sedition inasmuch as they clothe themselves in the public professions of the elite, which now stands accused of hypocrisy, if not the violation of a sacred trust. Having formulated the very terms of the argument and propagated them, the ruling stratum can hardly decline to defend itself on this terrain of its own choosing. The cowardly lion is a staple of pathos, if not humor, in the folklore of those who have regarded the lion as a metaphor for courage. An ascetic priestly caste is profoundly damaged if shown to be promiscuous and gluttonous; the benevolent czar is profoundly damaged if shown to have

---

68. See Ranajit Guha, *Elementary Aspects of Peasant Insurgency*, esp. chap 2.

ordered the troops to fire on his peacefully assembled, respectful subjects; the slave owner's claim to paternalism is hollow if he can be shown to whip his slaves *arbitrarily;* and the general is compromised if he abandons his troops in fear for his own life. Any dominant group is, in this respect, least able to take liberties with those symbols in which they are most heavily invested.[69]

Perhaps for this reason, as I indicated earlier, so many radical attacks originate in critiques within the hegemony—in taking the values of ruling elites seriously, while claiming that they (the elites) do not. To launch an attack in these terms is to, in effect, call upon the elite to take its own rhetoric seriously. Not only is such an attack a legitimate critique by definition, but it always threatens to appeal to sincere members of the elite in a way that an attack from outside their values could not. The Soviet dissident Vladimir Voinovich captures the critical force of disillusioned believers:

> I was a completely harmless member of society. It is the young people, those who display a serious interest in the theoretical foundations of communism and begin immersing themselves in Marx, Lenin and Stalin who pose a much greater danger to the regime. The Soviet authorities realize this. A person who takes theory seriously will, sooner or later, begin comparing it with practice, and will end up rejecting one or the other, and, later on, the two of them together. But a person who has not been seduced by the theory will view the practice as a common and immutable evil—one that can be lived with.[70]

The remarkable fact may be that it is when a would-be hegemonic ideology does manage to convince members of subordinate groups to take it to heart that a potentially radical chain of events is set into motion. That is, contrary to the usual wisdom and to Gramsci's analysis, radicalism may be less likely to arise among disadvantaged groups (the vast majority, it appears) who fail to take the dominant ideology seriously than among those who, in Marxist terms, might be considered falsely conscious. In a perceptive study of working-class secondary school students in England, Paul Willis discovered a strong counterculture that produced a cynical distance from dominant platitudes but not radicalism.[71] Paradoxically, it was the "conformists," who appeared, in form at least, to accept the values of the school (the hegemonic instrument par excellence in modern society), who posed the threat. Because they operated as if

---

69. Bourdieu, *Outline of a Theory of Practice,* 193–94. The constraint, I believe, is also self-imposed in part since these are claims that are rarely just a cynical facade for the dominant.

70. *The Anti-Soviet Soviet Union,* trans. Richard Lourie (New York: Harcourt Brace Jovanovich, 1985), 147.

71. *Learning to Labour,* 110–11.

they accepted the implicit promise of the dominant ideology (If you work hard, obey authority, do well in school, and keep your nose clean you will advance by merit and have satisfying work) they made sacrifices of self-discipline and control and developed expectations that were usually betrayed. Employers preferred not to hire them because they were pushy and hard to deal with as compared with the more typical working-class youth, who were realistic, expected little, and put in a day of work without too much grumbling. The system may have most to fear from those subordinates among whom the institutions of hegemony have been most successful.[72] The disillusioned mission boy (Caliban) is always a graver threat to an established religion than the pagans who were never taken in by its promises. The anger born of a sense of betrayal implies an earlier faith.

72. One might argue similarly that the institutional centers of the civil rights movement in the U.S. in the early 1960s were churches and universities precisely because the contradiction between the principles of equality and the reality of segregation was particularly striking in institutions making strong moral claims. See Evans, *Personal Politics*, 32.

CHAPTER FIVE

Making Social Space for a Dissident Subculture

Man is a being that aspires to equilibrium: he balances the weight of the evil piled on his back with the weight of his hatred.

—MILAN KUNDERA, *The Joke*

Men may . . . discourse flippantly from arm chairs of the pleasures of slave life; but let them toil with him in the field . . . behold him scourged, hunted, trampled on, and they will come back with another story in their mouths. Let them know the heart of the poor slave—learn his secret thoughts—thoughts he dare not utter in the hearing of the white man; let them sit by him in the silent watches of the night—converse with him in trustful confidence.

—SOLOMAN NORTHRUP, ex-slave

IN THE COURSE OF THIS CHAPTER I want to sketch out the dynamics of the link between the hidden transcript and the experience of domination. This entails showing how more or less compelled performances engender a reaction and the basic form that reaction takes. This work of negation, as I call it, can take quite simple or quite elaborate forms. An example of an elaborate negation is the reworking by slaves of Christian doctrine to answer their own experiences and desires.

The balance of the discussion explores the process by which particular social sites and particular actors come to represent the location and carriers, respectively, of the hidden transcript. Their significance is best attested to, I argue, by the unremitting efforts of elites to abolish or penetrate such sites and the corresponding efforts by subordinate groups to defend them. Finally, I raise the question of how cohesive or coherent a particular group's hidden transcript is likely to be. Providing an answer requires us to specify both the homogeneity of the domination and the intensity of mutuality among those subject to it.

The Reaction to Saying "Uncle"

Our common sense tells us that those who must routinely knuckle under to insults or physical beatings they consider unjust pay a heavy psychological price. Exactly what that price may be is another matter. There is, however, some tangential evidence from social psychology that attempts to specify the consequences of forced compliance.

The findings need to be treated carefully. Given the fact they are generated from a discipline that is largely experimental and that practices methodological individualism, I will be grossly slighting cultural and historical explanations. They may serve, nevertheless, to clarify the relationship between compliance and beliefs. Two general findings from a variety of experiments are of interest. First, they indicate that forced compliance not only fails to produce attitudes that would sustain that compliance in the absence of domination, *but produces a reaction against such attitudes.* Second, they show that individual beliefs and attitudes are likely to reinforce compliance with powerholders' wishes if, and only if, that compliance is perceived as freely chosen—as voluntary. Coercion, it would seem, can produce compliance but it virtually inoculates the complier against willing compliance.

A recent development in social psychology called reactance theory draws heavily on the findings of classical aggression theory. But instead of being rooted, as aggression theory was, in instinctual drives, reactance theory begins with the premise that there is a human desire for freedom and autonomy that, when threatened by the use of force, leads to a reaction of opposition.[1] Various experiments along these lines indicate that when threats are added to a persuasive communication they reduce the degree of attitude change that otherwise occurs. Providing the threat is sufficiently imposing, overt agreement and compliance may prevail but covert reactance will increase. Overt compliance in the presence of a threat was often secured only by close surveillance to detect and punish deviance. Once the surveillance was withdrawn, the compliance evaporated quickly, and it was found that the surveillance itself, as an emanation of compulsion, further increased the degree of reaction. As one summary of research concludes, "The literature on reactance theory attests to the fact that threatened choice alternatives tend to become more attractive, and threats to attitudes can produce boomerang attitude change."[2] The role of power relations in opening a gap between public and covert behavior is confirmed by other experimental evidence as well. In one case it was shown that dependent subordinates will agree more with an "irascible, malignant" supervisor than with a "benign and permissive one." Once the dependence—the domination—is eliminated, however, the results are reversed, implying that, covertly, the tyrannical supervisor was disliked all along and that this dislike

1. Sharon S. Brehm and Jack W. Brehm, *Psychological Reactance: A Theory of Freedom and Control.*
2. Ibid., 396.

was held back only through fear of punishment.[3] The greater the force majeure compelling the performance, the less the subordinate considers it representative of his "true self" and the more it seems merely a manipulative tactic having little or no bearing on his self-conception.

Unless the action appears to the subordinate as a more or less uncoerced choice, there is little chance that acting a mask will appreciably affect the face of the actor. And, if it does, there is a better chance that the face behind the mask will, in reaction, grow to look *less* like the mask rather than more like it. Put another way, the greater the extrinsic reasons compelling our action— here large threats and large rewards are comparable—the less we have to provide satisfactory reasons to ourselves for our conduct. Psychologists examining American prisoners after their release from camps in Korea, where they had been "broken" and had signed confessions and given propaganda talks, found that there were far fewer lasting consequences on their beliefs and attitudes than might have been supposed. The reasons for their collaboration were apparently so overwhelming that it could be seen instrumentally and have few consequences for beliefs.[4] To the degree such findings are germane to the more draconian and culturally elaborate forms of powerlessness we have examined, it helps us appreciate how compulsion and surveillance alone can generate a reaction that may lie in wait. It is little wonder, then, that those in involuntary service need close supervision, inasmuch as any lapse in surveillance is likely to result in a precipitous decline in the apparent enthusiasm of their performance.

3. Jones, *Ingratiation,* 47–51. For studies of aggression thwarted and released in much the same fashion, see Leonard Berkowitz, *Aggression: A Social Psychological Analysis.*

4. See Winn, *The Manipulated Mind.* Action that grows from what we see as a free choice works in the opposite way. When we commit ourselves voluntarily to actions that turn out to be at variance with our values, it is more likely that we will reassess our values to bring them more into line with our actions. This process was much in evidence in Stanley Milgram's famous experiment in which volunteers found themselves asked/commanded by experimental authorities to administer what they believed were severe electrical shocks to subjects apparently in pain. The rate of compliance was generally high, although it was clear that the volunteer subjects were reluctant; they showed obvious signs of tension like sweating and, when authority figures left the room, many only pretended to administer the shock. Evidently, the key to their compliance lay in their having volunteered in the first place. Those volunteers who were *less* well compensated for their participation produced *more* compelling reasons why the victims deserved to be shocked. They had more to justify to themselves. That there should be such sharp distinctions between the conscript and the volunteer is in line with our commonsense knowledge. The deprivations of the prison and of the austere monastery or convent may be roughly comparable. The inmates of the former, however, are alienated and hostile; they are there against their will. The inmates of the latter embrace their deprivations with dedication because it is a commitment freely chosen. See Philip G. Zimbardo, *The Cognitive Control of Motivation: The Consequences of Choice and Dissonance,* chap. 1.

The Work of Negation

In the contrived experimental world of reactance theory, the social facts being reacted to are comparatively trivial and thus the reaction itself is not elaborate. Slaves, serfs, untouchables, and peasants are, however, reacting to quite complex forms of historical domination, and thus their reaction is correspondingly elaborate as well.

By definition, we have made the public transcript of domination ontologically prior to the hidden, offstage transcript.[5] The result of proceeding in this fashion is to emphasize the reflexive quality of the hidden transcript as a labor of neutralization and negation. If we think, in schematic terms, of public transcript as comprising a domain of material appropriation (for example, of labor, grain, taxes), a domain of public mastery and subordination (for example, rituals of hierarchy, deference, speech, punishment, and humiliation), and, finally, a domain of ideological justification for inequalities (for example, the public religious and political world view of the dominant elite), then we may perhaps think of the hidden transcript as comprising the offstage responses and rejoinders to that public transcript. It is, if you will, the portion of an acrimonious dialogue that domination has driven off the immediate stage.

Just as traditional Marxist analysis might be said to privilege the appropriation of surplus value as the social site of exploitation and resistance, our analysis here privileges the social experience of indignities, control, submission, humiliation, forced deference, and punishment. The choice of emphasis is not to gainsay the importance of material appropriation in class relations. Appropriation is, after all, largely the purpose of domination. The very process of appropriation, however, unavoidably entails systematic social relations of subordination that impose indignities of one kind or another on the weak. These indignities are the seedbed of the anger, indignation, frustration, and swallowed bile that nurture the hidden transcript. They provided the energy, the passion, for Mrs. Poyser's year-long rehearsal of imaginary speeches to the squire (see chapter 1).

Resistance, then, originates not simply from material appropriation but

---

5. The point is also an important theme of Michel Foucault's work. "Where there is power, there is resistance, and yet, or rather consequently, this resistance is never in a position of exteriority in relation to power." *The History of Sexuality,* vol. 1, *An Introduction,* trans. R. Hurley, 95. This is a defensible way of proceeding, in my view, providing we keep two points in mind. The first is that the reverse of Foucault's statement is just as plausible: "Power is never in a position of exteriority in relation to resistance." Forms of domination are devised, elaborated, and justified *because* the effort to bend others to one's will always encounters resistance. The second point is that we ought not to assume that the real subjects of our analysis have absolutely nothing else to talk about except domination and resistance.

from the pattern of personal humiliations that characterize that exploitation. While the extraction of labor or grain from a subordinate population has something of a generic quality to it, the shape of personal domination is likely to be far more culturally specific and particular. The view urged here is not one that would ignore appropriation. Instead, it would enlarge the field of vision. In understanding the *experience* of slavery, for example, the coerced toil would be no more privileged than beatings, insults, sexual abuse, and forced self-abasement. In understanding serfdom, the grain and labor exacted from the peasantry would be no more privileged than the required gestures of homage and submission, forbidden terms of address, *ius primae noctis*, and public whippings.

My confidence in making this case for the kinds of domination we have examined is bolstered by studies of working-class values in liberal democracies. If the personal aspect of submission is crucial to relatively impersonal forms of wage labor performed by workers who enjoy political rights and who are formally free to quit their job, then it ought to be far more relevant to those forms of domination that are more direct and personal. Accounting for the way in which workers in the United States experience their working life, Richard Sennett emphasizes that having constantly to take commands arouses the greatest resentment. I offer two representative quotations from those to whom he spoke: "but then I went to work at the machine shop and like, it hit me. Life, people can order you around and you got to take it cause you need the job."[6] "All day, 'Yes, Sir,' 'Yes, Ma'am.' . . . I mean, I think work made me know how the little man has got to take it, you know?"[7] The other aspect of their jobs that breeds deep indignation is their belief that they are not accorded the minimal recognition they deserve as human beings on the job. As Sennett puts it, "At the same time, over and over again in our talks, people expressed a great resentment against 'being treated like nothing,' 'being treated like you was dirt,' 'like you are part of the woodwork.' How is man to make himself visible?"[8]

Public injury to one's dignity and standing as a person, Sennett argues, is at the very center of class experience for American workers. For while material appropriation may, in fact, be carried out quite impersonally (for example, work at a machine, piecework), domination is usually more individualized— one pays homage as a person, is punished as a person, is slighted as a person. It

6. Richard Sennett and Jonathan Cobb, *The Hidden Injuries of Class,* 97.

7. Ibid., 115. In each of these cases the men with whom Sennett is speaking recognize the logic or even the necessity of hierarchy in the plant, but it is still the most grating aspect of their work.

8. Ibid., 139.

is thus the domination, without which no appropriation takes place, that particularly leaves its mark on personal dignity—if not on the physical person.

Once we have named a condition of subordination such as *wage-laborer* or *slave*, it remains to specify the particular ways in which the subordination is experienced by those who occupy that status. We know relatively little about a Malay villager if we know only that he is poor and landless. We know far more about the cultural meaning of his poverty once we know that he is particularly in despair because he cannot afford to feed guests on the feast of Ramadan, that wealthy people pass him on the village path without uttering a greeting, that he cannot bury his parents properly, that his daughter will marry late if at all because he lacks a dowry, that his sons will leave the household early since he has no property to hold them, and that he must humble himself—often to no avail—to beg work and rice from wealthier neighbors. To know the cultural meaning of his poverty in this way is to learn the shape of his indignity and, hence, to gauge the content of his anger. To have said that he was poor and landless and to have stopped at that would merely have told us that he was short of income and the means of production. While the daily indignities we have listed all flow from his class position, they tell us far more about what it feels like to be a poor man in a particular culture with particular ritual decencies at a particular moment in history. It is these experienced indignities that form the bridge between his condition and his consciousness.

Dignity is at once a very private and a very public attribute. One can experience an indignity at the hands of another despite the fact that no one else sees or hears about it. What is reasonably clear, however, is that any indignity is compounded greatly when it is inflicted in public. An insult, a look of contempt, a physical humiliation, an assault on one's character and standing, a rudeness is nearly always far more injurious when it is inflicted before an audience. To gauge the added threat to personal dignity by a public injury, consider for a moment the difference between a dressing down (the term is itself suggestive) an employee may receive from his boss in the privacy of the boss's office and the same dressing down delivered before all of the employee's peers and subordinates. The latter, if I am not mistaken, will be viewed by the employee as a far more aggressive and humiliating act. In much the same fashion, it is a rare slave narrative that does not have a moving passage like the following: "Who can imagine what could be the feeling of a father and mother, when looking upon an infant child whipped and tortured with impunity, and then placed in a situation where they can afford it no protection?"[9] The direct harm in this case is inflicted upon the child; what the parents suffer is a

9. Osofsky, *Puttin' on Ole Massa*, 80–81.

devastating public display of their powerlessness to keep their child from harm. They lose, as Aggy did (see chapter 1), the public claim to be parents, above all in the eyes of their child and also in those of any onlookers. It is difficult to conceive a more damaging loss of standing as a person. The impact seems to be seared in the memory of those who suffer it.[10]

Who precisely, then, composes the audience before which an indignity is most damaging? It is, I believe, exactly that audience before whom one's dignity, one's standing as a person, is most important because it forms the social source for one's sense of self-esteem. In particular, this circle would include one's closest family, friends, neighbors, coworkers and peers, and, particularly, one's own subordinates toward whom one stands in a relationship of power.[11] Here it may be useful to distinguish between the standing enjoyed, say, by a slave with his master and the standing he enjoys with other slaves. Unless he is willing to court death, the slave can never effectively assert his personhood and dignity vis-à-vis his master. Correspondingly, he stands in little danger of losing much dignity in the master's eyes if for no other reason than that he has so little to begin with. The sphere within which a slave can, at least provisionally, more effectively establish his dignity and standing is that formed by his peers, among whom, correspondingly, he has most to lose by any public assault on that dignity.

Within this restricted social circle the subordinate is afforded a partial refuge from the humiliations of domination, and it is from this circle that the audience (one might say "the public") for the hidden transcript is drawn. Suffering from the same humiliations or, worse, subject to the same terms of subordination, they have a shared interest in jointly creating a discourse of dignity, of negation, and of justice. They have, in addition, a shared interest in concealing a social site apart from domination where such a hidden transcript can be elaborated in comparative safety.

The most elementary forms of negation found in the social sites of the hidden transcript represent nothing more than the safe articulation of the assertion, aggression, and hostility that is thwarted by the onstage power of the dominant. Discretion in the face of power requires that a part of the "self" that would reply or strike back must lie low. It is this self that finds expression in the safer realm of the hidden transcript. While the hidden transcript cannot be

10. See, for example, the account by untouchables of the humiliation of being insulted in front of one's own house and before one's family, children, and neighbors. Khare, *The Untouchable as Himself*, 124.

11. This last is clearly related to the exquisite pleasure derived by victimized subordinates in seeing their tormentor in turn publicly humiliated by his superior. Once a subordinate has seen his superior openly humbled, even if it does not essentially alter their power positions, something has, nonetheless, irretrievably changed.

described as the truth that contradicts the lies told to power, it is correct to say that the hidden transcript is a self-disclosure that power relations normally exclude from the official transcript.[12] No matter how elaborate the hidden transcript may become, it always remains a substitute for an act of assertion directly in the face of power. Perhaps for this reason the "many imaginary speeches" to the squire that Mrs. Poyser rehearsed backstage are unlikely to have yielded anything like the sense of satisfaction and release provided by her speech to the squire himself. A public insult, one suspects, is never fully laid to rest except by a public reply.

The negation found in the hidden transcript often takes back the speech or behavior that seemed unavoidable in power-laden encounters. A subordinate who has just received a public dressing down from his superior during which he behaved deferentially, and who now finds himself among his peers may curse his superior, make physical gestures of aggression, and talk about what he would like to say next time. ("Just wait until . . . .") But, in Mrs. Poyser's case and many others, it turns out to have been a dress rehearsal for a subsequent public negation. The collective hidden transcript of a subordinate group often bears the forms of negation that, if they were transposed to the context of domination, would represent an act of rebellion.

Ideological Negation

The work of negation, however, involves far more than the creation of a social realm in which the missing part of the subordinate's replies and assertions may be safely spoken. Inasmuch as the major historical forms of domination have presented themselves in the form of a metaphysics, a religion, a worldview, they have provoked the development of more or less equally elaborate replies in the hidden transcript.

How thoroughgoing this negation can be is evident from what we know about the difference between the public Christianity preached to the slaves by their masters in the antebellum U.S. South and the religion they practiced when they were not under surveillance.[13] In public religious services, con-

12. Jürgen Habermas bases his theory concerning the "ideal speech situation" on a similar assumption that any form of domination will prevent the free and equal discourse necessary for a just society. He claims, furthermore, that the ideal speech situation is nothing more than the practical assumptions that lie behind any effort to communicate and is therefore universal. My argument requires no such heroic assumptions, let alone Habermas's tendency to treat civil and political society as if it ought to be the perfect graduate student seminar. See Habermas, *The Theory of Communicative Action*, vol. 1, *Reason and the Rationalization of Society*, trans. Thomas McCarthy; see also Jürgen Habermas, chap. 4.

13. Unless otherwise noted, the material for this paragraph is drawn from Raboteau, *Slave Religion*, chaps. 4, 5.

ducted by the master or someone provided by him, the slaves were expected to control their gestures, facial expression, voice, and general comportment. Outside that surveillance and in the "hush arbors," where a whole series of devices were used to prevent the sound from carrying (for example, shouting into overturned pots), an entirely different atmosphere reigned—one of release from the constant guardedness of domination, permitting dancing, shouts, clapping, and participation. Autonomous slave religion was not merely a negation of the style of official services; it contradicted its content as well. Preachers with the interest of the masters at heart would emphasize New Testament passages about meekness, turning the other cheek, walking the extra mile, and texts like the following (from Ephesians 6 : 5–9), which, paraphrased, also appeared in a catechism for "Colored Persons": "Servant, be obedient to them that are your masters according to the flesh, with fear and trembling, in singleness of your heart, as unto Christ; not with eye service, as men pleasers; but as the servants of Christ, doing the will of God from the heart." In contrast to this plea for a sincere official transcript from slaves, the offstage Christianity, as we know, stressed the themes of deliverance and redemption, Moses and the Promised Land, the Egyptian captivity, and emancipation. The Land of Canaan, as Frederick Douglass noted, was taken to mean the North and freedom. When they could safely boycott or leave sermons that condemned theft, flight, negligent work, and insolence, the slaves did just that, as Charles Jones, who preached in the South in 1833, discovered:

> I was preaching to a large congregation on the Epistle of Philemon and when I insisted upon fidelity and obedience as Christian virtues in servants and upon the authority of Paul, condemned the practice of running away, one half of my audience deliberately rose up and walked off with themselves, and those that remained looked anything but satisfied with the preacher or his doctrine. After dismission, there was no small stir among them; some solemnly declared that "there was no such an Epistle in the Bible," others "that they did not care" if they ever heard me preach again.[14]

Slaves were rarely fortunate enough to be able to openly display their disagreement in this way. There is little doubt, however, that their religious beliefs were often a negation of the humility and forbearance preached to them by whites. Ex-slave Charles Ball noted that heaven for blacks was a place

14. Ibid., 294.

where they would be avenged of their enemies, and that the "cornerstone" of black religion was the "idea of a revolution in the conditions of the whites and blacks."[15] This idea took, we may assume, a form bearing some resemblance to the oath spoken by Aggy the cook after her daughter was punished.[16]

Among untouchables in India there is persuasive evidence that the Hindu doctrines that would legitimize caste-domination are negated, reinterpreted, or ignored. Scheduled castes are much less likely than Brahmins to believe that the doctrine of karma explains their present condition; instead they attribute their status to their poverty and to an original, mythical act of injustice. As a group, they have seized on those traditions, saints, and narratives within the Hindu tradition that ignore castes or elevate the status of those least privileged. As a public matter, of course, there have also been defections from Hinduism in the form of conversions on a large scale to Buddhism, Christianity, and Islam, all of which emphasize the equality of believers. Such negation goes on, it is important to add, at the same time as millions of untouchables continue in daily practice to observe the ritual avoidances and gestures of homage that are part and parcel of a caste order. As one writer aptly puts it, one has "orthopraxy" without any necessary "orthodoxy" from the lower castes.[17]

Practices of resistance may mitigate the daily patterns of material appropriation, and the gestures of negation in the hidden transcript may answer daily insults to dignity. But at the level of systematic social doctrine, subordi-

15. Ibid., 291.

16. We recover this pattern of negation in bits and shards—glimpses of a world that was largely concealed from whites. The testimony we have from after the Civil War makes it clear that many slaves prayed fervently for a Northern victory; few whites, however, knew this during the war. As it became apparent that the South was, in fact, losing the war, the boldness of slaves grew: they ran away in greater numbers, they shirked work with more tenacity, they spoke back more frequently. Thus a Georgia slave reported that when urged by his master and mistress near the end of the war to pray for a Confederate success, he said he was obedient to his owners but that he would not pray against his conscience and wanted his freedom and that of "all the Negroes." Only the crumbling power of the Confederacy made his open declaration possible. For, as Raboteau realizes, "He was shouting in public what had been repeated in the dead of night in the private place of prayer which the slave claimed as his own." *Slave Religion*, 309. Our attention is thus directed not simply to the capacity to negate the religious rationale for domination, but to the social sites in the recesses of the social order in which such negations can be spoken and acted.

17. J. F. Taal, "Sanskrit and Sanskritization." See also Bernard Cohn, "Changing Traditions of a Low Caste" in *Traditional India: Structure and Change*, ed. Milton Singer, 207; Gerald D. Berreman, "Caste in Cross Cultural Perspective," in *Japan's Invisible Race: Caste in Culture and Personality*, ed. George DeVos and Hiroshi Wagatsuma, 311, and Mark Jürgensmeyer, "What if Untouchables Don't Believe in Untouchability?" One of the standard sources that argues against the case made here and for "ideological incorporation" is Michael Moffat, *An Untouchable Community in South India: Structure and Consensus*.

nate groups confront elaborate ideologies that justify inequality, bondage, monarchy, caste, and so on. Resistance at this level requires a more elaborate riposte, one that goes beyond fragmentary practices of resistance. Better put, perhaps, resistance to ideological domination requires a counterideology—a negation—that will effectively provide a general normative form to the host of resistant practices invented in self-defense by any subordinate group.

The Importance of Mutuality

The external power that deprives man of the freedom to communicate his thoughts publicly deprives him at the same time of his freedom to think.
    —IMMANUEL KANT

Providing we take the term "publicly" to mean the social expression of thoughts in some context, however constrained, Kant's statement is an important truth about resistance to domination. The hidden transcript does require a public—even if that public necessarily excludes the dominant. None of the practices and discourses of resistance can exist without tacit or acknowledged coordination and communication within the subordinate group. For that to occur, the subordinate group must carve out for itself social spaces insulated from control and surveillance from above. If we are to understand the process by which resistance is developed and codified, the analysis of the creation of these offstage social spaces becomes a vital task. Only by specifying how such social spaces are made and defended is it possible to move from the individual resisting subject—an abstract fiction—to the socialization of resistant practices and discourses. It may seem reasonable to conjure up an individual subordinate who resents appropriation and resists it by pilfering, who is angered by an insult and dreams of striking back, who finds the rationale of his rulers unacceptable and dreams of a utopia where the last shall be first. The fact is, however, that even pilfering requires the complicity of fellow subordinates who will look the other way, that dreams of settling scores for an insult will necessarily take a social form satisfying to peers and appropriately provoking to superiors, and that the negation of a dominant religious ideology requires an offstage subculture in which the negation can be formed and articulated.

Social spaces of relative autonomy do not merely provide a neutral medium within which practical and discursive negations may grow. As domains of power relations in their own right, they serve to discipline as well as to formulate patterns of resistance. The process of socialization is much the same as with any stylized sentiment. If we can imagine, hypothetically, an unarticulated feeling of anger, the expression in language of that anger will necessarily impose a disciplined form to it. If this now-articulated anger is to become the property of a small group, it will be further disciplined by the shared experiences and power relations within that small group. If, then, it is to become the social property of a whole category of subordinates it must carry effective meaning for them and reflect the cultural meanings and distribution of power among them. In this hypothetical progression from "raw" anger to what we might call "cooked" indignation, sentiments that are idiosyncratic, unrepresentative, or have only weak resonance within the group are likely to be selected against or censored. Looked at from the vantage point of any society and culture, of course, our hypothetical progression makes no sense. Anger, humiliation, and fantasies are always experienced within a cultural framework created in part by offstage communication among subordinates. In this respect there is probably no such thing as completely raw anger, humiliation, or fantasy, even if it is never communicated to another; it has already been shaped by the cultural history of one's experience. The essential point is that a resistant subculture or countermores among subordinates is necessarily a product of mutuality.

As we turn to an examination of the social sites where the hidden transcript grows, it will be helpful to keep several points in mind. First, the hidden transcript is a social product and hence a result of power relations among subordinates. Second, like folk culture, the hidden transcript has no reality as pure thought; it exists only to the extent it is practiced, articulated, enacted, and disseminated within these offstage social sites. Third, the social spaces where the hidden transcript grows are themselves an achievement of resistance; they are won and defended in the teeth of power.[18]

18. Indirect support for the importance of resistant mutuality comes from social psychology experiments demonstrating how difficult it is to sustain *any* judgment without some social support. The simplest of such experiments involves judgments about the relative length of two straight lines, in which confederates of the experimenter all purposely affirm that the shorter of two lines is, in fact, the longer. When this happens, most subjects are unable to swim alone against the tide of (mistaken) opinion and concur openly with the others. When, however, even a single confederate of the experimenter disagrees with the rest, the subject reverts to what we imagine was his original perception and joins the dissent. A single companion often seems sufficient to break the pressure to conform. Although these experiments hardly replicate the conditions of domination with which we are directly concerned, they do suggest how extraordinarily difficult solitary dissent is and how even the smallest social space for dissent may allow a resistant subculture to form. See Winn, *The Manipulated Mind*, 110–11.

Sites and Carriers of the Hidden Transcript: Degrees of Freedom

That's why the cabaret is the parliament of the people.

—BALZAC, *Les Paysans*

The social sites of the hidden transcript are those locations in which the unspoken riposte, stifled anger, and bitten tongues created by relations of domination find a vehement, full-throated expression. It follows that the hidden transcript will be least inhibited when two conditions are fulfilled: first, when it is voiced in a sequestered social site where the control, surveillance, and repression of the dominant are least able to reach, and second, when this sequestered social milieu is composed entirely of close confidants who share similar experiences of domination. The initial condition is what allows subordinates to talk freely at all, while the second ensures that they have, in their common subordination, something to talk about.

For any relation of domination it ought to be possible to specify a continuum of social sites ranged according to how heavily or lightly they are patrolled by dominant elites. The least patrolled, most autonomous sites would presumably be the most likely locations for recovering the hidden transcript. In antebellum U.S. slavery, for example, control was clearly most pronounced in the organization of work life—the site of the direct appropriation of labor—and in public displays of mastery and deference. Social autonomy for slaves was thus minimized before whites, in the big house, and when working. Outside this heavily patrolled sphere there were domains of greater autonomy in the slave quarters, in the circles of family and friends, which found expression in folktales, dress, language, song, and religious expression. Further still from the center of close surveillance were those social spaces most effectively sequestered from domination, those that might, on that account, be considered the privileged sites for the hidden transcript. These might include the hidden hush arbors where protected speech, singing, religious enthusiasm, dreams of deliverance, schemes for escape, plots of rebellion, tactics for pilfering, and so on could be discussed in relative safety. In the words of Henry Cheatam, an ex-slave, "dat overseer was a devil. He wouldn't allow no meetin' on de place. Sometimes us would slip down de hill and turn de wash pot bottom upwards so de sound of our voices would go under de pot, and us'd have a singin' and prayin' right dere."[19]

The term *social site* may convey the wrong impression if we take it to mean only a sequestered physical location. It might, of course, be just that; slaves

19. From interview with Cheatam, in Norman Yetman, ed., *Voices from Slavery,* 56.

made use of secluded woods, clearings, gullies, thickets, ravines to meet and talk in safety. They might also conspire to transform a site that was not so intrinsically safe by actively sealing it off from surveillance. In the quarters at night slaves might hang up quilts and rags to deaden the sound, circle on their knees and whisper, and post a watch to ensure their seclusion. The creation of a secure site for the hidden transcript might, however, not require any physical distance from the dominant so long as linguistic codes, dialects, and gestures—opaque to the masters and mistresses—were deployed.[20]

If the social location par excellence of the public transcript is to be found in the public assemblies of subordinates summoned by elites, it follows that the social location par excellence for the hidden transcript lies in the unauthorized and unmonitored secret assemblies of subordinates. Thus, as noted earlier, Christopher Hill explains that the "heresy" of Lollardy was most rife in the pastoral, forest, moorland, and fen areas, where the social control of the church and the squirearchy did not effectively penetrate.[21] Three centuries later, E. P. Thompson makes much the same point about religious heterodoxy in a vastly changed England: "The countryside was ruled by the gentry, the towns by corrupt corporations, the nation by the corruptest corporation of all; but the chapel, the tavern, and the home were their own. In the 'unsteepled' places of worship there was room for free intellectual life and democratic experiments."[22] The unpatrolled, social spaces nurturing dissent are, for Thompson's working class, no longer the unsettled wilds where Lollardy flourished. Rather they may be found within the privacy of the home or in those public places such as the tavern and chapel that the working class can call its own.

In European culture at any rate, the alehouse, the pub, the tavern, the inn, the cabaret, the beer cellar, the gin mill were seen by secular authorities and by the church as places of subversion. Here subordinate classes met offstage and off-duty in an atmosphere of freedom encouraged by alcohol. Here was also a privileged site for the transmission of popular culture—embodied in games, songs, gambling, blasphemy, and disorder—that was usually at odds with official culture. Peter Burke writes that the evidence for the importance of the

20. The development of such secret signs and codes probably requires an offstage context in which they can be generated and given common meaning before they can be used under the noses of the dominant.

21. "From Lollards to Levellers," 87.

22. *The Making of the English Working Class*, 51–52. Thompson's account of eighteenth-century poaching and the struggle over rural property rights notes that scattered and sequestered habitations were always seen as favoring lawlessness, and there was a great effort made to enclose land so as to force the population into villages. E. P. Thompson, *Whigs and Hunters: The Origin of the Black Act*, 246.

tavern as a center for the development of English popular culture from 1500 to 1800 is overwhelming. A historian of religion goes so far as to talk of the nineteenth-century rivalry between the church and the pub.[23]

The importance of the tavern or its equivalent as a site of antihegemonic discourse lay less in the drinking it fostered or in its relative insulation from surveillance than in the fact that it was the main point of unauthorized assembly for lower-class neighbors and workers. Along with the market, which was larger and more anonymous, the tavern was the closest thing to a neighborhood meeting of subordinates. The development of the coffeehouse and club-room during the eighteenth century created a similar social space for a growing middle class and in turn fostered the growth of a distinctive middle-class culture, leaving the alehouse more exclusively to the working classes. Each site, owing to the social position of its habitués, generated a distinctive culture and pattern of discourse. Surveying such developing class cultures, Peter Stallybrass and Allon White conclude,

> Patterns of discourse are regulated through the forms of corporate assembly in which they are produced. Alehouse, coffee-house, church, law court, library, drawing room of a country mansion: each place of assembly is a different site of intercourse requiring different manners and morals. Discursive space is never completely independent of social place and the formation of new kinds of speech can be traced through the emergence of new public sites of discourse and the transformation of old ones. . . . And so, in large part, the history of political struggle has been the history of the attempts to control significant sites of assembly and spaces of discourse.[24]

For medieval Europe, according to Bakhtin's now-celebrated argument, the marketplace was the privileged site of antihegemonic discourse, and carnival was its most striking expression. Only in the marketplace did the population gather more or less spontaneously without ceremony being imposed from above. The anonymity of the crowd together with the buying and selling that served to put people on an equal footing marked out the marketplace as a domain where the rituals and deference required before lords and clergy did not apply. Privilege was suspended. This atmosphere, Bakhtin argues, encouraged forms of discourse excluded from the world of hierarchy and eti-

23. Burke, *Popular Culture in Early Modern Europe*, 109, and Colin Campbell, *Toward a Sociology of Religion*, 44.

24. *The Politics and Poetics of Transgression*, 80. For a discerning discussion of the cultural meaning of the alehouse in Shakespeare's time and in his plays, see Susanne Wofford, "The Politics of Carnival in *Henry IV*," in *Theatrical Power: The Politics of Representation on the Shakespearean Stage*, edited by Helen Tartar.

quette: parody, ridicule, blasphemy, the grotesque, scatology, revelry, and so on. For Bakhtin, the uninhibited license of the marketplace—and especially of carnival—was a black mass of official values. Here the piety, humility, servility, seriousness, respect, and poses[25] of official onstage conduct were replaced by patterns of speech and conduct that were otherwise disapproved.

The reasons the more unmediated versions of the hidden transcript should be encountered in taverns, alehouses, at the marketplace, during carnival, and at night in secluded spots are instructive. A dissident subculture "invests the weak points in a chain of socialization."[26] For the working class in Poland just prior to the riots in Poznan in 1956, those weak points came to be virtually all those settings where confidences might be shared. As Lawrence Goodwyn explains, "The organizing conversations at Cegielski [Railway Works] were conducted in places beyond the gaze of foremen—in trains and buses to and from work, in remote sections of the plant, at lunch breaks, and in the grossly inadequate cold water locker rooms which in themselves constituted one of the continuing grievances. . . . This space was not a gift; it had to be created by people who fought to create it."[27] Thus, to think of antihegemonic discourse as occupying merely the social space left empty by domination would be to miss the struggle by which such sites are won, cleared, built, and defended.

The elaboration of hidden transcripts depends not only on the creation of relatively unmonitored physical locations and free time but also on active human agents who create and disseminate them. The carriers are likely to be as socially marginal as the places where they gather. Since what counts as socially marginal depends so heavily on cultural definitions, the carriers will vary greatly by culture and over time. In early modern Europe, for example, it seems that the carriers of folk culture played a key role in developing the subversive themes of the carnivalesque. Actors, acrobats, bards, jugglers, diviners, itinerant entertainers of all kinds might be said to have made their living in this fashion. Other itinerants—journeymen, craftsmen on tour, tin-

25. By *poses* I mean to call attention to the physical gestures and posture of the public transcript. As Bakhtin understands, an essential element of carnival is the *physical release* from the strain of an onstage performance. I am struck, in this context, with the boisterousness and physical exuberance often noted in slave celebrations and religious ceremonies when slaves were safe from surveillance. Here the analogy of schoolchildren at recess may be instructive insofar as their performance as subordinates in the classroom is also severely physically confining. The control of the body, voice, and facial expression may, when it is imposed, create something of a physical hidden transcript that is released in movement.

26. Stuart Hall and Tony Jefferson, *Resistance Through Rituals: Youth Subcultures in Post-war Britain* (London: Hutchinson, 1976), 25–26.

27. "How to Make a Democratic Revolution: The Rise of *Solidarnosc in Poland*," MS, chap. 5, pp. 29, 34.

kers, colporteurs, shoemakers, petty traders, vagrants, healers, "tooth art-ists"—while perhaps less active in elaborating a dissident subculture, might be important vectors for its propagation. Since much of the resistance to the dominant culture took the form of religious heterodoxy and heresy, the role of what Max Weber has termed the "pariah-intelligentsia" should not be over-looked. Here we would include some of the renegade lower clergy, would-be prophets, pilgrims, marginal sects and monastic orders, mendicants, and so forth. Their critical distance from dominant values arises, Weber notes, from their skills and their marginality: "Groups which are at the lower end or altogether outside of the social hierarchy stand to a certain extent on the point of Archimedes in relation to social conventions, both in respect to the external order and in respect to common opinions. Since these groups are not bound by social conventions they are capable of an original attitude towards the meaning of the cosmos."[28]

If we step back slightly from specific groups in a particular cultural milieu, something more general may be said about the principal carriers of the hidden transcript. It is not simply a question of their anomalous or low social standing. They are also likely to follow trades or vocations that encourage physical mobility. As travelers they often serve as cultural brokers and social links between subordinate communities while remaining, themselves, less socially anchored and hence more autonomous. In the cases of guilds or sects, they may also have a corporate existence that provides its own social insulation from direct domination. Finally, a good many of these groups depend directly on the patronage of a lower-class public to make their living. The clergyman who must rely on popular charity or the bard who expects his audience to feed him and give small contributions is likely to convey a cultural message that is not at odds with that of his public.[29]

Social Control and Surveillance from Above: Preventing the Hidden Transcript

The strongest evidence for the vital importance of autonomous social sites in generating a hidden transcript is the strenuous effort made by dominant groups to abolish or control such sites. In Europe from the fifteenth through the seventeenth centuries, both secular and religious authorities understood

28. *The Sociology of Religion,* 126.
29. He may, of course, have many reasons for masking or disguising his message to avoid retaliation from above. Chapter 6 is largely devoted to this issue. Nevertheless the point here is that the bard who sings for an audience of subordinates will have a repertoire more in keeping with the hidden transcript than a bard who is retained exclusively to sing praise-songs to the prince.

the danger that autonomous sites of dissident folk culture could pose. Nowhere is this clearer than in the cultural conflicts that preceded the German Peasants' War on the eve of the Reformation. Lionel Rothkrug's analysis of the struggle over a pilgrimage site associated with the "drummer of Niklashausen" is a striking case in point.[30] The young drummer's prophetic vision in 1476 incorporated themes that were already part and parcel of an underground tradition of religious dissent. This tradition held that Christ's sacrifice had redeemed all humankind—including serfs—from bondage and that access to salvation was democratically distributed. The church where Boheim, the drummer, denounced the venality of the clergy (particularly over the sale of indulgences) and called for the removal of the pope attracted large, threatening crowds. After an initial skirmish in which commoner Swiss archers defeated the cream of the Burgundian nobility, Boheim was captured and put to death as a heretic and rebel. Two features of these events and their aftermath are instructive for our purposes. First, the Niklashausen church, which had been of no particular significance earlier, became a social magnet for pilgrimages and subversive discourse only because of the popular *response* to the prophecy. This autonomous site of the hidden transcript was a social creation, not a social given. Second, once the threat was established, the authorities spared no effort in abolishing this node of dissent. The church was razed, Boheim's ashes were strewn in the Tauber river, offerings left at the shrine were destroyed, all relics and monuments to him were confiscated, and pilgrimages to the now-empty site were prohibited. Simultaneously the bishop of Würzburg launched a cultural offensive aimed at anticlerical sentiment, commissioning verses that would defame Boheim and demonize the "insurgents" who heeded his call. It is difficult to imagine a more ambitious effort both to eliminate a physical site of subversive discourse and to erase its traces in popular oral culture.

The persistence of subversive popular heresies and the hostility of secular and religious authorities to their carriers and the sites at which they thrived is captured in David Sabean's account of Hans Keil in Lutheran Germany less than two centuries later, just at the end of the Thirty Years War.[31] Against a background of marauding troops, the plague, and extortionate taxes, Hans Keil received a sign from God and a message from an angel. His grapevines bled as they were pruned. The angel descended to promise collective punish-

30. "Icon and Ideology in Religion and Rebellion, 1300–1600: Bayernfreiheit and Réligion Royale," in *Religion and Rural Revolt: Papers Presented to the Fourth Interdisciplinary Workshop on Peasant Studies*, ed. Janos M. Bak and Gerhard Benecke, 31–61.

31. For a more detailed account, see David Warren Sabean, *Power in the Blood: Popular Culture and Village Discourse in Early Modern Europe*, chap. 2.

ment for man's wickedness. The sins the angel promised to punish were, most particularly, the crushing exactions of grain and labor by the nobility, the tithes of the high clergy, and the failure of avaricious, licentious, and vain elites to observe God's commands. In religious terms it was clear that God held the authorities responsible for the suffering of the war and intended to bring them low. Once again, as with the drummer of Niklashausen, the content of the prophecy was not surprising or new; it was amply prefigured in the circulating broadsheets, accounts of miracles, and popular biblical traditions. The danger posed by Hans Keil's message from God was that the peasantry took it as a sign that authorized them to resist taxation. As stories of the miracle circulated throughout the region via newly printed broadsheets and popular verses about Hans Keil's deeds, the authorities sensed the danger of a generalized tax revolt. The steps they took to prevent the diffusion of popular accounts are instructive. Broadsheets depicting the miracle were seized, and the printers, singers, and itinerant workers who disseminated them were detained. Anyone caught discussing the subject, especially in markets and inns, was to be arrested and questioned. What we have here is a systematic attempt by the authorities to sever the autonomous circuits of folk discourse and to deny this heterodox story any social site where it could be safely retold and interpreted.

We would not have had either of these episodes at hand had they not attracted official attention—and repression. That is how they made it into the archives, so to speak. Each prophecy spilled beyond the sequestered confines of the hidden transcript to pose a direct threat to powerholders. It is, however, the pattern of repression that highlights for us the circulatory system of the hidden transcript. For seventeenth-century central Europe, that system is composed of nothing more nor less than the producers, carriers, and consumers of popular culture together with the routes they travel and the sites they occupy or pass through. The importance of popular culture and its social vectors is not, moreover, of merely antiquarian interest for the study of feudal and early modern Europe. More than one student of modern working-class history has suggested that many of the circuits of popular culture were destroyed by conscious design in the late nineteenth century with ominous consequences for the disciplining and cultural domestication of the proletariat.[32]

Slave owners in both the West Indies and North America took great pains

32. The most forceful exponent of this argument is Frank Hearn. *Domination, Legitimation, and Resistance: The Incorporation of the 19th-Century English Working Class;* see also his "Remembrance and Critique: The Uses of the Past for Discrediting the Present and Anticipating the Future," *Politics and Society* 5:2 (1975):201–27. Much of the argument of Hoggart, *The Uses of Literacy,* though addressed to the twentieth century, may be read in the same sense.

to prevent the creation of sites where a hidden transcript could be created and shared. They were, of course, greatly aided by the fact that their subjects were a newly and traumatically assembled population torn from familiar contexts of social action.[33] To minimize communication plantation owners preferred to bring together a labor force of the greatest linguistic and ethnic diversity.[34] When a dialect of pidgin developed that was unintelligible to the planters, the slaves were required to converse at work only in a form of English their overseers could understand. Sunday and holiday gatherings, which planters understood as likely sites for sedition, were sharply restricted, and efforts were made to ensure that such assemblies rarely brought together slaves from several plantations. The standard use of slave informers served to further inhibit the establishment of safe sites for the hidden transcript. Finally, to break up secret nighttime gatherings of slaves, the owners organized mounted patrols—the dreaded patrollers—with dogs to apprehend and punish any slave found at large without authorization.

All these measures were part of a hopelessly utopian (a master's utopia, to be sure) project of eliminating any and all protected communication among slaves. Such aspirations were unrealizable in principle if for no other reason than the work itself required easy communication among the slaves. However hobbling the surveillance, it did not prevent the rapid development of linguistic codes impenetrable to outsiders, a popular slave culture of ridicule and satire, an autonomous religious vision emphasizing deliverance, actual patterns of arson and sabotage, not to mention free maroon communities in the hills.

Here, it is not the inevitable frustration of such plans that is most germane to our argument, but rather the effort, the aspiration, to atomize subordinates by removing or penetrating any autonomous domain of communication. The aspiration is encountered again and again, even in voluntary institutions that aim at commanding the undivided discipline and loyalty of their members. As Lewis Coser has argued, a close analysis of such "greedy" institutions as the jesuits, monastic orders, political sects, court bureaucracies using eunuchs or janissaries, or utopian communities brings to light social rules preventing the development of any subordinate loyalties or discourse that might compete with its hegemonic purpose.[35] To achieve their purpose, such rules would

---

33. In this respect they operated under handicaps similar in kind, but far more extreme in degree, to those of the new proletariat in the industrializing West shorn of their agrarian networks of social action.

34. This and subsequent points, unless otherwise noted, are drawn from Craton, *Testing the Chains*, chaps. 3–8.

35. *Greedy Institutions: Patterns of Undivided Commitment*, passim.

have to make subordinates entirely dependent upon their superiors, effectively isolated from one another, and more or less constantly under observation.

Imperial traditions of recruiting administrative staff from marginal, despised groups were designed precisely to create a trained cadre that was isolated from the populace and entirely dependent on the ruler for their status. In the case of celibacy or eunuchs, of course, the possibility of competing family loyalties was precluded in principle. In their training—which often began at a young age—and their service, they were frequently kept as isolated as possible from the civil population. Unlike that of serfs or slaves, the service of these elite staffs required a high degree of initiative, active loyalty, and cooperation, which in turn necessitated the horizontal links and training necessary to create a high esprit de corps. Even here, however, structured measures worked to minimize the generation of any purposes at odds with official aims. The more durable of the nineteenth-century utopian communities in the United States were those that insisted on either celibacy or free love within the community. Either option prevented the development of the dangerous dyadic and family ties that would create an alternative focus of loyalty. As Coser puts it, "The abolition of family life made it possible to assure that individuals always act in their public roles; that is, that they give up their right to privacy."[36] Transposed to the terminology we have been using, the abolition of family life was an effort to ensure that the onstage, public transcript exhausted the whole of social life. Accomplishing this also demanded a more or less complete pattern of surveillance to monitor any potentially subversive discourse. The Shakers, for example, had watchtowers, peepholes, and the social pressure of public confessions as part of their program of surveillance. Even voluntary, intentional communities, then, display an aspiration to total domination—an aspiration disclosed by their measures to eliminate all those small, autonomous social spaces and social ties in which some untoward, unauthorized hidden transcript might be born.

Social Control and Surveillance from Below: Defending the Hidden Transcript

If the logic of a pattern of domination is to bring about the complete atomization and surveillance of subordinates, this logic encounters a reciprocal resistance from below. Subordinates everywhere implicitly understand that if the logic of domination prevails, they will be reduced to a Hobbesian war of all

36. Ibid., 144. See also Rosabeth Moss Kanter, *Commitment and Community: Communes and Utopias in Sociological Perspective.*

against all. Individual strategies of preferment are a constant temptation to members of subordinate groups. It is, in part, to encourage normative and practical defection that elites call forth the public acts of compliance that represent their authority. Also by such means elites create the loyal retainers, "trustees," and informers on whom they can rely to patrol the sites of the hidden transcript. The mere presence of known or suspected trustees among subordinates is normally sufficient to disqualify the site as a safe place for the hidden transcript.

Members of a dissident subordinate subculture can act informally to foster a high degree of conformity to standards that violate dominant norms. A suggestive example drawn from sociolinguistic research on dialect use in England helps us to understand the process.[37]

Research into speech patterns of working-class men and women shows that women use a dialect significantly closer to Standard English (the dominant norm) than men. The difference is attributed to the fact that working-class men are more firmly embedded in an egalitarian workers' subculture than women, who are, by contrast, more anxious to avoid speech patterns (for example, double negatives) stigmatized by the dominant culture. More diagnostic for our purposes, however, is that women think they use more standard forms in their speech than they actually do, while men think they use more nonstandard forms than they actually do. The fact that men aspire, in a sense, to use working-class speech patterns even more frequently than is actually the case is testimony to the *covert prestige* of working-class usage among men. Against the pressures generated by the usage of their superiors, against the standardization fostered by the school system, by radio, and by television, the working-class culture has developed its own powerful sanctions that discourage a drift away from linguistic solidarity. Since both working-class English and Standard English are suitable for communicating most ideas, dialect here functions as a kind of moral discourse, expressing publicly a sense of identity and affiliation with one's working-class mates as against the middle and upper classes. Any sign of a linguistic betrayal of working-class dialect would be read as a telltale sign of a more general defection.

How does a subculture of subordinates with less social power, almost by definition, than the dominant culture achieve a high level of conformity? The answer surely lies in the social incentives and sanctions it can bring to bear to reward members who observe its norms and punish those who deviate. These sanctions must at least neutralize the pressures from above if the subordinate

---

37. Trudgill. *Sociolinguistics*, chap. 4. The central figure responsible for much of the research on issues of class, race, and dialect is William Labov.

subculture is to have any weight. Here, the vital social fact is that slaves, serfs, untouchables, and much of the working class historically have lived most of their lives in households and neighborhoods outside the direct gaze of elites. Even at work, providing they do not work individually, they are as much under observation from fellow workers as from the bosses. Subordinate groups do their own patrolling in this *kulturkampf*, singling out anyone who puts on airs, who denies his origins, who seems aloof, who attempts to hobnob with elites. These sanctions brought against them may run the gamut from small gestures of disapproval to a complete shunning and, of course, to physical intimidation and violence.

What is being policed by pressures for conformity within the subordinate group are not simply speech acts but a wide range of practices that damage the collective interest of subordinates as they see it. Among agricultural laborers in Franco's Spain, Juan Martinez-Alier reports that the concept of *union* expresses a shared ideal of solidarity.[38] Like the working-class dialect just discussed, it is not always religiously followed—given the temptations to break ranks—but nevertheless exerts a palpable influence on conduct. It dictates that those who agree to do piecework or to work for less than the minimum wage are held in open contempt, ostracized, and considered shameless. It dictates that workers will wait in their villages for work (rather than engaging in an unseemly scramble to beat one another to the estates), that they will not agree to sharecropping, and that they will not underbid a fellow laborer to gain work. Laborers who violate these injunctions fear not only the shame heaped upon them but physical retaliation as well.

As Alier points out in the case of Andalusian laborers, this conformity is created and maintained by shared linguistic practices. Landlords who are shown respect in public encounters are showered with abuse and given derisive nicknames behind their backs. The official, elite-imposed, public euphemism for sharecropping, *comparticipazione*, is privately mocked. Slanderous stories circulate about the local members of the *guardia civil* and priests. Class enmity is fanned not only by inequalities and domination but by the jokes, tales, and satirical verses that vividly convey injustice: "We eat the delicious thistle and tasty grass while they [the rich] eat the pestilent ham and the filthy sausage."[39] One can see in this linguistic practice and shared social outlook the unmistakable evidence of the *cultural work* performed by members of subordinate groups.

The military details of this skirmishing are not pretty. First, it must be

38. *Laborers and Landowners in Southern Spain*, chap. 4.
39. Ibid., 208.

remembered that in addition to engaging the enemy, one's own troops must be disciplined, particularly where the temptations of desertion are so large. While the dominant are likely to have more resort to open relations of force, intimidation, and economic power, the *mix* of incentives to conformity among subordinates is likely to include more peer pressure. Relations of force, however, are rarely absent, even among subordinates, when the costs of defection seem enormous. The assaulting of strikebreakers by workers on the picket line or the killing of suspected police agents in the black townships of South Africa are cases in point. For the most part, though, subordinates rarely have much in the way of coercive force to deploy among themselves, and what they do have depends typically on a modicum of popular assent—among subordinates—for it to be carried out. Conformity, instead, rests heavily on social pressure. Granting the *relatively* democratic aspect of social pressure among peers, these mechanisms of social control are painful and often ugly. Slander, character assassination, gossip, rumor, public gestures of contempt, shunning, curses, backbiting, outcasting are only a few of the sanctions that subordinates can bring to bear on each other. Reputation in any small, closely knit community has very practical consequences. A peasant household held in contempt by their fellow villagers will find it impossible to exchange harvest labor, to borrow a draft animal, to raise a small loan, to marry their children off, to prevent petty thefts of their grain or livestock, or even to bury their dead with any dignity. In aggregate, such sanctions have an obviously coercive weight, but they require, once again, a fair degree of popular assent to achieve their end of forcing the nonconformist back into line.

Solidarity among subordinates, if it is achieved at all, is thus achieved, paradoxically, only by means of a degree of conflict. Certain forms of social strife, far from constituting evidence of disunity and weakness, may well be the signs of an active, aggressive social surveillance that preserves unity. Nowhere has this principle been better illustrated than in Chandra Jayawardena's fine study of a Tamil plantation labor force in the Caribbean.[40] Their community was composed entirely of families employed by the plantation and therefore subject to the same structure of authority with few distinctions. They had developed a high degree of solidarity characterized by collective outbursts of violence involving tacit cooperation with no identifiable leadership or advance preparation. The solidarity was underwritten by an ideology of strictly egalitarian social relations termed *mati* (mate-ship). This ideology preserved a basic solidarity despite the desire of the management to cultivate collaborators and favorites from among the work force. The ideological work, in this case as

40. "Ideology and Conflict in Lower Class Communities."

in any other, was linked to a series of practices designed to prevent the growth of internal differentiation in status or income that might diminish the community's solidarity vis-à-vis the outside world.[41] These practices involved rumors, personal disputes, envy, and even court cases that had largely to do with violations of *mati*. As Jayawardena aptly puts it, "These disputes indicate the strength, not the weakness, of the bonds of community."[42] From our perspective the disputes do not simply indicate the bonds of community but are central in creating and reinforcing those bonds. It would thus be misleading to say that a form of domination creates social sites for a dissenting hidden transcript. It would be more accurate to claim that a form of domination creates certain possibilities for the production of a hidden transcript. Whether these possibilities are realized or not, and how they find expression, depends on the constant agency of subordinates in seizing, defending, and enlarging a normative power field.

The development of a thick and resilient hidden transcript is favored by the existence of social and cultural barriers between dominant elites and subordinates. It is one of the ironies of power relations that the performances required of subordinates can become, in the hands of subordinates, a nearly solid wall making the autonomous life of the powerless opaque to elites.

In its most striking form, an entire ersatz facade may be erected in order to shield another reality from detection. Hill villages in colonial Laos, for example, were required by the occasionally visiting French officials to have a village headman and elders with whom they could deal. The Laotians responded, it appears, by creating a set of bogus notables who had no local influence and who were presented to colonial functionaries as *the* local officials. Behind this ruse, the respected local figures continued to direct local affairs, including the performance of the bogus officials.[43] The Laotian case is but a dramatic instance of the age-old efforts of Southeast Asian villages to keep a threatening state at arm's length by keeping their land tenure, kinship, income, crop yields, livestock, and factions a closely guarded secret. This aim is often best accomplished by limiting contact with the state to the bare minimum, command performances.

More commonly, the use of a formulaic and seamless deference creates an impenetrable social barrier, which, because it employs the very observances

41. Social leveling, while it may contribute to solidarity, does involve a suppression of difference and hence of talent that is at odds with liberal ideology. This leveling often forces a worker to choose between excelling at work and keeping the friendship of his workmates, or the lower-class student to choose between good grades and the esteem of his classmates. See, for example, Sennett and Cobb, *The Hidden Injuries of Class*, 207–10.

42. "Ideology and Conflict," 441.

43. Jacques Dournes, "Sous couvert des maîtres."

insisted on by the dominant, is that much more durable. The willful use of submissiveness to this end can have a tone of aggression, as in this deathbed advice given by the grandfather in Ralph Ellison's *Invisible Man*: "Live with your head in the lion's mouth. I want you to overcome 'em with yesses, undermine 'em with grins, agree 'em to death and destruction, let 'em swoller you till they vomit or bust wide open. . . . Learn it to the young 'uns."[44] The wall of two-dimensional official performances by subordinate groups may often be supplemented by a feigned ignorance. As with performances, the dominant may grasp that the ignorance is a willful ignorance, intended to thwart demands or withhold information. An Afrikaner, speaking of the colored population in his district, understands the use value of such ignorance: "The coloureds have learned one thing: to play dumb. They can accomplish great things this way. I don't really know them myself. I don't think it is possible. They talk to me but there's always a wall between us—a point beyond which I have no understanding. I can know about them, but I can't know them."[45] In playing dumb, subordinates make creative use of the stereotypes intended to stigmatize them. If they are thought of as stupid and if a direct refusal is dangerous, then they can screen a refusal with ignorance. The systematic use of ignorance by the peasantry to thwart elites and the state prompted Eric Hobsbawm to claim, "The refusal to understand is a form of class struggle."[46]

It is tempting to generalize further about the ways in which the linguistic and social distance elites purposely put between themselves and their inferiors can be put to creative use by the latter. As an integral part of their claim to superiority, ruling castes are at pains to elaborate styles of speech, dress, consumption, gesture, carriage, and etiquette that distinguish them as sharply as possible from the lower orders. In racial, colonial, or status-based social orders, this cultural segregation also discourages unofficial contact between orders for fear of contamination. This combination of distinctiveness and apartheid creates, as Bourdieu has emphasized, an elite culture that is an illegible "hieroglyph," defying easy emulation by subordinates.[47] What he fails to note is that the same process that created an elite culture nearly impenetrable from below also encourages the elaboration of a subordinate culture that is opaque to those above it. In fact, it is precisely such a pattern of

44. Page 19.
45. Quoted by Vincent Crapanzano, *Waiting: The Whites of South Africa.* Compare with Balzac, *Les Paysans*— "'Lord, I do not know,' said Charles, with a stupid look a servant can assume to screen a refusal to his betters," 34.
46. "Peasants and Politics," *Journal of Peasant Studies* 1:1 (October 1973): 13.
47. *Distinction: A Social Critique of the Judgement of Taste,* 41.

dense social interaction among subordinates and very restricted, formal contact with superiors that fosters the growth of distinctive subcultures and the diverging dialects that accompany them.

A Sociology of Cohesion in the Hidden Transcript

How cohesive is the hidden transcript shared among members of a particular subordinate group? This question is not simply another way of asking how greatly at odds a given hidden transcript is from a subordinate group's onstage performance. The disparity between public action and offstage discourse depends heavily, as we have seen, on the severity of the domination. Other things equal, the more involuntary, demeaning, onerous, and extractive it is the more it will foster a counterdiscourse starkly at odds with its official claims.

Asking how unified a hidden transcript is amounts to asking about the resolving power of the social lens through which subordination passes. If subordinates are entirely atomized, of course, there is no lens through which a critical, collective account can be focused. Barring this limiting case, however, the cohesion of the hidden transcript would seem to rest on both the homogeneity of the domination and the social cohesion of the victims themselves.

In grasping the conditions that encourage the growth of a unified hidden transcript we may profit from a long tradition of research explaining differences in militancy and cohesion within the working class in the West. That research has demonstrated, to put it boldly, that workers who belong to "communities of fate" are most likely to share a clear, antagonistic view of their employers and to act with solidarity.[48] For example, an international comparison of workers' propensity to strike found that such occupational groups as miners, merchant seamen, lumberjacks, and longshoremen were far more militant than average in this respect. It is not difficult to see what distinguished such groups from the generality of the working class. Their labor was marked by an exceptionally high level of physical danger and required a commensurate degree of camaraderie and cooperation to minimize that danger. In a word, their very lives depended on their fellow workers. Second, miners, merchant seamen, and lumberjacks work and live in relative geographical isolation from other workers and other classes. In the case of lumberjacks and

48. Arthur Stinchcombe, "Organized Dependency Relations and Social Stratification," in *The Logic of Social Hierarchies*, ed. Edward O. Laumann et al., 95–99; Clark Kerr and Abraham Siegel, "The Inter-Industry Propensity to Strike: An International Comparison," in *Industrial Conflict*, ed. Arthur Kornhauser et al., 189–212; D. Lockwood, "Sources of Variation in Working-Class Images of Society"; Colin Bell and Howard Newby, "The Sources of Agricultural Workers' Images of Society."

merchant seamen, they are separated even from their families for much of the year. What marks these occupations, then, are the homogeneity and isolation of their community and work experience, their close mutual dependence, and, finally, a relative lack of differentiation within (and mobility out of) their trade. Such conditions are tailor-made to maximize the cohesion and unity of their subculture. They are nearly a race apart. They are all under the same authority, run the same risks, mix nearly exclusively with one another, and rely on a high degree of mutuality. We might say then, for them, all aspects of social life—work, community, authority, leisure—serve to amplify and sharpen a class focus. By contrast, a working class that lives in mixed neighborhoods, works at different jobs, is not highly interdependent, and takes its leisure in a variety of ways has a social life that serves powerfully to disperse their class interest and hence their social focus.

Little wonder, then, that communities of fate create a distinctive and unified subculture. They develop "their own codes, myths, heroes, and social standards."[49] The social site at which they develop a hidden transcript is itself uniform, cohesive, and bound by powerful mutual sanctions that hold competing discourses at arm's length. The process by which such high moral density develops is not unlike the way in which a distinctive dialect of a language develops. A dialect develops as a group of speakers mixes frequently with one another and rarely with others. Their speech patterns gradually diverge from those of the parent language and, indeed, if the process continues long enough, their dialect will become unintelligible to speakers of the parent language.[50]

In a similar fashion, isolation, homogeneity of conditions, and mutual dependence among subordinates favor the development of a distinctive subculture—often one with a strong "us vs. them" social imagery. Once this occurs, of course, the distinctive subculture itself becomes a powerful force for social unity as all subsequent experiences are mediated by a shared way of looking at the world. The hidden transcript, however, never becomes a language apart. The mere fact that it is in constant dialogue—more accurately, in argument—with dominant values ensures that the hidden and public transcripts remain mutually intelligible.

---

49. Kerr and Siegel, "The Inter-Industry Propensity to Strike," 191.

50. The process is akin to speciation among flora that, if sufficiently isolated from the genetic stock of the species as a whole, will gradually diverge to a point where the differences preclude cross-fertilization and a new species is created. It is thus the *relative* isolation of wildflowers, say, as compared with birds, that accounts for the greater local speciation among wildflowers.

CHAPTER SIX

Voice under Domination:
The Arts of Political Disguise

Hitting a straight lick with a crooked stick.

—JAMAICAN SLAVE SAYING

By stretching language, we'll distort it sufficiently to wrap ourselves in it and hide, whereas the masters contract it.

—GENET, *The Blacks*

Mes enfants, you mustn't go at things head-on, you are too weak; take it from me and take it on an angle. . . . Play dead, play the sleeping dog.

—BALZAC, *Les Paysans*

MOST OF THE POLITICAL LIFE of subordinate groups is to be found neither in overt collective defiance of powerholders nor in complete hegemonic compliance, but in the vast territory between these two polar opposites. The map of this territory between the two poles thus far provided risks giving the impression that it consists solely of convincing (but perhaps sham) performances onstage on the one hand and relatively uninhibited hidden discourse offstage. That impression would be a serious mistake. My aim in this chapter is to direct attention to the manifold strategies by which subordinate groups manage to insinuate their resistance, in disguised forms, into the public transcript.

If subordinate groups have typically won a reputation for subtlety—a subtlety their superiors often regard as cunning and deception—this is surely because their vulnerability has rarely permitted them the luxury of direct confrontation. The self-control and indirection required of the powerless thus contrast sharply with the less inhibited directness of the powerful. Compare, for example, the aristocratic tradition of the duel with the training for self-restraint in the face of insults found among blacks and other subordinate groups. Nowhere is the training in self-control more apparent than in the tradition of the "dozens" or "dirty dozens" among young black males in the United States. The dozens consist in two blacks trading rhymed insults of one another's family (especially mothers and sisters); victory is achieved by never losing one's temper and fighting, but rather in devising ever more clever insults so as to win the purely verbal duel. Whereas the aristocrat is trained to move every serious verbal insult to the terrain of mortal combat, the powerless are trained to absorb insults without retaliating physically. As Lawrence Levine observes, "The Dozens served as a mechanism for teaching and sharpening the ability to control emotions and anger; an ability which was often necessary for survival."[1] There is evidence that many subordinate groups have developed similar rituals of insult in which a loss of self-control means defeat.[2]

The training in verbal facility implied by rituals of this kind enables vulnerable groups not only to control their anger but to conduct what amounts to a veiled discourse of dignity and self-assertion within the public transcript. To sketch out fully the patterns of ideological struggle on this ambiguous terrain would require an elaborate theory of *voice under domination.*[3] While nothing like a full analysis of voice under domination is possible here, we can examine the ways in which ideological resistance is disguised, muted, and veiled for safety's sake.

The undeclared ideological guerrilla war that rages in this political space requires that we enter the world of rumor, gossip, disguises, linguistic tricks, metaphors, euphemisms, folktales, ritual gestures, anonymity. For good reason, nothing is entirely straightforward here; the realities of power for subordinate groups mean that much of their political action requires interpretation precisely because it is intended to be cryptic and opaque. Before the recent development of institutionalized democratic norms, this ambiguous realm of political conflict was—short of rebellion—*the* site of public political discourse. For much of the world's contemporary subjects, for whom citizenship is at best a utopian aspiration, this remains the case. Thus, in describing the

---

1. *Black Culture and Black Consciousness,* 358.

2. See, for example, Donald Brenneis, "Fighting Words," in *Not Work Alone: A Cross-cultural View of Activities Superfluous to Survival,* ed. Jeremy Cherfas and Roger Lewin, 168–80, on such patterns, as well as Roger Vailland *The Law,* trans. Peter Wiles (New York: Knopf, 1958), which makes the drinking games of *la legge/la passatella* in Italy into a metaphor for the patience required of the weak.

3. The term *voice* is adopted from Albert Hirschman's striking contrast between the classic economic response to consumer dissatisfaction with a firm's product—exit—and the classical political response to dissatisfaction with an institution's performance—voice. When exit (defection to an alternative) is unavailable or costly, Hirschman argues, dissatisfaction will likely take the form of open complaints, anger, and demands. For our purpose, however, the form that voice takes will vary according to the capacity of powerholders to severely punish open resistance. Albert O. Hirschman, *Exit, Voice, and Loyalty: Responses to Decline in Firms, Organizations, and States.*

distinctive Christian beliefs and practices among the Tswana peoples of South Africa, Jean Comaroff takes it as given that "such defiance had, of necessity, to remain concealed and coded."[4] As late as the eighteenth century in England, the historian E. P. Thompson notes, repression precluded direct political statements by lower classes; instead, "the expression of people's political sympathies was more often oblique, symbolic, and too indefinite to incur prosecution."[5] It remains to specify the techniques by which, against heavy odds, subordinate groups infiltrate the public transcript with dissent and self-assertion.

By recognizing the guises that the powerless must adopt outside the safety of the hidden transcript, we can, I believe, discern a political dialogue with power in the public transcript. If this assertion can be sustained, it is significant insofar as the hidden transcript of many historically important subordinate groups is irrecoverable for all practical purposes. What is often available, however, is what they have been able to introduce in muted or veiled form into the public transcript.[6] What we confront, then, in the public transcript, is a strange kind of ideological debate about justice and dignity in which one party has a severe speech impediment induced by power relations. If we wish to hear this side of the dialogue we shall have to learn its dialect and codes. Above all, recovering this discourse requires a grasp of the arts of political disguise. With that goal in mind I first examine the basic or elementary techniques of disguise: anonymity, euphemisms, and what I call grumbling. I then turn to more complex and culturally elaborate forms of disguise found in oral culture, folktales, symbolic inversion, and, finally, in rituals of reversal such as carnival.

Elementary Forms of Disguise

Like prudent opposition newspaper editors under strict censorship, subordinate groups must find ways of getting their message across, while staying somehow within the law. This requires an experimental spirit and a capacity to test and exploit all the loopholes, ambiguities, silences, and lapses available to them. It means somehow setting a course at the very perimeter of what the

---

4. *Body of Power, Spirit of Resistance,* 2.
5. *Whigs and Hunters,* 200.
6. This point has been made forcefully by Susan Friedman in "The Return of the Repressed in Women's Narrative." Citing Freud's analogy between political censorship and repression in the *Interpretation of Dreams,* in which "the stricter the censorship, the more far-reaching will be the disguise," she shows convincingly that women's narrative can be seen "as an insistent record—a trace, a web, a palimpsest, a rune, a disguise—of what has not or cannot be spoken directly because of the external and internalized censors of patriarchal social order."

authorities are obliged to permit or unable to prevent. It means carving out a tenuous public political life for themselves in a political order that, in principle, forbids such a life unless fully orchestrated from above. Below, we briefly explore some of the major techniques of disguise and concealment and suggest how they may be read.

At the most basic level, such techniques can be divided into those that disguise the message and those that disguise the messenger. The polar contrast here would be between, say, a slave whose tone of voice in saying, "Yes, Massa" seemed slightly sarcastic, on the one hand, to a direct threat of arson delivered anonymously by the same slave to the same master, on the other. In the first case the subordinate who is acting is identifiable, but his action is probably too ambiguous to be actionable by authorities. In the second case, the threat is all too unambiguous, but the subordinate(s) responsible for making it is concealed. Both messenger and message may, of course, be disguised, as when masked peasants deliver a cryptic, but threatening, insult to a nobleman during carnival. If both the messenger and the message in such a case are openly disclosed, then we are in the realm of direct confrontation (and perhaps, rebellion).

The practical modes of concealment are limited only by the imaginative capacity of subordinates. The degree of disguise, however, that elements of the hidden transcript and their bearers must assume to make a successful intrusion into the public transcript will probably increase if the political environment is very threatening and very arbitrary. Here we must above all recognize that the creation of disguises depends on an agile, firm grasp of the codes of meaning being manipulated. It is impossible to overestimate the subtlety of this manipulation.

Two contemporary examples from Eastern Europe serve to show how exaggerated compliance and perfectly ordinary behavior, when generalized and coded, can constitute relatively safe forms of resistance. In his (thinly disguised) autobiographical account of his time in a penal battalion for political prisoners, Czech writer Milan Kundera describes a relay race pitting the camp guards, who had organized it, against the prisoners.[7] The prisoners, knowing that they were expected to lose, spoiled the performance by purposely losing while acting an elaborate pantomime of excess effort. By exaggerating their compliance to the point of mockery, they openly showed their contempt for the proceedings while making it difficult for the guards to take action against them. Their small symbolic victory had real political conse-

7. *The Joke*, 83–88.

quences. As Kundera noted, "The good-natured sabotage of the relay race strengthened our sense of solidarity and led to a flurry of activity."[8]

The second example, from Poland, was both more massive and planned. In 1983, following General Wojciech Jaruzelski's declaration of martial law aimed at suppressing the independent trade union *Solidarnosc*, supporters of the union in the city of Lodz developed a unique form of cautious protest. They decided that in order to demonstrate their disdain for the lies propagated by the official government television news, they would all take a daily promenade timed to coincide exactly with the broadcast, wearing their hats backwards. Soon, much of the town had joined them. Officials of the regime knew, of course, the purpose of this mass promenade, which had become a powerful and heartening symbol for regime opponents. It was not illegal, however, to take a walk at this time of day even if huge numbers did it with an obvious political purpose in mind.[9] By manipulating a realm of ordinary activity that was open to them and coding it with political meaning, the supporters of Solidarity "demonstrated" against the regime in a fashion that was awkward for the regime to suppress.

I now turn to a few of the major forms of disguise.

Anonymity

"One member of the audience, explaining at the end of a carefully typed message why it was unsigned [wrote], 'This isn't the first winter this wolf has seen.'"

OPEN DISCUSSION OF CURRENT EVENTS, MOSCOW, NOVEMBER 1987

A subordinate conceals the hidden transcript from powerholders largely because he fears retaliation. If, however, it is possible to declare the hidden transcript while disguising the identity of the persons declaring it, much of the fear is dissipated. Recognizing this, subordinate groups have developed a large arsenal of techniques that serve to shield their identity while facilitating open criticism, threats, and attacks. Prominent techniques that accomplish this purpose include spirit possession, gossip, aggression through magic, rumor, anonymous threats and violence, the anonymous letter, and anonymous mass defiance.

8. Ibid., 86.

9. There was a sequel to this episode when the authorities shifted the hours of the Lodz curfew so that a promenade at that hour became illegal. In response, for some time, many Lodz residents took their televisions to the window at precisely the time the government newscast began and beamed them out at full volume into empty courtyards and streets. A passerby, who in this case would have had to have been an officer of the "security forces," was greeted by the eerie sight of working-class housing flats with a television at nearly every window blaring the government's message at him.

Spirit possession and cults of possession are common in a great many preindustrial societies. Where they exist, they frequently offer a ritual site at which otherwise dangerous expressions of hostility can be given comparatively free rein. I. M. Lewis, for example, argues persuasively that spirit possession in many societies represents a quasi-covert form of social protest for women and for marginal, oppressed groups of men for whom any open protest would be exceptionally dangerous.[10] Ultimately, Lewis's argument makes implicit use of the hydraulic metaphor we first encountered in the words of Mrs. Poyser; the humiliations of domination produce a critique that, if it cannot be ventured openly and at the site at which it arises, will find a veiled, safe outlet. In the case of spirit possession, a woman seized by a spirit can openly make known her grievances against her husband and male relatives, curse them, make demands, and, in general, violate the powerful norms of male dominance. She may, while possessed, cease work, be given gifts, and generally be treated indulgently. Because it is not she who is acting, but rather the spirit that has seized her, she cannot be held personally responsible for her words. The result is a kind of oblique protest that dares not speak its own name but that is often acceded to if only because its claims are seen to emanate from a powerful spirit and not from the woman herself.

Lewis extends his argument to many comparable situations in which any open protest by a subordinate group seems foredoomed. In particular, he examines episodes of possession among the low-caste servants of the higher-caste Nayars in the southern Indian state of Kerala, where he finds the same pattern of grievances and demands finding full voice under the cloak of possession. He makes a direct link between possession and deprivation:

> It is no surprise to find that the incidence of actual afflictions laid at the door of these spirits tends to coincide with episodes of tension and unjust treatment in relations between master and servant. Thus, as so often elsewhere, from an objective viewpoint, these spirits can be seen to function as a sort of "conscience of the rich." Their malevolent power reflecting the feelings of envy and resentment which peoples of high caste assume the less fortunate lower caste must harbour in relation to their superiors.[11]

Beyond spirit possession, strictly defined, Lewis claims that his analysis can often be applied to ecstatic cults, dionysian sects, rituals of drunkenness, hysteria, and the "hysteric" illnesses of Victorian women. What he finds

---

10. *Ecstatic Religion: An Anthropological Study of Spirit Possession and Shamanism.*
11. Ibid., 115.

comparable in these cases is a pattern of subordinate group expression of dissatisfaction in which personal responsibility may be disavowed. Whether or not it is plausible to call such acts protest is nearly a metaphysical question. On one hand, it is *experienced* as involuntary and as possession, never directly challenging the domination at which it is aimed.[12] It does, on the other hand, offer some practical redress, it gives voice to a critique of domination, and, in the case of cults of possession, it frequently creates new social bonds among those subject to such domination.

The great significance of the patterns Lewis finds is surely that they represent elements of a critique of domination that might otherwise have no public forum at all. Given the circumstances Lewis is examining, the choice would seem to be between fugitive forms of resistance such as possession and silence.

Gossip is perhaps the most familiar and elementary form of disguised popular aggression. Though its use is hardly confined to attacks by subordinates on their superiors, it represents a relatively safe social sanction. Gossip, almost by definition, has no identifiable author, but scores of eager retailers who can claim they are just passing on the news. Should the gossip—and here I have in mind malicious gossip—be challenged, everyone can disavow responsibility for having originated it. The Malay term for gossip and rumor, *khabar angin* (news on the wind), captures the diffuse quality of responsibility that makes such aggression possible.

The character of gossip that distinguishes it from rumor is that gossip consists typically of stories that are designed to ruin the reputation of some identifiable person or persons. If the perpetrators remain anonymous, the victim is clearly specified. There is, arguably, something of a disguised democratic voice about gossip in the sense that it is propagated only to the extent that others find it in their interest to retell the story.[13] If they don't, it disappears. Above all, most gossip is a discourse about social rules that have been violated. A person's reputation can be damaged by stories about his tight-fistedness, his insulting words, his cheating, or his clothing only if the public

12. Abu-Lughod, *Veiled Sentiments,* 102, reports a case in which a woman claims, to the ethnographer, that she purposely feigned possession in order to escape a hated marriage. In this case the tactic was successful.

13. The power to gossip is more democratically distributed than power, property, and income and, certainly, than the freedom to speak openly. I do not mean to imply that gossip cannot and is not used by superiors to control subordinates, only that resources on this particular field of struggle are relatively more favorable to subordinates. Some people's gossip is weightier than that of others, and, providing we do not confuse status with mere public deference, one would expect that those with high personal status would be the most effective gossipers.

among whom such tales circulate have shared standards of generosity, polite speech, honesty, and appropriate dress. Without an accepted normative standard from which degrees of deviation may be estimated, the notion of gossip would make no sense whatever. Gossip, in turn, reinforces these normative standards by invoking them and by teaching anyone who gossips precisely what kinds of conduct are likely to be mocked or despised.

We are more familiar with gossip as a technique of social control among relative equals—the stereotypical village tyranny of the majority—than from below. What is less often recognized, as emphasized in the previous chapter, is that much of the gossip, prying eyes, and invidious comparisons in such settings is precisely what helps maintain a conformity vis-à-vis dominating outsiders. In his analysis of social aggression in Andalusian villages—many with a radical, anarchist past—David Gilmore stresses the way in which they solidify a common front directed at rich landowners and the state.[14] When the victim is not too powerful, the gossiper makes sure that he knows he is being gossiped about; one might give people hard looks or perhaps cup one's hands to a friend's ear as the victim passes on the street. The purpose is to punish, chastise, or perhaps even drive out the offender. Gossip must take a more circumspect form against the rich and powerful for fear that the principal gossipers, if known, might well lose their jobs. Bitter criticism via gossip is also used routinely by those at the bottom of the caste system to destroy the reputation of their high-caste superiors.[15] Gossip, even in its strong form of character assassination, is a relatively mild sanction against the powerful. It presupposes not only a face-to-face community, but also one in which a reputation is still of some importance and value.[16]

Gossip might be seen as the linguistic equivalent and forerunner of witchcraft. In traditional societies, gossip is often reinforced by witchcraft: it is the next step, so to speak, in the escalation of social hostilities. The use of magic represents an attempt to move beyond gossip and turn "hard words" into an act of secret aggression that will bring direct harm to one's enemy, his family, his livestock, his crops. An aggressive wish to bring misfortune on someone ("May his crops wither!") becomes, through the performative act of magic, the

14. *Aggression and Community: Paradoxes of Andalusian Culture.* See also the classic analysis by J. A. Pitt-Rivers, *The People of the Sierra,* chap. 11.

15. Edward B. Harper, "Social Consequences of an Unsuccessful Low Caste Movement," in *Social Mobility in the Caste System in India: An Interdisciplinary Symposium, Comparative Studies in Society and History, Supplement #3,* ed. James Silverberg, 50.

16. It would be rare for a powerful person's standing to have no value whatever, if for no other reason than a climate of opinion that held him in contempt would encourage other forms of resistance.

agency of harm.[17] Like gossip and unlike an open verbal declaration of war, magical aggression is secret and can always be disavowed. Witchcraft is in many respects the classical resort of vulnerable subordinate groups who have little or no safe, open opportunity to challenge a form of domination that angers them. In a society that practices magic, those who perceive a lively resentment and envy directed at them from below will easily become convinced that any reverses they suffer are the result of malevolent witchcraft.

Rumor is the second cousin of gossip and magical aggression. Although it is not necessarily directed at a particular person, it is a powerful form of anonymous communication that can serve particular interests. Rumor thrives most, an early study emphasized, in situations in which events of vital importance to people's interests are occurring and in which no reliable information—or only ambiguous information—is available. Under such circumstances one would expect people to keep their ears close to the ground and to repeat avidly whatever news there was. Life-threatening events such as war, epidemic, famine, and riot are thus among the most fertile social sites for the generation of rumors. Before the development of modern news media and wherever, today, the media are disbelieved, rumor might be virtually the only source of news about the extralocal world. The oral transmission of rumor allows for a process of elaboration, distortion, and exaggeration that is so diffuse and collective it has no discernible author. The autonomy and volatility of politically charged rumor can easily spark violent acts. As Ranajit Guha notes, "An unmistakable, if indirect, acknowledgement of its power is the historically known concern for its repression and control on the part of those who, in all such societies, had the most to lose by rebellion. The Roman emperors were sensitive enough to rumor to engage an entire cadre of officials—*delatores*—in collecting and reporting it."[18]

The rapidity with which a rumor is propagated is astonishing. In part this derives from the mere mathematical logic of the chain letter phenomenon. If each hearer of a rumor repeats it twice, then a series of ten tellings will produce more than a thousand bearers of the tale. More astonishing than its speed, however, is the elaboration of rumor. In the great rebellion in India in 1857, touched off by a mutiny in the army, for example, Guha explains how an initial panic over greased cartridges grew quickly into rumors of forcible

---

17. See Annette B. Weiner, "From Words to Objects to Magic: 'Hard Words' and the Boundaries of Social Interaction," in *Dangerous Words: Language and Politics in the Pacific*, ed. Donald Lawrence Brenneis and Fred R. Myers, 161–91.

18. *Elementary Forms of Peasant Insurgency*, 251.

conversion, of the prohibition of agriculture, of a new law requiring everyone to eat bread.[19]

For our purposes the key fact is that the process of embellishment and exaggeration is not at all random. As a rumor travels it is altered in a fashion that brings it more closely into line with the hopes, fears, and worldview of those who hear it and retell it. Some ingenious experimental evidence has been developed to show that the transmission of rumor entails a loss of some information and the addition of elements that fit the general gestalt of the messengers.[20] Thus, U.S. experimenters showed a picture of a threatening crowd scene in which a white man holding a razor confronted an unarmed black man. In more than half of the retellings by whites, the razor was switched to the hand of the black man, in keeping with their fears and assumptions about blacks! The black subjects did not transfer the razor. The rumor, it appears, is not only an opportunity for anonymous, protected communication, but also serves as a vehicle for anxieties and aspirations that may not be openly acknowledged by its propagators. On this basis one must expect rumors to take quite divergent forms depending on what class, strata, region, or occupation they are circulating in.

The most elaborate study of historical rumor—that compiled by Georges Lefebvre in tracing the panic over a monarchist invasion in the summer following the storming of the Bastille—demonstrates in considerable detail the role of wish (and fear) fulfillment in "La Grande Peur."[21] The Revolution itself, civil strife, hunger, and roaming bands of dispossessed provided just the kind of unprecedented and charged atmosphere in which the extraordinary was commonplace and rumor thrived. Before the Revolution, for that matter, when the king summoned the Estates General for the first time since 1614 and initiated the compiling of complaints, it is not entirely surprising that the utopian hopes and direst fears of the peasantry colored their interpretation of its meaning:

19. Ibid., 255–59. It is not implausible to say that the rumors were the proximate cause of the Sepoy Mutiny.

20. Gordon W. Allport and Leo Postman, *The Psychology of Rumor*, esp. 75.

21. *The Great Fear of 1789: Rural Panic in Revolutionary France*, trans. Joan White. A striking recent parallel to Lefebvre's account can be seen in the grisly rumors that swept Rumania immediately after the fall of the Ceausescus. It was variously reported that sixty thousand had been killed by the Securitate in Timisoara, that the Securitate had poisoned the water supply there, and that thirty thousand die-hard Securitate officers had dug vast bunkers in the Carpathian mountains. See "Whispered No Longer, Hearsay Jolts Bucharest," Celestine Bohlen, *New York Times*, January 4, 1990, p. A14.

they were then invited not only to elect their representatives but also to draw up the *cahiers de doléances*: the king wished to hear the true voice of his people so that he might know their sufferings, their needs and their desires, presumably so that he could redress all wrongs. The novelty of the affair was truly astonishing. The king, the church's anointed, the lieutenant of God was all-powerful. Goodbye poverty and pain. But as hope sprang in the peoples' breasts, so did hatred for the nobility.[22]

It is not a simple matter to determine the proportions of wish fulfillment and willful misunderstanding that went into these utopian readings. What is certain, however, is that like Russian peasants interpreting the czar's wishes, their interpretations were very much in line with their interests. What are we to make of the following two contemporary reports by officials on the rumors then circulating?

> What is really tiresome is that these assemblies that have been summoned have generally believed themselves invested with some sovereign authority and that when they come to an end, the peasants went home with the idea that henceforth they were free from tithes, hunting prohibitions, and the payment of feudal dues.[23]

> The lower classes of the people are convinced that when the Estates General sat to bring about the regeneration of the kingdom we would see a total and absolute change, not only in present procedures, but also in conditions and income. . . . The people have been told [*sic*] that the king wishes every man to be equal, that he wants neither bishops nor lords; no more rank; no more tithes or seigneurial rights. And so these poor misguided people believe they are exercising their rights and obeying their king.[24]

The second observer appears to assume that the great expectations of the "lower classes" can be traced to outside agitators of some kind. In any event, clearly the lower classes believed what they chose to believe; they were, after all, free to disregard any utopian rumors. The rumors in this case, of course, had enormous consequences that impelled the revolution forward. Peasants, in fact, largely ceased paying feudal dues, withheld tithes, sent their cows and sheep to graze on the seigneurs' land, hunted and took wood as they pleased *before* these matters were resolved by the revolutionary legislature. When they

22. Ibid., 38.
23. Ibid., 39, quoting Desiré de Debuisson, lieutenant of the Saumur *baillage* during the elections.
24. Ibid., 39–40, quoting M. de Caraman (Aix).

were thwarted they complained about "the authorities who were concealing the king's orders and they said that he was willing for them to burn down the chateaux."[25] Knowing that all previous peasant risings had ended in a bloodbath, they were, at the same time, exceptionally alert to any rumor of an aristocratic counteraction, hoarding, or counterrevolutionary plots. The political impulse provided by rumor was integral to the revolutionary process.

Why is it that oppressed groups so often read in rumors promises of their imminent liberation? A powerful and suppressed desire for relief from the burdens of subordination seems not only to infuse the autonomous religious life of the oppressed but also to strongly color their interpretation of events. A few examples drawn from Caribbean slavery and the Indian caste system may serve to illustrate the pattern. In the slave rebellions in the late eighteenth and early nineteenth centuries, Craton shows, there was a fairly consistent belief that the king or British officials had set slaves free and that the whites were keeping the news from them.[26] Barbadan slaves in 1815 came to expect they would be freed on New Year's Day and took steps to prepare for that freedom. The colony of St. Domingue was shaken by a rumor that the king had granted slaves three free days a week and abolished the whip, but that the white masters had refused to consent.[27] Slaves treated the supposed decree as an accomplished fact, and incidents of insubordination and resistance to work routines increased, leading within a short time to the revolution that would culminate in Haiti's independence. Although we do not know much about the genesis of this particular rumor, most intimations of a coming liberation have some shard of substance behind them. The campaign for abolition, the Haitian Revolution, and the promises of freedom made by the British to any American slaves who would desert to them in the War of 1812 all proved incitements to imagine a coming freedom.

Untouchables, like slaves, are prone to read their hopes into rumor. As Mark Jürgensmeyer points out, at various times during colonial rule untouchables came to believe that the governor or his king had already raised them up and abolished untouchability.[28] Coupled with utopian expectations of the British was the common untouchable conviction that the Brahmins and other high-caste Hindus had stolen the secret, liberating texts they had once possessed.[29]

25. Ibid., 95.
26. Craton, *Testing the Chains*, 244 ff.
27. Carolyn Fick, "Black Peasants and Soldiers in the St. Domingue Revolution: Initial Reactions to Freedom in the South Province," in *History from Below*, ed. Krantz, 245.
28. *Religion as Social Vision*, esp. chap. 13.
29. Khare, *The Untouchable as Himself*, 85–86.

The parallels here between French peasants, slaves, untouchables, Russian serfs, and, for that matter, the cargo cults of peoples overwhelmed by Western conquest are too striking to ignore. The tendency to believe that an end to their bondage was at hand, that God or the authorities had granted their dreams, and that evil forces were keeping their freedom from them is a common, and usually tragic, occurrence among subordinated peoples.[30] By phrasing their liberation in such terms, vulnerable groups express their hidden aspirations in public in a way that both enables them to avoid individual responsibility and aligns them with some higher power whose express commands they are merely following. Such portents have, at the same time, helped fuel countless rebellions, almost all of which have miscarried. Social theorists who assume that a hegemonic ideology encourages a naturalization of domination in which no alternatives are imagined possible, will find it hard to account for these occasions on which subordinate groups seem to pick themselves up by the bootstraps of their own collective desires. If oppressed groups misconstrue the world, it is as often to imagine that the liberation they desire is coming as to reify domination.

We have hardly begun to exhaust the many forms of anonymity deployed by subordinate groups. Almost without exception they hide the individual identity of the actor and thereby make possible a far more direct expression of verbal or physical aggression.[31] In eighteenth-century Britain, for example, they are such a standard element in popular action that E. P. Thompson can speak convincingly of the

> *anonymous tradition.* The anonymous threat or even the individual terrorist act, is often found in a society of total clientage and dependency, on the other side of the medal of simulated deference. It is exactly in a society, where any open, identified resistance to the ruling power may result in instant retaliation, loss of home, employment, tenancy, if not victimisation

30. And perhaps for the early working class as well. As Ian McKay, discussing Bourdieu's work, writes, "Bourdieu notes with evident sorrow that workers are made incapable by the deep conditioning of their childhoods to seize historical opportunities, but he might also consider those historical instances of working classes who have been seized with a sense of historical possibility which was not objectively justified. Millenarian movements have not been unknown in the working class movement." "Historians, Anthropology, and the Concept of Culture," 238.

31. Or to make it possible at all. Sara Evans reports that the women in the Student Non-violent Coordinating Committee during the civil rights movement felt obliged to remain anonymous while raising issues about the treatment of women. Their memo made their concerns explicit: "This paper is anonymous. Think about the kinds of things the author, if made known, would have to suffer because of raising this kind of discussion. Nothing so final as being fired or outright exclusion, but the kinds of things which are killing to the insides, insinuations, ridicule, over-exaggerated compensations." *Personal Politics,* 234.

at law—that one tends to find acts of darkness; the anonymous letter, arson of the stock or outhouse, houghing of cattle, the shot or brick through the window, the gate off its hinges, the orchard felled, fish pond sluices opened at night. The same man who touches his forelock to the squire by day and who goes down to history as an example of deference may kill his sheep, snare his pheasants or poison his dogs at night.[32]

Thompson's juxtaposition of what I would term a public transcript of deferential performance with a hidden transcript of anonymous aggression in speech and act is compelling. In the anonymous, invariably threatening letters we may read what I imagine to be a fairly unvarnished rendition of what is said offstage and compare it with the official performance. Thus an anonymous letter provoked by the crop damage caused by gentry hunting minces no words: "[We will] not suffer such damned wheesing fat guted Rogues to Starve the Poor by Such hellish ways on purpose that they may follow hunting, horse-racing, etc. to maintain their families in Pride and extravagance."[33] Anonymous threats are not merely heartfelt expressions of anger. They are, above all, threats whether they take the form of a letter or an understood sign (the unlit torch stuck in the thatch, the bullet on the doorstep, the miniature cross and grave near the house) and are intended to modify the adversary's conduct. As Thompson sees it, such actions are episodes of a counter-theater. If the gentry's courts, hunts, clothing, and church appearances are intended to overawe their dependents, then the anonymous threat and violence of the rural poor are intended "to chill the spine of gentry, magistrates, and mayors."[34]

It goes without saying that when subordinates, individually or collectively, embark on direct attacks on the property or person of their superiors, they are likely to obscure their identity by precautions such as moving at night or wearing disguises. Poachers, arsonists, seditious messengers, and actual rebels take the same prudent steps as the highwayman. In the Catholic West the tradition of carnival provides, as we shall see, a ritual tradition that authorizes disguises coupled with direct speech and conduct that would otherwise not be tolerated. The men who dressed as women in the Rebecca Riots in Wales or in the *Demoiselles* protests against forest restrictions in France did not need to invent a new tradition.

These last two examples also illustrate the way in which the marginal and

32. "Patrician Society, Plebeian Culture," 399, emphasis added. For the details of another major nineteenth-century pattern of disguise and nighttime extortion by agricultural laborers adapting rituals of aggressive begging to their purposes, see Eric Hobsbawm and George Rudé, *Captain Swing*.

33. Ibid.

34. Ibid., 400.

apolitical status of women in a patriarchic order can be creatively exploited. In their desperate efforts to resist Stalin's collectivization program, the peasantry realized that if women took the lead in public opposition, the worst forms of punitive retaliation might be avoided. Men might then intervene with more safety on behalf of their threatened women. As Lynn Viola explains,

> peasant women's protest seems to have served as a comparatively safe outlet for peasant opposition in general and as a screen to protect the more politically vulnerable male peasants who could not oppose policy as actively or openly without serious consequences but who, nevertheless, could and did either stand silently and threateningly in the background or join in the disturbance once protest had escalated to a point where men might enter the fray as defenders of their female relations.[35]

In a larger sense, some of the basic forms of popular collective action that authorities would class as mob riots should almost certainly be seen as making strategic use of anonymity as well. The popular politics of the historical mob arises particularly in situations in which permanent opposition movements are impossible to sustain but where short-run collective action may succeed by virtue of its evanescence. Thus Thompson can write of the eighteenth-century English crowd's "capacity for swift direct action. To be of a crowd or a mob was another way of being anonymous, whereas to be a member of a continuing organization was bound to expose one to detection and victimisation. The 18th century crowd well understood its capacities for action, and its own art of the possible. Its successes must be immediate, or not at all."[36] Much the same point has been made about urban crowds in France from the mid-eighteenth to the mid-nineteenth centuries. The absence of any formal organization and the apparent impromptu nature of their actions wer exceptionally well adapted to an environment of power that precluded most alternative forms of direct action against the authorities. Looked at from this angle, to call such incidents spontaneous, as William Reddy notes, "is an irrelevant observation—unless we admit that the participants themselves appreciated, purposefully sought out spontaneity."[37]

The likelihood that subordinate groups may often deliberately choose spontaneous forms of popular action for the anonymity and other tactical advantages they provide would, if its implications were pursued, remake our perspective of popular politics. Traditionally, the interpretation of the crowd

35. "Babí bunty and Peasant Women's Protest during Collectivization," 39.
36. Thompson, "Patrician Society, Plebeian Culture," 401.
37. "The Textile Trade and the Language of the Crowd at Rouen, 1752–1871.

has emphasized the relative incapacity of lower classes to sustain any coherent political movement—a regrettable consequence of their short-run materialism and passions. In time, it was hoped, such primitive forms of class action would be replaced by more permanent and farsighted movements with a leadership (perhaps from the vanguard party) seeking fundamental political change.[38] If, however, a far more tactical reading is accurate, then the choice of fleeting, direct action by crowds is hardly a sign of some political handicap or incapacity for more advanced modes of political action. Such events as market riots, "price-setting" grain and bread riots, machine breaking, the burning of tax rolls and land records by swift mob action instead may represent a popular tactical wisdom developed in conscious response to the political constraints realistically faced. Spontaneity, anonymity, and a lack of formal organization then become enabling modes of protest rather than a reflection of the slender political talents of popular classes.[39]

The political advantages of impromptu action by a crowd conceal a deeper and more important form of disguise and anonymity without which such action would not be possible. While crowd action may not require formal organization, it most certainly does require effective forms of coordination and the development of an enabling popular tradition. In most respects the social coordination evident in traditional crowd action is achieved by the informal networks of community that join members of the subordinate group. Depending on the particular community, such networks may work through kinship, labor exchange, neighborhood, ritual practices, or daily occupational links (for example, fishing, pastoralism). What is important for our purposes is that these networks are socially embedded within the subordinate community and are therefore often as opaque to the authorities as they are "indispensable to sustained collective action."[40] Over time, naturally, such modes of collective action become part and parcel of popular culture, and the riot becomes something like a scenario, albeit a dangerous one, enacted by a large repertory company whose members know the basic plot and can step into the available roles. Anonymous mass action of this kind is thus entirely dependent on the existence of a social site for the hidden transcript, a site where social links and

38. I am referring particularly to Eric Hobsbawm's *Primitive Rebels: Studies in Archaic Forms of Social Movement in the 19th and 20th Centuries*. E. P. Thompson and George Rudé have written less in this vein because, I guess, they were less hobbled by a faith in the vanguard party.

39. For a path-breaking analysis of social protest in United States history that is sensitive to these issues, see Frances Fox Piven and Richard Cloward, *Poor People's Movements: Why They Succeed, How They Fail.*

40. See the argument of Frank Hearn claiming that the erosion of these "traditional" social structures was central to the political domestication of the English working class. *Domination, Legitimation, and Resistance,* 270.

traditions can grow with a degree of autonomy from dominant elites. In its absence, nothing of the kind would be possible.

One last form of anonymous mass action merits comment because it occurs under some of the direst forms of subordination. Here I have in mind the kind of collective protest often engaged in by prisoners rhythmically beating meal tins or rapping on the bars of their cells. Strictly speaking, the protesters are not anonymous but they nevertheless achieve a kind of anonymity by virtue of their numbers and the fact that it is seldom possible to identify who instigated or began the protest. While the form of expression is itself inherently vague, it is usually quite clear what the discontent is about from the context. Even in a total institution with little chance of creating a protected offstage site of discourse, a form of voice under domination that makes it next to impossible to single out individuals for retaliation is nevertheless achieved.

Euphemisms

If the anonymity of the messenger is often what makes it possible for the otherwise vulnerable to speak aggressively to power, one might imagine that without anonymity the performance of subordinates would revert to one of compliant deference. The alternative to complete deference, however, is to disguise the message just enough to skirt retaliation. If anonymity often encourages the delivery of an *un*varnished message, the veiling of the message represents the application of varnish.

The appropriate sociolinguistic analogy for this process of varnishing is the way in which what begins as blasphemy is transformed by euphemism into a hinted blasphemy that escapes the sanctions that open blasphemy would incur.[41] In Christian societies spoken oaths that "take the Lord's name in vain" have typically been altered to more innocuous forms in order that the speaker might avoid the anger of the Almighty, not to mention that of religious leaders and the pious. Thus, the oath "Jesus" becomes "Gee Whiz" or "Geez"; "Goddamned" becomes "G.D."; "by the blood of Christ" becomes "bloody." Even quite secular profanities such as "shit" are transformed into "shucks." In French the same process transforms "par Dieu" into "pardi" or "parbleu," "je renie Dieu" into "jarnibleu."

Euphemization is an accurate way to describe what happens to a hidden transcript when it is expressed in a power-laden situation by an actor who wishes to avoid the sanctions that direct statement will bring. Although subor-

41. Emile Benveniste, *Problèmes de linguistique générale*, 2:254–57.

dinate groups are by no means the only persons to use euphemisms, they resort to it frequently because of their greater exposure to sanctions. What is left in the public transcript is *an allusion to profanity without a full accomplishment of it;* a blasphemy with its teeth pulled. In time the original association between the euphemism and the blasphemy that it mimics may be lost altogether, and the euphemism becomes innocuous. So long as the association persists, however, all hearers understand it as taking the place of a real blasphemy. Much of the verbal art of subordinate groups consists of clever euphemisms that, as Zora Neale Hurston noted, "were characterized by indirect, veiled, social comment and criticism, a technique appropriately described as hitting a straight lick with a crooked stick."[42]

The use of euphemism as disguise is most striking in the pattern of folktales and folk culture generally among powerless groups. These more elaborate forms of veiling will be taken up later; here it is sufficient to note that euphemisms continually test the linguistic boundary of what is permissible and that often they depend for their intended effect on their being understood by powerholders. Slaves in Georgetown, South Carolina, apparently crossed that linguistic boundary when they were arrested for singing the following hymn at the beginning of the Civil War:

> We'll soon be free [repeated three times]
>   When the Lord will call us home.
> My brudder, how long [repeated three times]
>   'Fore we done suffering here?
> It won't be long [repeated three times]
>   'Fore the Lord call us home.
> We'll soon be free [repeated three times]
>   When Jesus sets me free.
> We'll fight for liberty [repeated three times]
>   When the Lord will call us home.[43]

Slave owners took the references to "the Lord" and "Jesus" and "home" to be too thinly veiled references to the Yankees and the North. Had their gospel hymn not been found seditious the slave worshippers would have had the satisfaction of having gotten away with an oblique cry for freedom in the public transcript. At the outset of the French Revolution, peasants might often make creative use of ambiguity in order to shield themselves either from the authorities of the ancien régime or the new revolutionary authorities. Inasmuch

42. "High John dè Conquer," in *Mother Wit*, ed. Alan Dundas, 543, cited in Raboteau, *Slave Religion*, 249–50.

43. Raboteau, *Slave Religion*, 245.

as democracy often meant the return of traditional rights, they would shout, "Ramenez la bonne" (Bring back the good) in which it was never clear to officials whether they meant "la bonne réligion," "la bonne révolution," "la bonne loi," or something else.[44]

Just as often, however, the euphemism may be intended as a threat whose force is lost unless it is taken as intended. The verbal formula of the threat, however, follows the path of euphemism in allowing the intention to be disavowed if challenged. André Abbiateci reports the following euphemisms actually used by arsonists in eighteenth-century France:

> I will have you awakened by a red cock.
> I will light your pipe.
> I'll send a man dressed in red who will pull everything down.
> I will fix you by sowing a seed that you will not soon regret.
> If you take away my land, you will see Damson plums.[45]

The purpose of these threats was virtually always to bring pressure to bear on the potential victim. If, the logic implied, he did what was required (for example, lower rents, restore forest rights, keep tenants, lower feudal dues) the arson could be avoided. So understood was the threat that it was typically delivered by an anonymous stranger or in a note. The peasants delivering the threat aimed to have their cake and eat it too; to deliver a clear threat in a form sufficiently ambiguous to escape prosecution.

Grumbling

Archibald: You're to obey *me*. And the text we've prepared.
Village: (banteringly) But I'm still free to speed up or draw out my recital and my performance. I can move in slow motion, can't I? I can sigh more often and more deeply.

    —GENET, *The Blacks*

We are all familiar with grumbling or muttering as a form of veiled complaint. Usually the intention behind the grumbling is to communicate a general sense of dissatisfaction without taking responsibility for an open, specific complaint. It may be clear enough to the listener from the context exactly what the complaint is, but, via the grumble, the complainer has avoided an incident and can, if pressed, disavow any intention to complain.

44. Maurice Agulhon, *La république au village: Les populations du Var de la Révolution à la seconde République*, 440.
45. "Arsonists in Eighteenth-Century France: An Essay in the Typology of Crime," from *Annales, E.S.C.* (Jan.–Feb. 1970), 229–48, trans. Elborg Forster and reprinted in *Deviants and the Abandoned in French Society: Selection from the Annales*, ed. Robert Forster and Orest Ranum, 4:158.

The grumble ought to be considered an instance of a broader class of thinly veiled dissent—a form that is particularly useful for subordinate groups. The class of events of which the grumble is an example would presumably include any communicative act intended to convey an indistinct and deniable sense of ridicule, dissatisfaction, or animosity. Providing such a message was imparted, almost any means of communication might serve the purpose: a groan, a sigh, a moan, a chuckle, a well-timed silence, a wink, or a stare. Consider this recent description by an Israeli officer of the stares he receives from Palestinian teenagers in the occupied West Bank: "Their eyes show hatred—no doubt. And it is a deep hatred. All the things they cannot say and all the things they feel inside of them, they put into their eyes and how they look at you."[46] The feeling conveyed in this case is crystal clear. Knowing they might be arrested, beaten, or shot for throwing rocks, the teenagers substitute looks, which are far safer but which, nonetheless, give nearly literal meaning to the expression, "If looks could kill. . . ."

Subordinates will naturally find it more often in their interest to grumble than superiors. Once they move beyond grumbling to direct complaints, they run far greater risks of open retaliation. Knowing the advantages they enjoy in an open confrontation, superiors will often try to insist on directness, asking the grumbler to state specifically what his complaint is. Just as often, the subordinate, wishing to remain in the more favorable arena of ambiguity, will disavow having made a complaint. Much of the day-to-day political communication from highly vulnerable subordinates to their superiors is, I believe, conducted in terms of just such grumbling. Over time a pattern of muttering may develop that has much of the communicative force of a quite refined language as the timing, tune, and nuances of the complaints become quite definitely understood. This language exists alongside the language of deference without necessarily violating its prescriptions. As Erving Goffman, echoing Genet, notes, "And of course in scrupulously observing the proper forms he [the actor] may find that he is free to insinuate all kinds of disregard by carefully modifying intonation, pronunciation, pacing, and so forth."[47] What is preserved through all of this is the facade of the public transcript. The point of grumbling is that it stops short of *in*subordination—to which it is a prudent

---

46. Thomas L. Friedman, "For Israeli Soldiers, 'War of Eyes' in West Bank," *New York Times*, January 5, 1988, p. A10. Such acts themselves, for that matter, need not be vague, only their meanings. Thus, Arlie Russell Hochschild describes how an angry flight attendant purposely spills a drink on the lap of a rude passenger, then apologizes, describing the event as an accident—with perhaps a suspicious hint of lightheartedness. The attendant has managed to perform what might be seen as an act of aggression and, at the same time, to control its possible consequences for her by claiming that it was inadvertent. *The Managed Heart*, 114.

47. "The Nature of Deference and Demeanor," 478.

alternative. Because the intention of making an explicit statement is denied, the need for a direct reply is also denied: officially, nothing has happened. Looked at from above, the dominant actors have permitted subordinates to grumble providing that they never infringe on the public etiquette of deference. Looked at from below, those with little power have skillfully manipulated the terms of their subordination so as to express their dissent publicly, if cryptically, without ever providing their antagonists with an excuse for a counterblow.

As with thinly veiled threats expressed in euphemisms, the message must not be so cryptic that the antagonist fails, utterly, to get the point. The purpose of grumbling is often not simply self-expression, but the attempt to bring the pressure of discontent to bear on elites. If the message is too explicit, its bearers risk open retaliation; if it is too vague, it passes unnoticed altogether. Quite often, however, what is intentionally conveyed by grumbling is an unmistakable tone, be it one of anger, contempt, determination, shock, or disloyalty. So long as the tone itself is effectively communicated, a certain vagueness may strategically heighten its impact on dominant groups. The effect of fear on one's antagonist, for example, may be heightened if he is left free to imagine the worst. An analysis of Rastafarian dress, music, and religion suggests, along these lines, that such indirect forms of communication with Jamaican white society had certain advantages over the more straightforward language of rebellion: "Paradoxically, 'dread' only communicates so long as it remains incomprehensible to its intended victims, suggesting the unspeakable rites of an insatiable vengeance."[48] Here the diffuseness of the Rastafarian menace amplifies its effect while at the same time providing an avenue of retreat for its adherents, who, after all, have made no particular threat.

Only on the rarest and most incendiary occasions do we ever encounter anything like an unadorned hidden transcript in the realm of public power relations. The realities of power require that it either be spoken by anonymous subordinates or be protected by disguise as rumor, gossip, euphemism, or grumbling that dares not speak in its own name.

Elaborate Forms of Disguise: The Collective Representations of Culture

If ideological sedition were confined to the ephemeral forms of gossip, grumbling, rumor, and the occasional hostility of masked actors, it would have a

48. Dick Hebdige, "Reggae, Rastas, and Rudies," in *Resistance Through Rituals,* ed. Hall and Jefferson, 152.

marginal life indeed. The fact is that ideological insubordination of subordinate groups also takes a quite public form in elements of folk or popular culture. Given the political handicaps under which the bearers of this folk culture habitually operate, however, its public expression typically skirts the bounds of impropriety. The condition of its public expression is that it be sufficiently indirect and garbled that it is capable of two readings, one of which is innocuous. As with a euphemism, it is the innocuous meaning—however tasteless it may be considered—that provides an avenue of retreat when challenged. These ambiguous, polysemic elements of folk culture mark off a relatively autonomous realm of discursive freedom on the condition that they declare no *direct* opposition to the public transcript as authorized by the dominant.

Major elements of popular (as distinct from elite) culture may come to embody meanings that potentially undercut if not contradict their official interpretation. There are at least three reasons why the culture of subordinate groups should reflect the smuggling of portions of the hidden transcript, suitably veiled, onto the public stage.

Insofar as folk or popular culture is the property of a social class or strata whose social location generates distinctive experiences and values, we should expect those shared characteristics to appear in their ritual, dance, drama, dress, folktales, religious beliefs, and so forth. Max Weber was not the only social analyst to notice that the religious convictions of the "disprivileged" reflected an implicit protest against their worldly fate. In a sectarian spirit fostered by their resentments, they were likely to envision an eventual reversal or leveling of worldly fortunes and rank, to emphasize solidarity, equality, mutual aid, honesty, simplicity, and emotional fervor. The distinctiveness of subordinate group cultural expression is created in large part by the fact that in this realm at least, the process of cultural selection is relatively democratic. Their members, in effect, select those songs, tales, dances, texts, and rituals that they choose to emphasize, they adopt them for their own use, and they of course create new cultural practices and artifacts to meet their felt needs. What survives and flourishes within the folk culture of serfs, slaves, and peasants is largely dependent on what they decide to accept and transmit. This is not to imply that the realm of cultural practices is unaffected by the dominant culture; only that it is less effectively patrolled than, say, the realm of production.

The second reason why subordinate groups might wish to find ways of expressing dissonant views through their cultural life is simply as a riposte to an official culture that is almost invariably demeaning. The culture of the aristocrat, lord, slave masters, and higher castes is, after all, largely designed to distinguish these ruling groups from the mass of peasants, serfs, slaves, and untouchables beneath them. In the case of peasant societies, for example, the existing cultural hierarchy holds out a model of behavior for civilized man that the peasantry lacks the cultural and material resources to emulate. Whether it is a matter of knowing the sacred texts, of speaking and dressing properly, of table manners and gestures, of performing elaborate ceremonies of initiation, marriage, or burial, of patterns of taste and cultural consumption, peasants are asked, in effect, to worship a standard that is impossible for them to achieve. In traditional China, for example, literacy was a critical means of stratification and implied, as a Sung encyclopaedist pointed out, that "people who know ideographs are wise and worthy, whereas those who do not know ideographs are simple and stupid."[49] Inasmuch as the cultural dignity and status of ruling groups are typically established through the systematic denigration and indignities imposed on subordinate classes, it is not surprising that commoners are not likely to share these assumptions with quite the same fervor.

Finally, what permits subordinate groups to undercut the authorized cultural norms is the fact that cultural expression by virtue of its polyvalent symbolism and metaphor lends itself to disguise. By the subtle use of codes one can insinuate into a ritual, a pattern of dress, a song, a story, meanings that are accessible to one intended audience and opaque to another audience the actors wish to exclude. Alternatively, the excluded (and in this case, powerful) audience may grasp the seditious message in the performance but find it difficult to react because that sedition is clothed in terms that also can lay claim to a perfectly innocent construction. Astute slaveholders undoubtedly realized that the attention to Joshua and Moses in slave Christianity had something to do with their prophetic roles as liberators of the Israelites from bondage. But, since they were, after all, Old Testament prophets, slaves could hardly be punished for revering them as part of their—authorized—Christian faith.

Two brief examples may help suggest how such coding might take place. The first concerns the cult of the Japanese village elder and martyr Sakura Sagoro as it grew from his execution in 1653 until the eighteenth century.[50] Sakura was crucified by the lords of the Narita area for having presented a petition on behalf of his oppressed villagers, petitioning being a capital crime. Presumably because he was martyred in their interests, the peasantry celebrated his spirit (with a vengeance!), and he became the most famous case of the "righteous man (*gimin*) who sacrifices himself for the welfare of his

49. Jack Goody, *Literacy in Traditional Societies*, 24.
50. Nagita and Scheiner, *Japanese Thought in the Tokugawa Period*, 39–62. See also Ann Walthall, "Narratives of Peasant Uprisings in Japan," *Journal of Asian Studies* 43, no. 3 (May 1983), 571–87.

people." The cult of Sakura through its shrine, through tales told by minstrels and troupes of puppeteers, plays, and the worship of his spirit as a Buddhist savior became something of a focus of popular solidarity and resistance. Thus far, the disguise here seems minimal except for the fact that it takes the form of a cult rather than direct political resistance. The more public manifestations of the cult in, say, public drama were, however, very carefully phrased in terms of the virtues of benevolent government. If peasants demanded land, they demanded it in order to be able to pay the taxes of the lord. What was new, and implicitly seditious, was that the achievement of justice was now shifted to peasant action rather than being left to noblesse oblige. The cult and its elaborations apparently played a vital role in creating and maintaining a peasant subculture of collective resistance to impositions from above.

Filipino use of the Christian tradition of the passion play to convey a general, yet guarded, dissent from elite culture is another striking example of the pattern. As Reynaldo Ileto has deftly shown, a cultural form that might have been taken to represent the submission of the Filipinos to the religion of their colonial masters and resignation before a cruel fate was infused with quite divergent meaning.[51] In its many variants performed throughout Tagalog society during Holy Week, the vernacular *pasyon* managed to negate much of the cultural orthodoxy of the Spanish and their local, Hispanicized *illustrado* allies. Traditional authority figures were ignored or repudiated, horizontal solidarity replaced loyalty to patrons, those placed most lowly (the poor, servants, victims) were shown to be most noble, the institutional church was criticized, and millennial hopes were entertained. Quite apart from the thematic ideas embedded in the performances, the actual organization and performance of the play was a powerful social tie uniting ordinary Filipinos. The vehicle for all of this was, of course, a church ritual authorized from above—a fact that made it a more sheltered social site for subversive meanings. This is not at all to claim a premeditated and cynical manipulation of the passion play; rather it was simply that the religious experience of ordinary Filipinos gradually infused this folk ritual which came to represent their sensibilities—within the limits of what might be ventured in comparative safety. Ileto shows how the ideology implicit in the *pasyon* appears in militant garb in a large number of violent uprisings, including, most notably, the popular movements associated with the revolution against Spain and local tyrants at the end of the nineteenth century. Nor is it a question of a mere affinity between the two. More accurately, one would have to say that the *pasyon*, appropriated by ordinary Filipinos, help create a shared subordinate

51. The material for this discussion is drawn from Ileto, "Pasyon and Revolution," passim.

ethos through its public—if disguised—enactment in folk ritual. Far from being confined to the social sites of the hidden transcript, the Tagalog population, like other subordinate groups, continued to give their deviant and resistant social visions a fugitive existence in public discourse.[52]

Oral Culture as Popular Disguise

The great bulk of lower-class cultural expression has typically taken an oral rather than a written form. Oral traditions, due simply to their means of transmission, offer a kind of seclusion, control, and even anonymity that make them ideal vehicles for cultural resistance. To appreciate how the folk song, the folktale, the joke, and of course, Mother Goose rhymes have borne a heavy weight of seditious meanings, the structure of oral traditions merits brief elaboration.[53]

We are all aware that speech, particularly informal speech between friends or intimates, is likely to take greater liberties in syntax, grammar, and allusions than formal speech, let alone print. What is less often appreciated is how even modern, print-dominated societies contain a large contemporary oral tradition that is generally ignored by cultural historians. As Robert Graves trenchantly observed,

> When a future historian comes to treat of the social taboos of the 19th and 20th centuries in a fourteen volume life work, his theories of the existence of an enormous secret language of bawdry and an immense oral literature of obscene stories and rhymes known, in various degrees of initiation, to every man and woman in the country, yet never consigned to writing or openly admitted as existing will be treated as a chimerical notion by the enlightened age in which he writes.[54]

If this much can be said about a relatively literate and socially integrated industrial country, how much more vast and significant would be the oral culture of subordinate groups whose culture directly concerns us?

The anonymity possible within oral culture derives from the fact that it exists in only impermanent forms through being spoken and performed. Each

52. For a valuable account of how rituals can be adapted to take on new, subversive meanings that are opaque to the powerful, see Robert Weller's analysis of the Festival of the Hungry Ghosts in Taiwan during the Japanese occupation. "The Politics of Ritual Disguise: Repression and Response in Taiwanese Popular Religion."

53. See William S. Baring-Gould and Cecil Baring-Gould, *The Annotated Mother Goose: Nursery Rhymes New and Old* (New York: C. W. Potter, 1962).

54. *Lars Porsena, or the Future of Swearing and Improper Language,* 55.

enactment is thus unique as to time, place, and audience as well as different from every other enactment. Like gossip or rumor, the folk song is taken up and performed or learned at the option of its listeners and, in the long run, its origins are lost altogether. It becomes impossible to recover some *ur* version from which all subsequent renditions are deviations. In other words, there is no orthodoxy or center to folk culture since there is no primary text to serve as the measure of heresy. The practical result is that folk culture achieves the anonymity of collective property, constantly being adjusted, revised, abbreviated, or, for that matter, ignored. The multiplicity of its authors provides its protective cover, and when it no longer serves current interests sufficiently to find performers or an audience, it simply vanishes forever.[55] Individual performers and composers can take refuge, like the originator of a rumor, behind this anonymity. A collector of Serbian folk songs thus complained, "Everyone denies responsibility [for having composed a new song], even the true composer and says he heard it from someone else."[56]

Strictly speaking, written communication is more effectively anonymous than spoken communication. Anonymous circulars can be prepared in secret, delivered in secret, and unsigned, whereas oral communication (before the telephone) is exchanged between at least two known individuals—unless they are themselves in disguise. From the point of view of concealment, however, the disadvantage of writing is that once a text is out of the author's hands, control over its use and dissemination is lost.[57] The advantage of communication by voice (including gestures, clothes, dance, and so on) is that the communicator retains control over the manner of its dissemination—the audience, the place, the circumstances, the rendition. Control, then, of oral culture is irretrievably decentralized. A given folktale, for example, may be retold or ignored and, if retold, may be abbreviated, enlarged, changed, spoken in completely different forms or dialects according to the interests, tastes, and also the fears of the speaker. For this reason the realm of private conversation is the most difficult for even the most persistent police apparatuses to penetrate. Part of the relative immunity of the spoken word from surveillance

55. In societies in which a literate class exists, a version may, of course, survive, and the form may be recovered. Once a written version of an oral text is collected (for example, Homer's *Odyssey*), it may take on a fundamentally different life.

56. Burke, *Popular Culture in Early Modern Europe*, 115.

57. The secrecy of oral communication can of course serve elite interests as well: gentlemens' agreements, oral instructions that can be disavowed, and so on. Max Weber notes that the sacred knowledge of the Brahmin was transmitted orally for centuries and it was forbidden to set it down in writing for fear lower castes would break their monopoly of esoteric knowledge. Weber, *The Sociology of Religion*, 67. The "disavowability" of oral communication is undoubtedly the reason behind the contemporary adage to "get it in writing."

springs from its low technological level. Printing presses and copying machines may be seized, radio transmitters may be located, even typewriters and tape recorders may be taken, but short of killing its bearer, the human voice is irrepressible.

The most protected format of spoken communication is a conversation between two persons; the level of security diminishes as the number of people reached in a single encounter (for example, a public rally) increases. Oral communication, then, is safe only when it is a petty retail operation. Two important factors circumvent this apparent disadvantage. First, this account fails to allow for the geometrical progression of serial tellings, which may reach thousands in a short time, as we have seen in the case of rumors. The second factor is that each oral performance can be nuanced, disguised, evasive, and shaded in accordance with the degree of surveillance from authorities to which it is exposed. A possibly seditious folk song can, in this sense, be performed in hundreds of ways: from the apparently innocuous before hostile audiences to the openly seditious before a friendly and secure audience. Those who have earlier been privy to the more seditious interpretations will appreciate the hidden meaning of the innocuous version. Thus it is the particularity and elasticity of oral culture that allows it to carry fugitive meanings in comparative safety.

Folktales, the Trickster

Nothing illustrates the veiled cultural resistance of subordinate groups better than what have been termed trickster tales. It would be difficult, I think, to find a peasant, slave, or serf society without a legendary trickster figure, whether in animal or human form. Typically the trickster makes his successful way through a treacherous environment of enemies out to defeat him—or eat him—not by his strength but by his wit and cunning. The trickster is unable, in principle, to win any direct confrontation as he is smaller and weaker than his antagonists. Only by knowing the habits of his enemies, by deceiving them, by taking advantage of their greed, size, gullibility, or haste does he manage to escape their clutches and win victories. Occasionally the fool and trickster figures are combined, and the guile of the underdog may consist in playing dumb or in being so clever in the use of words that his enemy is misled.[58]

It doesn't require a great deal of subtle analysis to notice that the structural

58. For an account of the Central Sulawesi trickster *Pantenggel,* who is admired for his ability to clothe even the simplest statements in elaborate, elusive imagery, see Jane Mannig Atkinson, "Wrapped Words: Poetry and Politics among the Wana of Central Sulawesi, Indonesia," in *Dangerous Words,* ed. Brenneis and Myers.

position of the trickster hero and the stratagems he deploys bear a marked resemblance to the existential dilemma of subordinate groups. The motto of the trickster hero is, in fact, captured by a common slave saying from South Carolina: "De bukrah [whites] hab scheme, en de nigger hab trick, en ebery time de bukrah scheme once, de nigger trick twice."[59] As a genre of tales (for example, the mouse-deer Sang Kanchil stories in the Malay world, the Siang Miang tales from northeast Thailand, the spider stories from West Africa, the Till Eulenspiegel tales in Western Europe) trickster stories also contain a great deal of violence and aggression. There is some evidence linking fantasy aggression of this kind with severely punitive situations and, in particular, aggressive folktales with societies that repress open aggression.[60] Without insisting on psychological theories of projection and displacement, it is sufficient to recognize that the underdog who outwits his normally dominant antagonist in such tales is likely to exploit his advantage to exact physical revenge.

The Brer Rabbit tales of North American slaves are among the best-known examples of an oral tradition of trickster tales, many variants of which have been collected. Any collected version, naturally, represents a single performance—without the nuances of pacing and emphasis—and it is quite possible that those variants transcribed by slaveholding whites or outside folklorists represent the most sanitized or prudent tellings. The origins of the tales are, as we might expect, uncertain, although similar stories in West African oral traditions as well as in the Indian *jataka* tales of Buddha as a young man suggest a possible lineage. Brer Rabbit is generally pitted against Brer Fox or Brer Wolf, whom he defeats by relying on his endless store of dissimulation, guile, and agility. Often his exploits mimicked the survival strategies of the slaves who elaborated these tales. "Significantly, one of the trickster's greatest pleasures was eating food he had stolen from his powerful enemies."[61]

Rabbit's road to victory is not entirely smooth, but his setbacks are usually attributable to rashness (for example, in the tarbaby stories) or trust in the sincerity of the strong. When victory comes, it is often savored in some detail. Rabbit not only kills Wolf but "mounts him, humiliates him, reduces him to servility, steals his woman and, in effect, takes his place."[62]

The disguises that the Brer Rabbit tales afforded were multiple. Any

59. Cited in Levine, *Black Culture and Black Consciousness*, 81.
60. G. O. Wright, "Projection and Displacement: A Cross-cultural Study of Folk-tale Aggression," cited in Berkowitz, *Aggression*, 121–23.
61. Alex Lichtenstein, "That Disposition to Theft with which they have been Branded: Moral Economy, Slave Management, and the Law," 418.
62. Levine, *Black Culture and Black Consciousness*, 111–16.

raconteur could claim simply to be passing on a story for which he or she had no responsibility—in the way one may distance oneself from a joke that one claims to have overheard. The story in this case is obviously a story about animals, a fantasy story at that, which has nothing to do with human society. A teller of a Brer Rabbit tale could also select from among a host of stories and could adjust any particular tale to suit the circumstances.

Within this relatively veiled context, however, the slave could identify with the protagonist, who managed to outwit, ridicule, torture, and destroy his more powerful enemy while at the same time inserting the narrative into an apparently innocuous context. It goes without saying, as well, that these tales had an instructive, cautionary side. Identifying with Brer Rabbit, the slave child learned, as he or she learned in other ways, that safety and success depended on curbing one's anger and channeling it into forms of deception and cunning, where one's chances of success were greater. What they taught, the tales also celebrated as a source of pride and satisfaction. What is being celebrated is not adequately captured by the loaded English term *cunning*.[63]

The celebration of guile and cleverness was hardly confined to the Brer Rabbit tales. It can be found in the High John (or Old John) tales[64] and the Coyote tales, not to mention proverbs and songs, all of which were the public face of an oral culture that reinforced a certain hatred of the powerful and a worship of the persistence and agility of the underdog.

It is customary to treat oral traditions like the Brer Rabbit tales as communication among slaves and then to gauge their role in the socialization of a spirit of resistance. What this ignores is the publicness of the Brer Rabbit stories. They were not told just offstage in the slave quarters. The place of such tales as part of the public transcript suggests a line of interpretation. It suggests that, for any subordinate group, there is tremendous desire and will to express publicly what is in the hidden transcript, even if that form of expression must use metaphors and allusions in the interest of safety. The hidden transcript, as it were, presses against and tests the limits of what may be safely ventured in terms of a reply to the public transcript of deference and

63. As Detienne and Vernant have explained at great length, the ancient Greeks greatly admired this quality, which they called *mêtis* and which "combine[s] flair, wisdom, forethought, subtlety of mind, deception, resourcefulness, vigilance, opportunism, various skills and experience acquired over the years. It is applied in situations which are transcient, shifting, disconcerting, and ambiguous, situations which do not lend themselves to precise measurement, exact calculation, or rigorous logic." Marcel Detienne and Jean-Pierre Vernant, *Cunning Intelligence in Greek Culture and Society,* trans. Janet Lloyd, 3–4; see also p. 44. For a thirteenth-century Arabic compilation of thousands of clever tricks known to have been successfully used to outwit enemies, see René B. Khawam, trans., *The Subtle Ruse: The Book of Arabic Wisdom and Guile.*

64. Hurston, "High John de Conquer," 541–48.

conformity. Analytically, then, one can discern a dialogue with the dominant public culture in the public transcript as well as in the hidden transcript. Reading the dialogue from the hidden transcript is to read a more or less *direct* reply, with no holds barred, to elite homilies. The directness is possible, of course, only because it occurs offstage, outside the power-laden domain. Reading the dialogue from the public oral traditions of subordinate groups requires a more nuanced and literary reading simply because the hidden transcript has had to costume itself and speak more warily. It succeeds best— and one imagines is most appreciated too—when it dares to preserve as much as possible of the rhetorical force of the hidden transcript while skirting danger.

The slaves' dialogue with the masters, then, proceeds on three levels. First, there is the official public culture, which might be represented by this extract from a catechism prepared for slaves in the antebellum U.S. South:

Q. Are not servants bound to obey their masters?

A. Yes, the Bible exhorts servants to be obedient to their masters, and to please them well in all things. . . .

Q. If the master is unreasonable, may the servant disobey?

A. No, the Bible says, "Servants, be subject to your masters in all fear, not only to the good and gentle, but also to the forward. . . ."

Q. If servants suffer unjustly, what are they to do?

A. They must bear it patiently.[65]

At this level, in the midst of a ritual of subordination monitored by those in authority, slaves had little choice but to deliver up the performance required of them—though they might by small gestures indicate their lack of enthusiasm. Offstage, on the other hand, they might directly repudiate their command performance. If we examine the narratives of slaves who came North, we can find evidence of this offstage negation. Two plausible replies might have been, "But I did not regard it [pilfering] as stealing then; I do not regard it as such now. I hold that a slave has a moral right to eat, drink, and wear all that he needs . . . because it was the labor of my own hands."[66] Or, a direct cry of vengeance rather than humility might be apparent from the actual religious convictions of slaves: "They are deceived who imagine that he arises from his knees, with back lacerated and bleeding cherishing only a spirit of meekness and forgiveness. A day may come—it will come if his prayer is heard—a terrible day of vengeance when the master in his turn will cry for mercy."[67]

65. Osofsky, *Puttin' on Ole Massa*, 32–33.
66. From the narrative of William Wells Brown in ibid., 166.
67. From the narrative of Solomon Northrup in ibid., 363.

Allowing for the formality of writing and an audience of white northerners, we can imagine the unvarnished oral versions of these replies that might have been voiced in the slave quarters.

What the Brer Rabbit stories represent, I believe, is the muffled, oblique version of the direct replies quoted above. The same would hold true for much of the oral culture of subordinate groups.[68] It may seem that the heavy disguise this reply wears must all but eliminate the pleasure it gives. While it is surely less satisfying than an open declaration of the hidden transcript it nevertheless achieves something the backstage can never match. It carves out a public, if provisional, space for the autonomous cultural expression of dissent. If it is disguised, it is at least not hidden; it is spoken to power.[69] This is no small achievement of voice under domination.[70]

Symbolic Inversion, World-Upside-Down Prints

If the slaves' oral tradition of Brer Rabbit stories was sufficiently opaque and innocuous to allow public telling, the pan-European tradition of "world-upside-down" drawings and prints must be counted as rather more daring.

68. Burke notes that the Catholic Indexes of the late fifteenth century banned the publication of some ballads and chapbooks, notably *Till Eulenspiegel* and *Reynard the Fox. Popular Culture in Early Modern Europe*, 220.

69. See, in this context, Lila Abu-Lughod's striking analysis of Bedouin women's poetry as a disguised counterpoint to official, male values of honor. As she notes, "Poetry cloaks statements in the veils of formula, convention, and tradition, thus suiting it to the task of carrying messages about the self that contravene the official cultural ideals." "As noted, the ghinnawa (poem) is a highly formulaic and stylized verbal genre." "Formula renders content impersonal or non-individual, allowing people to dissociate themselves from the sentiments they express, if revealed to the wrong audience, by claiming that 'it was just a song.'" *Veiled Sentiments*, 239.

70. One of the most effective and common ways subordinates may express resistance is by embedding it in a larger context of symbolic compliance. This pattern relates directly to the earlier discussion of the use-value of hegemony but merits brief comment here as a form of disguise. The pattern to which I wish to call attention was apparent in the weekly protests by Argentine mothers in Buenos Aires's Plaza de Mayo demanding that the military regime account for the disappearance of their children. Here was, in effect, an act of open defiance against a repressive regime responsible for the extrajudicial murder of thousands of opponents. And yet the protests continued and grew into a key antiregime ritual. Their *relative* immunity from summary violence sprang, I believe, from their structural appeal to just those patriarchal values of religion, family, morality, and virility to which the right-wing regime gave constant lip service. In a public ideology that implicitly respected women, above all, in their roles as mothers or virginal daughters, these women were demonstrating as mothers on behalf of their children. An open attack on women acting in this particular capacity and disavowing any other motive would have been quite awkward for the public standing of the regime. As any dominant ideology does, this ideology not only excluded certain forms of activity as illegitimate, it also, perhaps inadvertently, created a small niche of opportunity that was utilized by the mother of the *desaparecidos*. By clothing their defiance in hegemonic dress, these women were able to challenge the regime in other respects.

Enormously popular throughout Europe, especially after the advent of printing in the sixteenth century made them accessible to the lower classes, these
prints depicted a topsy-turvy world in which all the normal relations and
hierarchies were inverted. Mice ate cats, children spanked parents, the hare
snared the hunter, the cart pulled the horse, fishermen were pulled from the
water by fish, the wife beat the husband, the ox slaughtered the butcher,
the poor man gave alms to the rich man, the goose put the cook into the pot,
the king on foot led a peasant on horseback, fish flew in the air, and so on in
seemingly endless profusion. By and large each of these broadsheets, standard items in the sacks of colporteurs, reversed a customary relationship of
hierarchy or predation or both.[71] The underdog took revenge, just as he did in
the Brer Rabbit tales.

Before turning to the vital question of how the world-upside-down broadsheets should be interpreted, I must stress that they did not stand by themselves, but nested in a popular culture brimming over with images of reversal.
Such themes could be found in satirical songs, in popular theater where the
lower-class clown and commentator (for example, Falstaff) might exchange
clothes and roles with his master, in the rich traditions of carnival (a ritual of
reversal), and widespread millennial expectations. The symbolic opulence of
popular culture was such that a single symbol could represent virtually an
entire worldview. Thus Le Roy Ladurie notes that any one of several carnival
symbols—the green bough, the rake, the onion, or the Swiss trumpet—was
understood to represent leveling—whether of food, property, status, wealth,
or authority.[72] Popular sayings that implicitly questioned the distinction between commoner and noble were popular and widely disseminated. The
seditious couplet usually linked to John Ball and the Peasants' Revolt of 1381,
"When Adam delved and Eve span, / Who was then the gentleman?" could be
found in nearly identical form in other Germanic languages (for example,
German, Dutch, Swedish) and, slightly altered, in Slavic and romance languages as well.[73]

The world-upside-down tradition can, of course, be taken to have no
political significance whatever. As a trick of a playful imagination—a simple
jeu d'esprit—it may mean nothing more than that. More commonly, the
tradition is occasionally seen in functionalist terms as a safety-valve or vent

71. The bulk of my discussion here is drawn from the fine analysis by David Kunzle, "World
Upside Down." For a fascinating account of the reversal of gender roles in roughly the same
period, see Natalie Zemon Davis, "Women on Top: Symbolic Sexual Inversion and Political
Disorder in Early Modern Europe," in *The Reversible World: Symbolic Inversion in Art and Society,*
ed. Barbara A. Babcock, 129–92.

72. *Carnival in Romans,* 77.

73. Burke, *Popular Culture in Early Modern Europe,* 53–54.

that, like carnival, harmlessly drains away social tensions that might otherwise become dangerous to the existing social order. In a slightly more ominous version of this argument, it is suggested that world-upside-down prints and other rituals of reversal are something of a conspiracy of the dominant, actually devised by them as a symbolic substitute for the real thing. Functional arguments of this kind, especially when they rely on conspiracies that would have every reason to remain concealed, cannot be refuted directly. What can be done, I think, is to show how implausible such a perspective is and how the circumstantial evidence leads firmly in the opposite direction.

Admittedly, it is impossible to envision a world upside down without beginning with a world right side up of which it is the mirror image. The same is true by definition for any cultural negation; the hippie's life-style represents a protest only by being seen against the background of middle-class conformity; the proclamation of one's atheism makes sense only in a world filled with religious believers. Inversions of this kind do, however, play an important imaginative function, even if they accomplish nothing else. They do, at least at the level of thought, create an imaginative breathing space in which the normal categories of order and hierarchy are less than completely inevitable. It is not obvious why dominant groups would want to encourage anything that didn't entirely reify or naturalize the existing social distinctions they benefit from. And if it is claimed that this is a cultural concession they must make to ensure order, it suggests that such inversions are less something granted than something insisted on from below. When we manipulate any social classification imaginatively—turning it inside out and upside down—we are forcibly reminded that it is to some degree an arbitrary human creation.

Far from encouraging the production and circulation of world-upside-down broadsheets, the authorities did what they could to limit their circulation. A popular series of prints called "the war of the rats against the cat" was considered a particularly subversive inversion. In 1797 in a Holland recently occupied by French revolutionary troops, authorities seized both the publisher and his stock of such prints. Under Peter the Great, Russian censors insisted on changes in prints of the cat so that it wouldn't be seen to resemble their czar. In 1842 czarist officials seized all known copies of a very large print depicting an ox slaughtering the butcher.[74] Its seditious import, apparent to those in charge of preventing protest, would not, we must imagine, have been lost on the wider public who came across it. Not content with restricting potentially subversive popular culture, the authorities not uncommonly pro-

74. Kunzle, "World Upside Down," 78.

duced and disseminated the popular culture they thought appropriate for the lower orders. Books of proverbs reminiscent of the slaves' catechism were circulated. Given their content, for example, "Hunger costs little, anger much," "Poverty is good for many (all) things," "Too much justice is injustice," "Each should behave according to his rank," it is not surprising that they found a readier audience among those of higher status.[75] When nothing was readily at hand to reply to a threatening popular culture, defamatory verse might be commissioned for the occasion. That, as noted in the previous chapter, was how the bishop of Würzburg attempted to undercut the anticlerical appeal of the drummer of Niklashousen in late fifteenth-century Germany. And in their cultural offensive against the heresies of William Tell, they produced woodcuts that gave the peasant an animal's face and depicted his moral viciousness. The point of these brief illustrations is simply that world-upside-down imagery was not endorsed as a form of cultural anesthesia by elites but rather was made the object of suppression and counteroffensives.

What are we to make, however, of the mixture of implicit social critique with inversions that either have no obvious social content or that actually violate the physical laws of nature? It takes no interpretive leap of faith to see the subversive import of the following sorts of broadsheets: the lord serves a peasant at table; the poor man hands his sweat and blood to the rich; Christ wears a crown of thorns while, next to him, the pope wears a triple gold tiara; the peasant stands over the lord, who is digging or hoeing. Such imagery is, however, typically combined with two other kinds of prints. First, prints in which, say, two geese turn a human on a spit over a fire. Here, the meaning is not obvious, although who normally roasts and eats whom is being reversed. The common use—far more common than today—of analogies from the barnyard and agrarian life to describe human relations makes a seditious reading of the print that much more plausible. After all, when Winstanley, in the English Civil War, wanted to describe the relationship between property law and the poor, he dramatized it in familiar terms: "The law is the fox, poor men are the geese; he pulls off their feathers and feeds upon them."[76] A seditious reading of the geese roasting a man is, of course, disavowable; that is why it is cast in equivocal terms. Given the codes and imagery then in circulation, a subversive interpretation is also available.

The prints depicting scenes such as fish flying in the air and birds under the water pose a somewhat different problem. At one level they simply com-

75. Ibid., 74.
76. Burke, *Popular Culture in Early Modern Europe*, 160.

plete or extend a series of inversions. At another level one might claim that their purpose is to make a mockery of all the inversions by implying that they are at least as preposterous as fish flying in the air. On this reading, the aggregate effect of the upside-down broadsheets would be symbolically to rule out any reversals of the social hierarchy. Here, I believe, the element of disguise plays a vital role. As *public* popular culture the world-upside-down prints are disguised by the anonymity of their authorship, by the ambiguity of their meaning, and by the addition of obviously harmless material. The wish for a reversal of the social hierarchy becomes public, in such conditions, only on condition that it is Janus-faced. As David Kunzle, the most searching student of this genre of popular culture, concludes,

> The essential ambivalence of WUD [world upside down] permits, according to the circumstances, those satisfied with the existing or traditional social order to see the theme as a mockery of the idea of changing that order around, and at the same time, those dissatisfied with that order to see the theme as mocking it in its present perverted state.
>
> . . .
>
> The truly impossible, the "purely playful" fantasies involving animals . . . *functions as a masking mechanism* for the dangerous, vindictive, anarchic, "childish," but otherwise suppressed or unconscious desires which are embedded in the less than impossible human reversals.[77]

Kunzle's interpretation, moreover, coincides with other readings of how heretical messages might be successfully coded at this time. The potentially inflammatory prophecies of the sixteenth-century abbot Joachim of Fiore, which were to play a role in many millennial movements, were disseminated in part by a series of ambiguous pictures. An empty throne might thus be taken as an endorsement of the hermit-pope Celestine or as the beginning of a spiritual revolution; a representation of the pope holding his miter over a crowned or horned animal that has a human face might be taken as the lamb of God, as a secular ruler, or as the anti-Christ. Viewing them in historical context, however, Marjorie Reeves claims, "the main thrust of the prophesies is clear. These Joachites were able through these symbols, to make *veiled* but bitter commentary on the contemporary papacy and then to highlight the Joachite expectation."[78] Reeves might, more accurately perhaps, have written, "bitter

---

77. "World Upside Down," 82, 89, emphasis added.
78. Reeves, "Some Popular Prophesies from the 14th to 17th Centuries," in *Popular Belief and Practice: Papers Read at the 9th Summer Meeting and 10th Winter Meeting of the Ecclesiastical History Society*, ed. G. J. Cuming and Derek Baker, 107–34.

because veiled" inasmuch as it was the veiling that permitted the prophecies to be disseminated in this public fashion at all.[79]

If world-upside-down broadsheets were either innocuous or soporific, we would not expect to find them figuring so prominently in actual rebellions and in the imagery and actions of the insurgents themselves. In the Reformation and in the subsequent Peasants' War, the prints play an undeniably major role in disseminating the spirit of revolution. As the conflict became open and violent, the imagery became more direct: a Lutheran cartoon showed a peasant defecating into the papal tiara. The prints associated with the peasant revolutionaries under Thomas Münzer pictured "peasants disputing with learned theologians, ramming the scriptures down the throat of priests, and pulling down the tyrant's castle."[80] When a captured rebel was asked (rhetorically) what kind of beast he was, he replied, "A beast that usually feeds on roots and wild herbs but, when driven by hunger, sometimes consumes priests, bishops, and fat citizens."[81] Not only did such radical ideas—an end to status distinctions, the abolition of differences in wealth, popular justice, and popular religion, revenge on exploiting priest, nobles, and wealthy townsmen—play a rhetorical role in the Peasants' War, but there are instances in which the rebels turned the images of inversion into tableaux vivants. One peasant leader thus dressed a countess up like a beggar and sent her off in a dung cart; knights, now in rags, were obliged to serve their vassals at table while peasants dressed up in knightly garb and mocked their noble rituals.[82] This once, briefly, peasants had the opportunity to live their fantasies and dreams of revenge, and those fantasies might have been read from the world-upside-down prints.

Many of the same aspirations among serfs and the lower classes generally can be found in the context of the English Civil War and the French Revolution. The popular movement in the English Civil War, among other popular goals, sought to eliminate honorific forms of address and the status distinctions that

79. There appears to be something of a Japanese equivalent to the world-upside-down tradition. Nagita and Scheiner write, "In Edo, for example, the spirit of *yonaoshi* [Buddhist new world—a millennial vision] and hostility toward the rich become associated with the *namazu* (catfish). Immediately after the great Edo earthquake in 1855, a series of unsigned prints depicted the *namazu* which supported the world as avenging itself on the rich and crafty who had exploited the poor. . . . Prints now showed him propped on the bodies of the rich as he forced them to excrete and vomit forth coins and jewels for the poor. Such prints also depicted the *uchi kowashi* [wrecking the homes of rich or officials]. . . . 'Herewith we, the people, attained our cherished desire,' read the caption under one of the prints." *Japanese Thought in the Tokugawa Period*, 58.

80. Kunzle, "World Upside Down," 64.

81. Ibid., 63.

82. Ibid., 64.

generated them, to divide up the land, eliminate lawyers and priests, and so on.[83] During the French Revolution, sansculottes scouring the countryside for provisions would occasionally bivouac in a chateau and insist on being served by the nobility: "The *commissaires* would get their victims to cook them copious meals, which they had then to serve standing up, while the *commissaires* themselves sat down with the local *gendarmes* and artisan members of the local *comité*—a Passion Play in Food egalitarianism that was performed over and over again in the areas subjected to ultra-revolutionism."[84] As if to generalize such new rituals, a revolutionary print showed a peasant riding a nobleman and carried the inscription, "I knew our turn was coming."[85]

All this evidence suggests such traditions as world-upside-down prints represent the public portion of the reply, the counterculture in a quite literal sense, to a dominant transcript of hierarchy and deference. If it is muted or ambiguous, this is because it must be evasive if it is to be public at all. The vision it propagates is reinforced by a utopian reading of religious texts, folktales and songs and, of course, by the large and uncensored realm of the hidden transcript. When the conditions that constrain this evasive popular culture are, as occasionally happens, relaxed, we may expect to see the disguises become less opaque as more of the hidden transcript shoulders its way onto the stage and into action.

Rituals of Reversal, Carnival and Fêtes

I never heard the proclamations of generals before battle, the speeches of führers and prime-ministers . . . national anthems, temperance tracts, papal encyclicals and sermons against gambling and contraception without seeming to hear in the background a chorus of raspberries from all the millions of common men to whom these high sentiments make no appeal.

—GEORGE ORWELL

Laughter contains something revolutionary. In the church, in the palace, on parade, facing the department head, the police officer, the German administration, nobody laughs. The serfs are deprived of the right to smile in the presence of the landowners. Only equals may laugh. If inferiors are permitted to laugh in front of their superiors, and if they cannot suppress their hilarity, this would mean farewell to respect.

—ALEXANDER HERZEN

If the raspberries to which Orwell refers have a privileged social and temporal location, it is surely in the pre-Lenten tradition of carnival. As the

83. The best description of this movement is still Christopher Hill's remarkable *The World Turned Upside Down*, passim.
84. Cobb, *The Police and the People*, 174–75.
85. Burke, *Popular Culture in Early Modern Europe*, 189 and pl. 20.

occasion for rituals of reversal, satire, parody, and a general suspension of social constraints, carnival offers a unique analytical vantage point from which to dissect social order. Precisely because carnival has generated such a large and often-distinguished literature, we can assess it as an institutionalized form of political disguise. The availability of this literature makes the choice of carnival a matter of analytical convenience only. For there are scores of festivals, fairs, and ritual occasions that share many of the essential features of carnival itself. The Feast of Fools, charivari, coronations, periodic market fairs, harvest celebrations, spring fertility rights, and even traditional elections share something of the carnivalesque. Furthermore, it is difficult to find any culture that does not have something on the order of a carnival event in its ritual calendar. Thus there is the Feast of Krishna (Holi) in Hindu society, the water festival in much of mainland Southeast Asia, the Saturnalia in ancient Roman society, and so on.

What all these occasions seem to share is that they are socially defined in some important ways as being out of the ordinary. Normal rules of social intercourse are not enforced, and either the wearing of actual disguises or the anonymity conferred by being part of a large crowd amplifies a general air of license—licentiousness. Much of the writing on carnival emphasizes the spirit of physical abandon, its celebration of the body through dancing, gluttony, open sexuality, and general immodesty. The classical carnival figure is a fat, lusty eater and drinker; the spirit of Lent, which follows, is a thin, old woman.

For our purposes, what is most interesting about carnival is the way it allows certain things to be said, certain forms of social power to be exercised that are muted or suppressed outside this ritual sphere. The anonymity of the setting, for example, allows the social sanctions of the small community normally exercised through gossip to assume a more full-throated voice. Among other things, carnival is "the people's informal courtroom"[86] in which biting songs and scolding verse can be sung directly to the disrespected and malefactors. The young can scold the old, women can ridicule men, cuckholded or henpecked husbands may be openly mocked, the bad-tempered and stingy can be satirized, muted personal vendettas and factional strife can be expressed. Disapproval that would be dangerous or socially costly to vent at other times is sanctioned during carnival. It is the time and place to settle, verbally at least, personal and social scores.

Carnival, then, is something of a lightning rod for all sorts of social tensions and animosities. In addition to being a festival of the physical senses it

86. Gilmore, *Aggression and Community,* 99.

is a festival of spleen and bile. Much of the social aggression within carnival is directed at dominant power figures, if for no other reason than the fact that such figures are, by virtue of their power, virtually immune from open criticism at other times. Any local notables who had incurred popular wrath—merciless usurers, soldiers who were abusive, corrupt local officials, priests who were avid or lascivious—might find themselves the target of a concerted carnival attack by their erstwhile inferiors. Satirical verses might be chanted in front of their houses, they might be burned in effigy, and they might be extorted by masked and threatening crowds to distribute money or drink and made to publicly repent. Institutions as well as persons came under attack. The church, in particular, was an integral part of the ritual mockery of carnival. In fact, every conceivable sacred rite had its counterpart in a carnival parody: sermons in praise of thieves or of St. Hareng (the fish), travesties of the catechism, the creed, the Psalms, the Ten Commandments, and so forth.[87] Here was something of an open dialogue, suitably elusive, between a heterodox popular religion and an official hierarchy of piety. Hardly any pretension to superior status—legal knowledge, title, classical learning, high tastes, military prowess, or property—went unscathed by the leveling techniques of carnival.

As one might reasonably expect, class and political antagonisms could also be aired through carnival techniques. David Gilmore's account of how the growing animosity in twentieth-century Andalusia between agricultural laborers and landowners affected carnival is instructive.[88] Initially, both classes participated in carnival, the landowners tolerating the ridicule and satirical verses sung to them. As agrarian conditions worsened, the abuse and threats drove the landowners to withdraw and watch carnival from their balconies. For some time now the landowners actually leave town for the duration of carnival, abandoning it to their antagonists. Two aspects of this schematic account bear emphasis. First, it reminds us that such rituals are far from static but are rather likely to reflect the changing structure and antagonisms within a society. Second, carnival is, par excellence, an occasion for recriminations from subordinate groups, presumably because normal power relations operate to silence *them*. As Gilmore notes, "In particular, the poor and the powerless used the occasion to express their accumulated resentments against the rich and powerful, to indict social injustice, as well as to chastise peasant offenders against the moral traditions of the pueblo, its ethics, its norms of

87. Burke, *Popular Culture in Early Modern Europe*, 123.
88. *Aggression and Community*, chap. 6.

honesty."[89] The privileged outspokenness of carnival might even come to constitute a kind of national politics in societies in which direct commentary might be treasonous or lèse-majesté. Thus, the carnival effigy might be made up to look like whoever was the municipal enemy of the day—for example, Mazarin, the pope, Luther, Louis XVI, Marie Antoinette, Napoleon III. But always these forays into the public transcript were politically sheltered by the license and anonymity of carnival and "a way of scoffing at authority by allusions which are simultaneously evident and innocent, by an insolence sufficiently ambiguous to disarm or ridicule the repression."[90]

The great contribution of Bakhtin to the study of the carnivalesque was to treat it, through Rabelais's prose, as *the* ritual location of uninhibited speech. It was the only place where *undominated discourse* prevailed, where there was no servility, false pretenses, obsequiousness, or etiquettes of circumlocution. If, in carnival and the marketplace, profanities and curses prevailed, that was because the euphemisms required by official discourse were unnecessary. If so much of the carnivalesque was focused on the functions we share with lower mammals—eating and drinking, defecation, fornication, flatulence—that is because this is the level at which we are all alike and no one can claim a higher status. Above all, these free zones were places where one could relax and breathe easily, not having to worry about committing a costly faux pas. For the lower classes, who spent much of their lives under the tension created by subordination and surveillance, the carnivalesque was a realm of release:[91] "Officially the palaces, churches, institutions and private homes were dominated by hierarchy and etiquette, but in the marketplace a special kind of speech was heard, almost a language of its own, quite unlike the language of the church, palace, courts, and institutions. It was also unlike the tongue of official literature or of the ruling classes—the aristocracy, the nobles, the high-rank clergy, the top burghers."[92] Bakhtin wants us to take carnival speech as something of a shadow society in which the distortions created by

---

89. Ibid., 98. It is useful in this context to recall that during carnival the use of social sanctions against members of one's own class may have the purpose of disciplining those who are trying to curry favor with elites at the expense of their peers.

90. Yves-Marie Berée, *Fêtes et révolte: Des mentalités populaires du XVIᵉ au XVIIIᵉ siècles*, 83.

91. As with carnival itself, Bakhtin was playing a cat and mouse game with high Stalinism as he was writing his study of Rabelais. It doesn't take much in the way of inference to equate the realm of official mendacity and dominated discourse with the Stalinist state and the carnivalesque of Rabelais as an offstage negation and skepticism that will survive repression. But, again like carnival, because Bakhtin's text also has a perfectly innocent meaning, it has a chance of slipping through. It is at least not obviously treasonous.

92. Mikhail Bakhtin, *Rabelais and His World*, trans. Helene Iswolsky, 154.

domination were absent. Compared to official speech, this realm of free speech was the closest approximation to a Socratic dialogue or, in terms of contemporary social theory, the "ideal speech situation" envisaged by Jürgen Habermas.[93] Among the implicit operating assumptions that, Habermas argues, must lie behind any communicative act are that the speaker means what he says and that he speaks truly. Dominated discourse is, of necessity, distorted communication because power relations encourage "strategic" forms of manipulation that undermine genuine understanding.[94]

From our perspective, treating carnival speech as true speech or as approaching the ideal speech situation is too idealist a reading of social reality. So long as speech occurs in any social situation it is saturated with power relations; there is no single privileged vantage point from which the distance of a speech act from "true" speech can be measured. In brief, we all measure our words. What one can do, however, is to compare different speech situations for the relative light they shed on one another. Bakhtin is, in this sense, comparing the speech found where anonymity and a festive atmosphere evade certain everyday relationships of power and replace them with a different relationship of power. Social power in carnival may be less asymmetrical; but reciprocal power is still power.

The other difficulty of a view derived from Bakhtin or Habermas is that it misses the extent to which the speech characteristic of one realm of power is, in part, a product of the speech that is blocked or suppressed in another realm of power. Thus, the grotesquerie, profanity, ridicule, aggression, and character assassination of carnival make sense only in the context of the effect of power relations the rest of the year. The profoundness of the silences generated in one sphere of power may be proportional to the explosive speech in another sphere. Who can fail to recognize this linkage in the following statement about carnival by an Andalusian peasant? "We come alive. We cover our faces and no one recognizes us, and then, watch out! The sky's the limit."[95] The anticipation of carnival and the pleasure derived from it are due largely to the fact that, in anonymity, one can say to one's antagonists precisely what one has had to choke back all year. Great inequalities in status and power generate a rich hidden transcript. In a society of equals there would still be room for carnival for there would still be power relations, but one imagines that it would

93. *The Theory of Communicative Action.* See also Thomas McCarthy's helpful exegesis, *The Critical Theory of Jürgen Habermas,* 273–352.

94. Habermas argues that strategic lying and deception are parasitic on "genuine" speech acts since the deception and lying work only if they're mistakenly accepted as the truth by one's interlocutor.

95. Gilmore, *Aggression and Community,* 16.

be less ferocious, and certainly the pleasures of carnival would not be so heavily concentrated in one segment of the society.

Accepting, for the moment, the place of suppressed speech and acting in carnival, we must still consider whether it ritually serves to displace and relieve social tensions and hence restore social harmony. This is a familiar variant of the safety-valve theory—the idea that once the people get the hidden transcript off their chest, they'll find the routines of domination easier to return to. We must take this argument more seriously perhaps for the case of carnival than for the world-upside-down prints because of the symbolic subordination and institutionalization of carnival. By symbolic subordination, I mean that carnival is ritually timed to fall just before and to be replaced by Lent; Mardi Gras gives way to Ash Wednesday. Gluttony, carousing, and drinking are superseded by fasting, prayer, and abstinence. In most carnival rituals, as if to emphasize the ritual hierarchy, a figure representing the spirit of carnival is ritually killed by a figure representing Lent, almost as if to say, "Now that you've had your fun we shall return to the sober, pious life." The institutionalization of carnival might also be taken to support the safety-valve theory. If carnival is disorder, it is a disorder within the rules, perhaps even a ritual lesson in the consequences and folly of violating the rules. The rules or conventions of carnival—including the rule that no one may remove another's mask—are, rather like the Geneva Convention for armed conflict, what allow carnival to proceed. As Terry Eagleton, quoting Shakespeare's Olivia, notes, "There is no slander in an allowed fool."[96]

If issues of interpretation like this were resolved on the basis of a majority vote of scholars who had looked at the matter, the safety-valve theory would almost surely prevail.[97] Most of them would agree with Roger Sales that the authorities "removed the stopper to stop the bottle being smashed altogether."[98] The partisans of carnival historically were not above making precisely this kind of appeal to their superiors. Witness this letter that circulated in 1444 in the Paris School of Theology arguing that the Feast of Fools be celebrated:

> So that foolishness, which is our second nature and seems to be inherent in man might freely spend itself at least once a year. *Wine barrels burst if from time to time we do not open them and let in some air.* All of us men are

96. *Walter Benjamin, Towards a Revolutionary Criticism,* 148, quoted in Stallybrass and White, *Politics and Poetics of Transgression,* 13.

97. See, for example, Max Gluckman, *Order and Rebellion in Tribal Africa;* Victor Turner, *The Ritual Process: Structure and Anti-Structure;* and Roger Sales, *English Literature in History, 1780–1830: Pastoral and Politics.*

98. *English Literature in History,* 169.

barrels poorly put together, which would burst from the wine of wisdom, if this wine remains in a state of constant fermentation of piousness and fear of God. We must give it air in order not to let it spoil. *This is why we permit folly on certain days so that we may later return with greater zeal to the service of God.*[99]

Using Mrs. Poyser's hydraulic figure of speech to make their case, the authors manage nicely to combine both an appeal to the hegemonic value of carnival and an implicit threat about what might happen if their request is not granted.

The view that carnival is a mechanism of social control authorized by elites is not entirely wrong, but it is, I believe, seriously misleading. It risks confusing the intentions of elites with the results they are able to achieve. Here, as we shall see, the view ignores the actual social history of carnival, which bears directly on this issue. Setting aside social history for the moment, however, we may discern also an untenable essentialism embedded in this functionalist perspective. A complex social event such as carnival cannot be said to be simply this or that as if it had a given, genetically programed, function. It makes far greater sense to see carnival as the ritual site of various forms of social conflict and symbolic manipulation, none of which can be said, prima facie, to prevail. Carnival, then, may be expected to vary with culture and historic circumstances and is likely to be serving many functions for its participants. This brings us to a further difficulty with the functionalist view: namely, that it ascribes a unique agency to elites. It is surely not accurate to proceed as if carnival were set up exclusively by dominant groups to allow subordinate groups to play at rebellion lest they resort to the real thing. The existence and the evolving form of carnival have been the outcome of social conflict, not the unilateral creation of elites. It would be just as plausible to view carnival as an ambiguous political victory wrested from elites by subordinate groups. Finally, one wonders what sort of psychological law lies behind the safety-valve theory. Why is it that a ritual modeling of revolt should necessarily diminish the likelihood of actual revolt? Why couldn't it just as easily serve as a dress rehearsal or a provocation for actual defiance? A ritual feint at revolt is surely less dangerous than actual revolt, but what warrant have we for assuming it is a substitute, let alone a satisfactory one?

At this point it is instructive to turn to the actual struggles over carnival. If, in fact, the safety-valve theory guided elite conduct, one would expect elites to encourage carnival, especially when social tensions were running high. The opposite is more nearly the case. In any event, even if elites did believe in the safety-valve theory, they were never so confident as to assume that its opera-

99. Bakhtin, *Rabelais and His World,* 75, emphasis added.

tion was automatically assured. For much of its history the church and secular elites have seen carnival as a potential if not actual site of disorder and sedition that required constant surveillance. Rudwin has written at some length about the persistent efforts of church authorities in German-speaking Europe to prohibit or replace the carnival comedies (*ludi*) that mercilessly satirized them.[100] In place of the burlesques of the mass and the pranks of Till Eulenspiegel, the church attempted to promote passion and mystery plays in direct competition. Carnivals in France that were originally permitted or even sanctioned by church officials and municipalities were later proscribed after they had been appropriated and turned to suspect purposes by the populace. Bakhtin, for example, notes that the popular societies formed to create farces, *soties*, and satires for carnival (for example, the *Basochiens* and the *Enfants sans souci*) were often "the object of prohibitions and repressions, the Basochiens being eventually suspended."[101]

Where it has survived, the twentieth-century carnival retains its social bite. One of the first pieces of legislation passed during the Spanish Civil War by General Francisco Franco's government was an act outlawing carnival. For the remainder of the war, anyone caught in non-Republican-held areas wearing a mask was liable to harsh penalties, and carnival was much abated, but not eliminated. Once martial law was lifted, however, "people in Fuenmajor would not give it up, and so they sang their insults from jail." "'No one could take away carnival from us, not the Pope, not Franco, not Jesus himself,' they say in Fuenmajor."[102] As Franco understood, carnival and masks are always a potential threat. Rabelais, himself a Jesuit, after all, had to flee France for a time for writing in a carnivalesque vein, and his friend Etienne Dolet, who said much the same thing but disguised it less, was burned at the stake.

The possible conjunction between carnival and revolt is nowhere better illustrated than in Emmanuel Le Roy Ladurie's account of the bloody carnival of 1580 in the town of Romans, to the southeast of Lyons.[103] A recent history of class and religious strife fed into the carnival spirit; Romans had had its own St. Bartholemew's Day massacre in 1572. A newly wealthy urban patriciate

---

100. *The Origin of the German Carnival Comedy.* Pre-Reformation authorities also objected to the pagan fertility rites embedded in carnival, while post-Reformation authorities in Protestant areas associated carnival with Roman paganism. Both thought it potentially subversive of public order. In municipalities where the burghers took over carnival it might contain satires of the peasantry.

101. *Rabelais and His World,* 97. For a much later attempt in England to prohibit fairs, which were sites for the carnivalesque and disorder, see R. W. Malcolmson, *Popular Recreations in English Society, 1700–1850.*

102. Gilmore, *Aggression and Community,* 100, 99.

103. *Carnival in Romans.*

was buying land from ruined peasants and acquiring titles that exempted them from taxes, with the result that the tax burden on the remaining smallholders and artisans was greatly increased. In this context, Ladurie explains, carnival became, in Romans, a site of conflict between an upper crust of merchants, landowners, and bourgeois patricians against a "small property-owning sector in the middle ranges of common craftsmen."[104] In the countryside, it became a struggle between peasants and nobles.

The first sign of trouble was the failure of carnival to flow in the ritual channel designated for it by the town's elite. Since various elements of the carnival festivities were organized by neighborhood and by craft, fiscal and class tensions coincided to some extent with carnival societies. The craftsmen and tradesmen, for example, refused to participate in the initial parade, in which the order of march represented a precise marking of relative status. Instead they held their own parades in their quarters. As Jean Bodin had warned, "[A] procession of all the ranks and all the professions carries the risk . . . of conflicts of priority and the possibility of popular revolts. Let us not overdo, . . . except in case of dire need ceremonies of this kind."[105] Each of three so-called Animal Kingdoms, those of the hare (Huguenots), the Capon (Leaguers or rebels), and the Partridge (Catholics and patriciate), was entitled to a day when their ritual kingdoms were enacted.[106] In this case, however, the Capon procession was particularly threatening. The dancers proclaimed that the rich had grown wealthy at the expense of the poor and demanded restitution via door-to-door collections of food and cash, which were traditional but in this case openly menacing. When time came, ritually speaking, for the Capon kingdom to give way to the Partridge kingdom, it defiantly continued, thereby making something of a symbolic declaration of war. In this ritual defiance the authorities read an apocalyptic omen: "The poor want to take all our earthly goods and our women, too; they want to kill us, perhaps even eat our flesh."[107] Fearing not just a figurative but a literal world upside down, the elite moved first, assassinating league leader Paumier and touching off a small civil war that took thirty lives in Romans and more than one thousand in the surrounding countryside.

However much the aristocrats and property owners of Romans may have wished to orchestrate carnival into a ritual reaffirmation of existing hier-

104. Ibid., 19.
105. Quoted in *ibid.*, 201.
106. The equations with strata and religious confession are crude but will suffice for our purposes here.
107. Ibid., 163.

archies, they failed. Like any ritual site, it could be infused with the signs, symbols, and meanings brought to it by its least advantaged participants as well. It might symbolize the folly of disorder or it might, if appropriated from below, break out of its ritual straightjacket to symbolize oppression and defiance. What is striking historically about carnival is not how it contributed to the maintenance of existing hierarchies, but how frequently it was the scene of open social conflict. As Burke summarizes his own survey, "At all events, between 1500 and 1800 rituals of revolt did coexist with serious questioning of the social, political, and religious order, and the one sometimes turned into the other. Protest was expressed in ritual forms, but the ritual was not always sufficient to contain the protest. The wine barrel sometimes blew its top."[108]

In 1861, when the czar decided on the abolition of serfdom, the ukase was signed in the midst of carnival week. Fearing "the orgies of villagers so frequent during that week would degenerate into an insurrection," officials delayed the actual proclamation for another two weeks so that the news might have a less incendiary impact.

I do not mean to imply that carnival or rituals of reversal cause revolt; they most certainly do not. The point is rather about the relation between symbolism and disguise. Carnival, in its ritual structure and anonymity, gives a privileged place to normally suppressed speech and aggression. It was, in many societies, virtually the only time during the year when the lower classes were permitted to assemble in unprecedented numbers behind masks and make threatening gestures toward those who ruled in daily life. Given this unique opportunity and the world-upside-down symbolism associated with carnival, it is hardly surprising that it would frequently spill over its ritual banks into violent conflict. And if one were, in fact, planning a rebellion or protest, the legitimate cover of anonymous assembly provided by carnival might suggest itself as a likely venue. The authorized element of carnival, rather like the relatively innocent world-upside-down prints of flying fish, furnished a setting in which it was relatively safe to insert less-than-innocuous messages. This is why, I think, that it is virtually impossible to dissociate the carnivalesque from politics until quite recently.[109] It is why actual rebels mimic carnival—they dress as women or mask themselves when breaking machinery or making political demands; their threats use the figures and symbolism of carnival; they extort cash and employment concessions in the manner of crowds expecting gifts during carnival; they use the ritual planning

108. *Popular Culture in Early Modern Europe,* 203.
109. Ibid., chap. 8.

and assembly of the carnival or fair to conceal their intentions. Are they playing or are they in earnest? It is in their interest to exploit this opportune ambiguity to the fullest.

And, of course, if the immediate aftermath of a successful revolt looks very much like carnival, that too is understandable because both are times of license and liberty when the hidden transcript may be disclosed, the latter with masks, the former in full view. Short of these "moments of madness" nearly all public action by subordinate groups is pervaded by disguise.[110]

110. Zolberg, "Moments of Madness."

CHAPTER SEVEN

The Infrapolitics of
Subordinate Groups

The cultural forms may not say what they know, nor know what they say, but they mean what they do—at least in the logic of their praxis.

—PAUL WILLIS, *Learning to Labour*

[The supervision of gleaning] exasperated morale to the limit; but there is such a void between the class which was angered and the class that was threatened, that words never made it across; one only knew what happened from the results; [the peasants] worked underground the way moles do.

—BALZAC, *Les Paysans*

IN A SOCIAL SCIENCE already rife—some might say crawling—with neologisms, one hesitates to contribute another. The term *infrapolitics*, however, seems an appropriate shorthand to convey the idea that we are dealing with an unobtrusive realm of political struggle. For a social science attuned to the relatively open politics of liberal democracies and to loud, headline-grabbing protests, demonstrations, and rebellions, the circumspect struggle waged daily by subordinate groups is, like infrared rays, beyond the visible end of the spectrum. That it should be invisible, as we have seen, is in large part by design—a tactical choice born of a prudent awareness of the balance of power. The claim made here is similar to the claim made by Leo Strauss about how the reality of persecution must affect our reading of classical political philosophy: "Persecution cannot prevent even public expression of the heterodox truth, for a man of independent thought can utter his views in public and remain unharmed, provided he moves with circumspection. He can even utter them in print without incurring any danger, provided he is capable of *writing between the lines*."[1] The text we are interpreting in this case is not Plato's

---

1. *Persecution and the Art of Writing*, 24. It should be abundantly clear that my analysis is fundamentally at cross purposes with much else of what passes as "Straussianism" in contemporary philosophy and political analysis (e.g., its unwarranted claim of privileged access to the true interpretation of the classics, its disdain for the 'vulgar multitude' as well as for dim-witted tyrants). The attitude of Straussians toward nonphilosophers strikes me as comparable to Lenin's attitude toward the working class in *What is to Be Done*. What I do find instructive, however, is the premise that the political environment in which Western political philosophy was written seldom permits a transparency in meaning.

Symposium but rather the veiled cultural struggle and political expression of subordinate groups who have ample reason to fear venturing their unguarded opinion. The meaning of the text, in either case, is rarely straightforward; it is often meant to communicate one thing to those in the know and another to outsiders and authorities. If we have access to the hidden transcript (analogous to the secret notes or conversations of the philosopher) or to a more reckless expression of opinion (analogous to subsequent texts produced under freer conditions) the task of interpretation is somewhat easier. Without these comparative texts, we are obliged to search for noninnocent meanings using our cultural knowledge—much in the way an experienced censor might!

The term *infrapolitics* is, I think, appropriate in still another way. When we speak of the infrastructure for commerce we have in mind the facilities that make such commerce possible: for example, transport, banking, currency, property and contract law. In the same fashion, I mean to suggest that the infrapolitics we have examined provides much of the cultural and structural underpinning of the more visible political action on which our attention has generally been focused. The bulk of this chapter is devoted to sustaining this claim.

First, I return briefly to the widely held position that the offstage discourse of the powerless is either empty posturing or, worse, a substitute for real resistance. After noting some of the logical difficulties with this line of reasoning, I try to show how material and symbolic resistance are part of the same set of mutually sustaining practices. This requires reemphasizing that the relationship between dominant elites and subordinates is, whatever else it might be, very much of a material struggle in which both sides are continually probing for weaknesses and exploiting small advantages. By way of recapitulating some of the argument, I finally try to show how each realm of open resistance to domination is shadowed by an infrapolitical twin sister who aims at the same strategic goals but whose low profile is better adapted to resisting an opponent who could probably win any open confrontation.

The Hidden Transcript as Posing?

A skeptic might very well accept much of the argument thus far and yet minimize its significance for political life. Isn't much of what is called the hidden transcript, even when it is insinuated into the public transcript, a matter of hollow posing that is rarely acted out in earnest? This view of the safe expression of aggression against a dominant figure is that it serves as a substitute—albeit a second-best substitute—for the real thing: direct aggression. At best, it is of little or no consequence; at worst it is an evasion. The prisoners who spend their time dreaming about life on the outside might instead be digging a tunnel; the slaves who sing of liberation and freedom might instead take to their heels. As Barrington Moore writes, "Even fantasies of liberation and revenge can help to preserve domination through dissipating collective energies in relatively harmless rhetoric and ritual."[2]

The case for the hydraulic interpretation of fighting words in a safe place is, as we have noted, perhaps strongest when those fighting words seem largely orchestrated or stage-managed by dominant groups. Carnival and other ritualized and, hence, ordinarily contained rites of reversal are the most obvious examples. Until recently, the dominant interpretation of ritualized aggression or reversal was that, by acting to relieve the tensions engendered by hierarchical social relations, it served to reinforce the status quo. Figures as diverse as Hegel and Trotsky saw such ceremonies as conservative forces. The influential analyses of Max Gluckman and Victor Turner argue that because they underline an essential, if brief, equality among all members of a society and because they illustrate, if only ritually, the dangers of disorder and anarchy, their function is to emphasize the necessity of institutionalized order.[3] For Ranajit Guha the order-serving effects of rituals of reversal lie precisely in the fact that they are authorized and prescribed from above.[4] Allowing subordinate groups to play at rebellion within specified rules and times helps prevent more dangerous forms of aggression.

In his description of holiday festivities among slaves in the antebellum U.S. South, Frederick Douglass, himself a slave, resorts to the same metaphor. His reasoning, however, is slightly different:

> Before the holidays, there are pleasures in prospect; after the holidays, they become pleasures of memory, and they serve to keep out thoughts and wishes of a more dangerous character . . . these holidays are conductors or safety-valves to carry off the explosive elements inseparable from the human mind, when reduced to the condition of slavery. But for those, the rigors and bondage would become too severe for endurance, and the slave would be forced to dangerous desperation.[5]

Douglass's claim here is not that some ersatz rebellion takes the place of the real thing but simply that the respite and indulgence of a holiday provide just

2. *Injustice,* 459n.

3. Max Gluckman, *Rituals of Rebellion in South-East Africa,* and Turner, *The Ritual Process,* esp. chap. 2.

4. *Aspects of Peasant Insurgency,* 18–76. "It is precisely in order to prevent such inversions from occurring in real life that the dominant culture in all traditional societies *allows* these to be simulated at regular calendric intervals," 30, emphasis added.

5. *My Bondage and My Freedom,* edited and with an introduction by William L. Andrews, 156.

enough pleasure to blunt the edge of incipient rebellion. It is as if the masters have calculated the degree of pressure that will engender desperate acts and have carefully adjusted their repression to stop just short of the flashpoint.

Perhaps the most interesting thing about the safety-valve theories in their many guises is the most easily overlooked. They all begin with the common assumption that systematic subordination generates pressure of some kind from below. They assume further that, if nothing is done to relieve this pressure, it builds up and eventually produces an explosion of some kind. Precisely how this pressure is generated and what it consists of is rarely specified. For those who live such subordination, whether Frederick Douglass or the fictional Mrs. Poyser, the pressure is a taken-for-granted consequence of the frustration and anger of being unable to strike back (physically or verbally) against a powerful oppressor. That pressure generated by a perceived but unrequited injustice finds expression, we have argued, in the hidden transcript—its size, its virulence, its symbolic luxuriance. In other words, the safety-valve view implicitly accepts some key elements of our larger argument about the hidden transcript: that systematic subordination elicits a reaction and that this reaction involves a desire to strike or speak back to the dominant. Where they differ is in supposing that this desire can be substantially satisfied, whether in backstage talk, in supervised rituals of reversal, or in festivities that occasionally cool the fires of resentment.

The logic of the safety-valve perspective depends on the social psychological proposition that the safe expression of aggression in joint fantasy, rituals, or folktales yields as much, or nearly as much, satisfaction (hence, a reduction in pressure) as direct aggression against the object of frustration. Evidence on this point from social psychology is not altogether conclusive but the preponderance of findings does not support this logic. Instead, such findings suggest that experimental subjects who are thwarted unjustly experience little or no reduction in the level of their frustration and anger unless they are able to directly injure the frustrating agent.[6] Such findings are hardly astonishing. One would expect retaliation that actually affected the agent of injustice to provide far more in the way of catharsis than forms of aggression that left the source of anger untouched. And, of course, there is much experimental evidence that aggressive play and fantasy increase rather than decrease the

6. Berkowitz, *Aggression*, 204–27. In one experiment, for example, two groups of subjects were insulted by a powerful figure in identical ways. Some of the "victims" were then allowed to give an electric shock to their victimizer, while others were not. Those who struck back then felt less hostile toward their victimizer and also experienced a decline in blood pressure. Those who were not permitted to strike back, even though they could fully voice their aggressive fantasies indirectly in interpreting a thematic apperception test, experienced no decline in blood pressure. Indirect aggression, then, seems a poor substitute for direct retaliation.

likelihood of actual aggression. Mrs. Poyser felt greatly relieved when she vented her spleen directly to the squire but presumably was not relieved—or not sufficiently—by her rehearsed speeches and the oaths sworn behind his back. There is, then, as much, if not more, reason to consider Mrs. Poyser's offstage anger as a preparation for her eventual outburst than to see it as a satisfactory alternative.

If the social-psychological evidence provides little or no support for catharsis through displacement, the historical case for such an argument has yet to be made. Would it be possible to show that, other things equal, dominant elites who provided or allowed more outlets for comparatively harmless aggression against themselves were thereby less liable to violence and rebellion from a subordinate group? If such a comparison were undertaken, its first task would be to distinguish between the effect of displaced aggression per se and the rather more material concessions of food, drink, charity, and relief from work and discipline embedded in such festivities. In other words, the "bread and circuses" that, on good evidence, are often political concessions *won* by subordinate classes may have an ameliorating effect on oppression quite apart from ritualized aggression.[7] An argument along these lines would also have to explain an important anomaly. If, in fact, ritualized aggression displaces real aggression from its obvious target, why then have so many revolts by slaves, peasants, and serfs begun precisely during such seasonal rituals (for example, the carnival in Romans described by Le Roy Ladurie) designed to prevent their occurrence?[8]

The Hidden Transcript as Practice

The greatest shortcoming of the safety-valve position is that it embodies a fundamental idealist fallacy. The argument that offstage or veiled forms of aggression offer a harmless catharsis that helps preserve the status quo assumes that we are examining a rather abstract debate in which one side is handicapped rather than a concrete, material struggle. But relations between masters and slaves, between Brahmins and untouchables are not simply a clash of ideas about dignity and the right to rule; they are a process of

7. This perspective is suggested by the monumental work of Paul Veyne, *Le pain et le cirque.* Veyne treats the bread and circuses of classical Rome as something as much *wrung* from elites as conferred by them to neutralize anger. As he claims, "The government does not provide the circus to the people to depoliticize them but, certainly, they would be politicized against the government if it refused them the circus" (94).

8. The coincidence by itself does not, of course, prove that such rituals, as rituals, were a provocation to revolt. Here one would have to distinguish between the effects of ritual symbolism on the one hand, and the mass assembly of subordinates on the other.

subordination firmly anchored in material practices. Virtually every instance of personal domination is intimately connected with a process of appropriation. Dominant elites extract material taxes in the form of labor, grain, cash, and service in addition to extracting symbolic taxes in the form of deference, demeanor, posture, verbal formulas, and acts of humility. In actual practice, of course, the two are joined inasmuch as every public act of appropriation is, figuratively, a ritual of subordination.

The bond between domination and appropriation means that it is impossible to separate the ideas and symbolism of subordination from a process of material exploitation. In exactly the same fashion, it is impossible to separate veiled symbolic resistance to the ideas of domination from the practical struggles to thwart or mitigate exploitation. Resistance, like domination, fights a war on two fronts. The hidden transcript is not just behind-the-scenes griping and grumbling; it is enacted in a host of down-to-earth, low-profile stratagems designed to minimize appropriation. In the case of slaves, for example, these stratagems have typically included theft, pilfering, feigned ignorance, shirking or careless labor, footdragging, secret trade and production for sale, sabotage of crops, livestock, and machinery, arson, flight, and so on. In the case of peasants, poaching, squatting, illegal gleaning, delivery of inferior rents in kind, clearing clandestine fields, and defaults on feudal dues have been common stratagems.

To take the question of slave pilfering as an illustration, how can we tell what meaning this practice had for slaves?[9] Was the taking of grain, chickens, hogs, and so on a mere response to hunger pangs, was it done for the pleasure of adventure,[10] or was it meant to chasten hated masters or overseers? It could be any of these and more. Publicly, of course, the master's definition of *theft* prevailed. We know enough, however, to surmise that, behind the scenes, theft was seen as simply taking back the product of one's labor. We also know that the semiclandestine culture of the slaves encouraged and celebrated theft from the masters and morally reproved any slave who would dare expose such a theft: "[To] steal and not be detected is a merit among [slaves]. . . . And the vice which they hold in the greatest abhorrence is that of telling upon one another."[11] Our point is not the obvious one that behaviors are impenetrable

9. I have benefited greatly here from Alex Lichtenstein, "That Disposition to Theft, with which they have been Branded."

10. As Charles Joyner, *Down by the Riverside*, 177, notes, the trickster in Afro-American folktales took particularly great satisfaction in taking his food from more powerful animals. Cited in ibid., 418.

11. Charles C. Jones, *The Religious Institution of the Negroes in the United States*, 131, 135, cited by Lichtenstein, "That Disposition to Theft," 422.

until given meaning by human actors. Rather, the point is that the discourse of the hidden transcript does not merely shed light on behavior or explain it; it helps constitute that behavior.

The example of forest crimes in eighteenth- and nineteenth-century Europe, since the historical evidence is comparatively rich, provides a way of further demonstrating how practices of resistance and discourses of resistance were mutually sustaining. At a time when property law and state control were being imposed, direct assertion of opposition was ordinarily very dangerous. Since the difficulties of effectively policing the forests were enormous, however, low-grade forms of resistance there promised success at comparatively little risk. Following the French Revolution, Maurice Agulhon notes, the peasants of Var, taking advantage of the political vacuum, stepped up their offenses against the forest laws.[12] With greater impunity they exercised what, to judge from customary claims, they assumed to be their privileges—taking dead wood, making charcoal, pasturing animals, gathering mushrooms, and so on—though the new national laws prohibited it. Agulhon nicely captures the way in which these practices implied and, in fact, sprang from a consciousness of rights to the forest that could not safely take the form of a public claim: "From then on, [there was] an evolution already under way at the level of infra-politics, which led from the consciousness of rights to the woods to rural offenses, and from this to prosecution, which in turn led to hatred against gendarmes, bailiffs, and prefects and finally from this hatred to a desire for a new revolution more or less libertarian."[13]

A penetrating study of forest poaching in early eighteenth-century England and the draconian death penalties enacted to curb it reveals the same link between a sense of popular justice that cannot be openly claimed and a host of practices devised to exercise those rights in clandestine ways.[14] In this period, the titled owners of estates and the Crown began in earnest to restrict local customary rights to forest pasturage, hunting, trapping, fishing, turf and heath cutting, fuel wood gathering, thatch cutting, lime burning, and quarrying on what they now insisted was exclusively their property. That yeomen, cottagers, and laborers considered this breach of customary law to be an injustice is abundantly clear. Thompson can thus write of yeomen with a "tenacious tradition of memories as to rights and customs . . . and a sense that they and not the rich interlopers, owned the forest."[15] The term *outlaws* as applied to those who continued to exercise these now-proscribed rights has a

12. *La république au village*, 81.
13. Ibid., 375.
14. Thompson, *Whigs and Hunters*.
15. Ibid., 108.

strange ring when we recall that they were certainly acting within the norms and hence with the support of most of their community.

And yet, we have no direct access to the hidden transcript of cottagers as they prepared their traps or shared a rabbit stew. And of course there were no public protests and open declarations of ancient forest rights in a political environment in which all the cards were stacked against the villagers in any sustained, open confrontation. At this level we encounter almost total silence—the plebeian voice is mute. Where it does speak, however, is in everyday forms of resistance in the increasingly massive and aggressive assertion of these rights, often at night and in disguise. Since a legal or political confrontation over property rights in the forest would avail them little and risk much, they chose instead to exercise their rights piecemeal and quietly—to take in fact the property rights they were denied in law. The contrast between public quiescence and clandestine defiance was not lost on contemporary authorities, one of whom, Bishop Trelawny, spoke of "a pestilent pernicious people . . . such as take oaths to the government, but underhand labor its subversion."[16]

Popular poaching on such a vast scale could hardly be mounted without a lively backstage transcript of values, understandings, and popular outrage to sustain it. But that hidden transcript must largely be inferred from practice— a quiet practice at that. Once in a while an event indicates something of what might lie beneath the surface of public discourse, for example, a threatening anonymous letter to a gameskeeper when he continued to abridge popular custom or the fact that the prosecution couldn't find anyone with a radius of five miles to testify against a local blacksmith accused of breaking down a dam recently built to create a fish pond. More rarely still, when there was nothing further to lose by a public declaration of rights, the normative content of the hidden transcript might spring to view. Thus two convicted "deer-stealers," shortly to be hanged, ventured to claim that "deer were wild beasts, and that the poor, as well as the rich, might lawfully use them."[17]

The point of this brief discussion of poaching is that any argument which assumes that disguised ideological dissent or aggression operates as a safety-valve to weaken "real" resistance ignores the paramount fact that such ideological dissent is virtually always expressed in practices that aim at an unobtrusive renegotiation of power relations. The yeomen and cottagers in question were not simply making an abstract, emotionally satisfying, backstage case for what they took to be their property rights; they were out in the

16. Ibid., 124.
17. Ibid., 162.

forests day after day exercising those rights as best they could. There is an important dialectic here between the hidden transcript and practical resistance.[18] The hidden transcript of customary rights and outrage *is* a source of popular poaching providing that we realize, at the same time, that the practical struggle in the forests is also the source for a backstage discourse of customs, heroism, revenge, and justice. If the backstage talk is a source of satisfaction, it is so in large part owing to practical gains in the daily conflict over the forests. Any other formulation would entail an inadmissible wall between what people think and say, on the one hand, and what they do, on the other.

Far from being a relief-valve taking the place of actual resistance, the discursive practices offstage sustain resistance in the same way in which the informal peer pressure of factory workers discourages any individual worker from exceeding work norms and becoming a rate-buster. The subordinate moves back and forth, as it were, between two worlds: the world of the master and the offstage world of subordinates. Both of these worlds have sanctioning power. While subordinates normally can monitor the public transcript performance of other subordinates, the dominant can rarely monitor fully the hidden transcript. This means that any subordinate who seeks privilege by ingratiating himself to his superior will have to answer for that conduct once he returns to the world of his peers. In situations of systematic subordination such sanctions may go well beyond scolding and insult to physical coercion, as in the beating of an informer by prisoners. Social pressure among peers, however, is by itself a powerful weapon of subordinates. Industrial sociologists discovered very early that the censure of workmates often prevailed over the desire for greater income or promotion. We can, in this respect, view the social side of the hidden transcript as a political domain striving to enforce, against great odds, certain forms of conduct and resistance in relations with the dominant. *It would be more accurate, in short, to think of the hidden transcript as a condition of practical resistance rather than a substitute for it.*

One might argue perhaps that even such practical resistance, like the discourse it reflects and that sustains it, amounts to nothing more than trivial coping mechanisms that cannot materially affect the overall situation of domination. This is no more real resistance, the argument might go, than veiled symbolic opposition is real ideological dissent. At one level this is perfectly true but irrelevant since our point is that these are the forms that political

18. A comparable dialectic, moreover, joins the practices of domination to the hidden transcript. The predations of game wardens, arrests and prosecutions, new laws and warnings, the losses of subsistence resources would continually find their way into the normative discourse of those whose earlier rights to the forest were being curtailed.

struggle takes when frontal assaults are precluded by the realities of power. At another level it is well to recall that the aggregation of thousands upon thousands of such "petty" acts of resistance have dramatic economic and political effects. In production, whether on the factory floor or on the plantation, it can result in performances that are not bad enough to provoke punishment but not good enough to allow the enterprise to succeed. Repeated on a massive scale, such conduct allowed Djilas to write that "slow, unproductive work of disinterested millions . . . is the calculable, invisible, and gigantic waste which no communist regime has been able to avoid."[19] Poaching and squatting on a large scale can restructure the control of property. Peasant tax evasion on a large scale has brought about crises of appropriation that threaten the state. Massive desertion by serf or peasant conscripts has helped bring down more than one ancien regime. Under the appropriate conditions, the accumulation of petty acts can, rather like snowflakes on a steep mountainside, set off an avalanche.[20]

Testing the Limits

In any stratified society there is a set of limits on what . . . dominant and subordinate groups can do. . . . What takes place, however, is a kind of continual probing to find out what they can get away with and discover the limits of obedience and disobedience.

—BARRINGTON MOORE, *Injustice*

Rarely can we speak of an individual slave, untouchable, serf, peasant, or worker, let alone groups of them, as being either entirely submissive or entirely insubordinate. Under what conditions, however, do veiled ideological opposition and unobtrusive material resistance dare to venture forth and speak their name openly? Conversely, how is open resistance forced into increasingly furtive and clandestine expression?

The metaphor that promises to serve us best in understanding this process is that of guerrilla warfare. Within relations of domination, as in guerrilla warfare, there is an understanding on both sides about the relative strength and capacities of the antagonist and therefore about what the likely response to an aggressive move might be. What is most important for our purposes, though, is that the actual balance of forces is never precisely known, and estimates about what it might be are largely inferred from the outcomes of previous probes and encounters. Assuming, as we must, that both sides hope

19. *The New Class,* 120. One is also reminded of the East European adage, "They pretend to pay us and we pretend to work."
20. This argument is made at much greater length in Scott, *Weapons of the Weak,* chap. 7.

to prevail, there is likely to be a constant testing of the equilibrium. One side advances a salient to see if it survives or is attacked and, if so, in what strength. It is in this no-man's-land of feints, small attacks, probings to find weaknesses, and not in the rare frontal assault, that the ordinary battlefield lies. Advances that succeed—whether against opposition or without challenge—are likely to lead to more numerous and more aggressive advances unless they meet with a decisive riposte. The limits of the possible are encountered only in an empirical process of search and probing.[21]

The dynamic of this process, it should be clear, holds only in those situations in which it is assumed that most subordinates conform and obey *not* because they have internalized the norms of the dominant, but because a structure of surveillance, reward, and punishment makes it prudent for them to comply. It assumes, in other words, a basic antagonism of goals between dominant and subordinates that is held in check by relations of discipline and punishment. We may, I believe, routinely suppose this assumption holds in slavery, serfdom, caste domination, and in those peasant–landlord relations in which appropriation and status degradation are joined. Such assumptions may also hold in certain institutional settings between wardens and prisoners, staff and mental patients, teachers and students, bosses and workers.[22]

The vicissitudes of the relationship between gameskeepers and woodwardens on the one hand and poachers on the other is a useful example of how limits are probed, tested, and occasionally breached. E. P. Thompson's account of early eighteenth-century poaching details the stepwise progression of poaching as plebeian encroachments nibbled steadily at private and Crown land.[23] Once a practice was established it could be considered a custom, and a

21. The initiation of some forms of rebellion can be understood along these lines. Imagine, for example, that a subordinate peasantry appears to have been effectively intimidated by their overlords, to judge from their deferential manner. On closer inspection one may find occasional, if rare, acts of aggression from below (e.g., a tenant who loses his temper and strikes back when the work is too onerous, the rents too high, or his pride too insulted). These acts will typically have been met quickly with severe sanctions (e.g., beatings, jailings, hut burnings) thus establishing a frontier of intimidation. Imagine now that after some years a distant political event (e.g., a government with reformist sympathizers) neutralized the rural police authorities who had applied these sanctions. In this case, the occasional acts of aggression from below might, for the first time in living memory, go unpunished. As the realization spread that, say, a tenant who slapped a landlord actually went unpunished, I suspect that other tenants would be tempted to risk acting on their own anger. Assuming these new expectations about the balance of power were confirmed, it is not hard to see how, like the process by which rumor is propagated, open acts of aggression could quickly become generalized. As the aggression from below becomes generalized it also fundamentally changes the balance of power that prevailed earlier.

22. The most obvious empirical test of this assumption is to observe what happens when surveillance or punishment is relaxed.

23. *Whigs and Hunters*, chaps. 1, 2.

custom, steadily exercised, was nearly as good as a right in law. The process was, however, nearly imperceptible under ordinary circumstances so as not to provoke an open confrontation. For example, villagers might secretly girdle the bark of trees just below ground level and then, when the tree inevitably died, openly take the dead tree, to which they were entitled. Alternatively, they might conceal green boughs in the center of a bundle of dead wood. Gradually, they might, if not checked, increase the proportion of green wood till it made up most of the load. This incremental process might accelerate precipitously whenever forest enforcement was lax, as those who had held back now rushed in to take the wood, game, pasturage, and peat to which they all along thought they had a right. Thus, when a bishopric with substantial woodland "fell vacant . . . for six months the tenants . . . appear to have made a vigorous assault on the timber and deer."[24] The preponderance of force was, in overall terms, obviously in the hands of the Crown and large property holders, but the poachers were not entirely without resources. The terrain favored their kind of infrapolitics, and they were frequently able to intimidate justices of the peace and gameskeepers with anonymous threats, beatings, arson, and so on. As poaching became more generalized, aggressive, and open, the issue was no longer simply the de facto control of property in game and wood but the implicit provocation represented by open insubordination from below. As Thompson explained,

> What made the "emergency" was the repeated public humiliation of the authorities, the simultaneous attacks upon royal and private property, the sense of a confederated movement which was enlarging its special demands . . . the symptoms of something close to class warfare with the royalist gentry in the disturbed areas objects of attack and pitifully isolated in their attempts to enforce order. . . . It was this displacement of authority and not the ancient abuse of deer-stealing, which constituted, in the eyes of the Government, an emergency.[25]

The Black Acts, providing capital punishment for those found abroad at night with blackened faces, were one of the decisive ripostes by the state.

The impetus behind forms of infrapolitical resistance like poaching is not only influenced by the counterforce of surveillance and punishment brought to bear by the authorities. It is greatly affected as well by the level of need and indignation among the subordinate population. The theft of wood in mid

24. Ibid., 123.
25. Ibid., 190.

nineteenth-century Germany was, as Marx noted in some early articles in the *Rheinische Zeitung,* a form of class struggle.[26] The overall volume of offenses varied as much with the subsistence needs of the population as with the vigor of enforcement. Forest encroachments ballooned when provisions were expensive, when wages were low, when unemployment grew, when the winter was severe, where emigration was difficult, and where dwarf-holdings prevailed. In the bad year of 1836, 150,000 out of a total of 207,000 prosecutions in Prussia were for forest crimes. In 1842 alone in the state of Baden there was one conviction for every four inhabitants.[27] The virtual invasion of the forest for a time overwhelmed the enforcement apparatus of the state.

While the pressure driving everyday resistance varies with the needs of subordinate groups it is rarely likely to disappear altogether. The point is that any weakness in surveillance and enforcement is likely to be quickly exploited; any ground left undefended is likely to be ground lost. Nowhere is this pattern more evident than in the case of repetitive appropriations such as rents or taxes. Le Roy Ladurie and others, for example, have charted the fortunes of tithe collections (in principle, one-tenth of the grain harvest of cultivators) over nearly four centuries.[28] Because it was so rarely devoted to the local religious and charitable purposes for which it was originally intended, the tithe was bitterly resented. Resistance, however, was less to be found in the open protests, petitions, riots, and revolts that did occasionally erupt but rather in a quiet but massive pattern of evasion. Peasants secretly harvested grain before the tithe collector arrived, opened unregistered fields, interplanted titheable and nontitheable crops, and took a variety of measures to ensure that the grain taken by the titheman was inferior and less than one-tenth of the crop. The pressure was constant, but at those rare moments when enforcement was lax, the peasantry would take quick advantage of the opportunity. When a war stripped a province of its local garrison, tithe collections would plummet; full advantage would be taken of a new tithe collector, unfamiliar with all the techniques of evasion. The most dramatic example of exploiting the openings available came with the redemption payments accorded the clergy just after the French Revolution in order to phase out the tithe gradually. Sensing the political opening and the inability of the revolutionary government to enforce

26. Peter Linebaugh, "Karl Marx, the Theft of Wood, and Working-class Composition: A Contribution to the Current Debate."

27. Ibid., 13.

28. For a review of this literature and an argument about the importance of this form of resistance, see my "Resistance without Protest and without Organization," 417–52.

the payments, the peasantry so effectively evaded payment as to abolish the tithe forthwith.[29]

Ideological and symbolic dissent follows much the same pattern. Metaphorically we can say, I believe, that the hidden transcript is continually pressing against the limit of what is permitted on stage, much as a body of water might press against a dam. The amount of pressure naturally varies with the degree of shared anger and indignation experienced by subordinates. Behind the pressure is the desire to give unbridled expression to the sentiments voiced in the hidden transcript directly to the dominant. Short of an outright rupture, the process by which the limit is tested involves, say, a particularly intrepid, angry, risk-taking, unguarded subordinate gesturing or saying something that slightly breaches that limit. If this act of insubordination (disrespect, cheek) is not rebuked or punished, others will exploit that breach and a new, de facto limit governing what may be said will have been established incorporating the new territory. A small success is likely to encourage others to venture further, and the process can escalate rapidly. Conversely, the dominant may also breach the limit and move it in the opposite direction, suppressing previously tolerated public gestures.[30]

Ranajit Guha has argued convincingly that open acts of desacralization and disrespect are often the first sign of actual rebellion.[31] Even seemingly small acts—for example, lower castes wearing turbans and shoes, a refusal to bow or give the appropriate salutation, a truculent look, a defiant posture—signal a public breaking of the ritual of subordination. So long as the elite treat such assaults on their dignity as tantamount to open rebellion, symbolic defiance and rebellion do amount to the same thing.

The logic of symbolic defiance is thus strikingly similar to the logic of everyday forms of resistance. Ordinarily they are, by prudent design, unob-

29. Revolutionary vacuums have aided more than one peasantry in this fashion. In the months after the Bolshevik seizure of power but before the new state made its presence felt in the countryside, the Russian peasantry did on a larger scale what they had always attempted on a smaller scale. They opened up new fields in what had earlier been woodland, gentry pastures, and state land and didn't report it; they inflated local population figures and *de*flated arable acreage in order to make the village seem as poor and untaxable as possible. A remarkable study of this period by Orlando Figes suggests that as a result of these self-help measures the 1917 census underestimated the arable land in Russia by 15 percent. *Peasant Revolution, Civil War: The Volga Countryside in Revolution*, chap. 3.

30. Primary and secondary school teachers share a lore about how important it is to establish a firm line and enforce it lest a pattern of verbal disrespect become established, leading, presumably, to more daring acts of lèse-majesté. Similarly, referees of basketball games may punish even trivial fouls at the outset of a game simply to establish a line that they may later relax slightly.

31. *Elementary Forms of Peasant Insurgency*, chap. 2.

trusive and veiled, disowning, as it were, any public defiance of the material or symbolic order. When, however, the pressure rises or when there are weaknesses in the "retaining wall" holding it back, poaching is likely to escalate into land invasions, tithe evasions into open refusals to pay, and rumors and jokes into public insult. Thus, the offstage contempt for the Spanish church hierarchy that was, before the Civil War, confined to veiled gossip and humor, took, at the outset of the war, the more dramatic form of the public exhumation of the remains of archbishops and prioresses from the crypts of cathedrals, which were then dumped unceremoniously on the front steps.[32] *The process by which Aesopian language may give way to direct vituperation is very much like the process by which everyday forms of resistance give way to overt, collective defiance.*

The logic of the constant testing of the limits alerts us to the importance, from the dominant point of view, of making an example of someone. Just as a public breach in the limits is a provocation to others to trespass in the same fashion, so the decisive assertion of symbolic territory by public retribution discourages others from venturing public defiance. One deserter shot, one assertive slave whipped, one unruly student rebuked; these acts are meant as public events for an audience of subordinates. They are intended as a kind of preemptive strike to nip in the bud any further challenges of the existing frontier (as the French say, "pour encourager les autres") or perhaps to take new territory.

Finally, a clear view of the "micro" pushing and shoving involved in power relations, and particularly power relations in which appropriation and permanent subordination are central, makes any static view of naturalization and legitimation untenable. A dominant elite under such conditions is ceaselessly working to maintain and extend its material control and symbolic reach. A subordinate group is correspondingly devising strategies to thwart and reverse that appropriation and to take more symbolic liberties as well. The material pressure against the process of appropriation is, for slaves and serfs, nearly a physical necessity, and the desire to talk back has its own compelling logic. No victory is won for good on this terrain: hardly has the dust cleared before the probing to regain lost territory is likely to begin. The naturalization of domination is always being put to the test in small but significant ways, particularly at the point where power is applied.[33]

---

32. Bruce Lincoln, "Revolutionary Exhumations in Spain, July 1936."

33. This, I believe, is the missing element in the theories of legitimation to be found in John Gaventa's otherwise perceptive book, *Power and Powerlessness,* esp. chap. 1. See also Lukes, *Power: A Radical View.*

Resistance below the Line

We are now in a position to summarize a portion of the argument. Until quite recently, much of the active political life of subordinate groups has been ignored because it takes place at a level we rarely recognize as political. To emphasize the enormity of what has been, by and large, disregarded, I want to distinguish between the open, declared forms of resistance, which attract most attention, and the disguised, low-profile, undeclared resistance that constitutes the domain of infrapolitics (see accompanying table). For contemporary liberal democracies in the West, an exclusive concern for open political

Domination and Resistance

	Material Domination	*Status Domination*	*Ideological Domination*
Practices of Domination	appropriation of grain, taxes, labor, etc.	humiliation, disprivilege, insults, assaults on dignity	justification by ruling groups for slavery, serfdom, caste, privilege
Forms of Public Declared Resistant	petitions, demonstrations, boycotts, strikes, land invasions, and open revolts	public assertion of worth by gesture, dress, speech, and/or open desecration of status symbols of the dominant	public counter-ideologies propagating equality, revolution, or negating the ruling ideology
Forms of Disguised, low profile, Undisclosed resistance, INFRA-POLITICS	everyday forms of resistance, e.g. poaching, squatting, desertion, evasion, foot-dragging Direct Resistance by Disguised Resisters, e.g. masked appropriations, threats, anonymous threats	hidden transcript of anger, aggression, and disguised discourses of dignity e.g., rituals of aggression, tales of revenge, use of carnival symbolism, gossip, rumor, creation of autonomous social space for assertion of dignity	development of dissident subcultures e.g., millennial religions, slave "hush-arbors," folk religion, myths of social banditry and class heroes, world-upside-down imagery, myths of the "good" king or the time before the "Norman Yoke"

action *will* capture much that is significant in political life. The historic achievement of political liberties of speech and association has appreciably lowered the risks and difficulty of open political expression. Not so long ago in the West, however, and, even today, for many of the least privileged minorities and marginalized poor, open political action will hardly capture the bulk of political action. Nor will an exclusive attention to declared resistance help us understand the process by which new political forces and demands germinate before they burst on the scene. How, for example, could we understand the open break represented by the civil rights movement or the black power movement in the 1960s without understanding the offstage discourse among black students, clergymen, and their parishioners?

Taking a long historical view, one sees that the luxury of relatively safe, open political opposition is both rare and recent. The vast majority of people have been and continue to be not citizens, but subjects. So long as we confine our conception of *the political* to activity that is openly declared we are driven to conclude that subordinate groups essentially lack a political life or that what political life they do have is restricted to those exceptional moments of popular explosion. To do so is to miss the immense political terrain that lies between quiescence and revolt and that, for better or worse, is the political environment of subject classes. It is to focus on the visible coastline of politics and miss the continent that lies beyond.

Each of the forms of disguised resistance, of infrapolitics, is the silent partner of a loud form of public resistance. Thus, piecemeal squatting is the infrapolitical equivalent of an open land invasion: both are aimed at resisting the appropriation of land. The former cannot openly avow its goals and is a strategy well suited to subjects who have no political rights. Thus, rumor and folktales of revenge are the infrapolitical equivalent of open gestures of contempt and desecration: both are aimed at resisting the denial of standing or dignity to subordinate groups. The former cannot act directly and affirm its intention and is thus a symbolic strategy also well suited to subjects with no political rights. Finally, millennial imagery and the symbolic reversals of folk religion are the infrapolitical equivalents of public, radical, counterideologies: both are aimed at negating the public symbolism of ideological domination. Infrapolitics, then, is essentially the strategic form that the resistance of subjects must assume under conditions of great peril.

The strategic imperatives of infrapolitics make it not simply different in degree from the open politics of modern democracies; they impose a fundamentally different logic of political action. No public claims are made, no open symbolic lines are drawn. All political action takes forms that are designed to obscure their intentions or to take cover behind an apparent meaning. Virtually no one acts in his own name for avowed purposes, for that would be self-defeating. Precisely because such political action is studiously designed to be anonymous or to disclaim its purpose, infrapolitics requires more than a little interpretation. Things are not exactly as they seem.

The logic of disguise followed by infrapolitics extends to its organization as well as to its substance. Again, the form of organization is as much a product of political necessity as of political choice. Because open political activity is all but precluded, resistance is confined to the informal networks of kin, neighbors, friends, and community rather than formal organization. Just as the symbolic resistance found in forms of folk culture has a possibly innocent meaning, so do the elementary organizational units of infrapolitics have an alternative, innocent existence. The informal assemblages of market, neighbors, family, and community thus provide both a structure and a cover for resistance. Since resistance is conducted in small groups, individually, and, if on a larger scale, makes use of the anonymity of folk culture or actual disguises, it is well adapted to thwart surveillance. There are no leaders to round up, no membership lists to investigate, no manifestos to denounce, no public activities to draw attention. These are, one might say, the elementary forms of political life on which more elaborate, open, institutional forms may be built and on which they are likely to depend for their vitality. Such elementary forms also help explain why infrapolitics so often escapes notice. If formal political organization is the realm of elites (for example, lawyers, politicians, revolutionaries, political bosses), of written records (for example, resolutions, declarations, news stories, petitions, lawsuits), and of public action, infrapolitics is, by contrast, the realm of informal leadership and nonelites, of conversation and oral discourse, and of surreptitious resistance. The logic of infrapolitics is to leave few traces in the wake of its passage. By covering its tracks it not only minimizes the risks its practitioners run but it also eliminates much of the documentary evidence that might convince social scientists and historians that real politics was taking place.

Infrapolitics is, to be sure, real politics. In many respects it is conducted in more earnest, for higher stakes, and against greater odds than political life in liberal democracies. Real ground is lost and gained. Armies are undone and revolutions facilitated by the desertions of infrapolitics. De facto property rights are established and challenged. States confront fiscal crises or crises of appropriation when the cumulative petty stratagems of its subjects deny them labor and taxes. Resistant subcultures of dignity and vengeful dreams are created and nurtured. Counterhegemonic discourse is elaborated. Thus infrapolitics is, as emphasized earlier, always pressing, testing, probing the boundaries of the permissible. Any relaxation in surveillance and punishment and foot-dragging threatens to become a declared strike, folktales of oblique aggression threaten to become face-to-face defiant contempt, millennial dreams threaten to become revolutionary politics. From this vantage point infrapolitics may be thought of as the elementary—in the sense of foundational—form of politics. It is the building block for the more elaborate institutionalized political action that could not exist without it. Under the conditions of tyranny and persecution in which most historical subjects live, it *is* political life. And when the rare civilities of open political life are curtailed or destroyed, as they so often are, the elementary forms of infrapolitics remain as a defense in depth of the powerless.

CHAPTER EIGHT

A Saturnalia of Power: The First Public Declaration of the Hidden Transcript

Altogether, this time of trouble was rather a Saturnalian time to Kazia [a domestic servant of a family recently fallen on hard times]: she could scold her betters with unreproved freedom.

—GEORGE ELIOT, *The Mill on the Floss*

You'll bring me to speak the unspeakable, very soon.

—SOPHOCLES, *Antigone*

The best, most exciting wrestling matches . . . are those which arise out of a history of injustice, betrayal, and injury, and which promise retribution. As wrestlers are fond of saying, and as their fans learn to expect, "what goes around comes around."

—DONALD NONINI and ARLENE AKIKO TERAOKA, "Class Struggle in the Squared Circle"[1]

IN THIS FINAL CHAPTER we take up what happens when the frontier between the hidden and the public transcripts is decisively breached. What concerns us particularly is the charged political impact of the first public declaration of the hidden transcript. It would be unfortunate if the analysis of these exceptional moments were to preempt our earlier discussion. The main thrust of my argument thus far has been to demonstrate how an appreciation of the public and backstage transcripts of the dominant and the weak can illuminate power relations in a novel way. As we now turn to rarer occasions of open confrontation, there is some danger that the hidden transcript of subordinate groups will seem significant only as a prologue—as the groundwork—to public clashes, social movements, and rebellion. If that were the case, my insistence that most of the political struggle of subordinate groups is conducted in much more ambiguous territory would have been in vain.

With this necessary qualification in mind, it is nonetheless evident that an analysis of the hidden transcript can tell us something about moments that

---

1. To appear in *Critical Anthropology: The Ethnology of Stanley Diamond*, ed. Ward Gailey and Viana Muller, forthcoming.

carry the portent of political breakthroughs. The first step in understanding such moments is to place the tone and mood experienced by those who are speaking defiantly for the first time near the center of our analysis. Insofar as their excitement and energy are part of what impels events, they are as much a part of the situation as structural variables. They are, furthermore, an essential force in political breakthroughs—a force that resource-mobilization theories of social movements, let alone public choice theory, cannot remotely hope to capture. After illustrating the initial elation (mixed with fear) that acts of defiance generate, I try to account for the fact that the reversal of a public humiliation, to be fully savored, needs to be public as well. This leads to a consideration of how charismatic acts gain their social force by virtue of their roots in the hidden transcript of a subordinate group. It is this prehistory that makes such charismatic acts possible and helps us understand how a political breakthrough can escalate so rapidly that even revolutionary elites find themselves overtaken and left in its wake.

The Refusal to Reproduce Hegemonic Appearances

Any public refusal, in the teeth of power, to produce the words, gestures, and other signs of normative compliance is typically construed—and typically intended—as an act of defiance. Here the crucial distinction is between a *practical failure* to comply and a *declared refusal* to comply. The former does not necessarily breach the normative order of domination; the latter almost always does.

When a practical failure to comply is joined with a pointed, public refusal it constitutes a throwing down of the gauntlet, a symbolic declaration of war. It is one thing to fail to greet a superior with the appropriate formula. Such a failure might be construed as an inadvertent lapse of attention having no symbolic significance. It is another to refuse boldly to greet a superior. In some respects the behavior may be nearly identical, but the former is either a harmless or ambiguous act while the latter is an implicit threat to the relation of domination itself. Thus there is likely to be all the difference in the world between bumping against someone and openly pushing that person, between pilfering and the open seizure of goods, between failing to sing the national anthem and publicly sitting while others stand during its performance, between gossip and a public insult, between machine breaking that could be the result of carelessness and machine breaking that is the result of evident sabotage. The Catholic hierarchy, for example, understands that if large numbers of their adherents have chosen to live together out of wedlock, such a choice, however regrettable it might be, is of less institutional significance than if these same adherents openly repudiated the sacrament of marriage itself and the Church's authority to bestow it.

The distinction dominant elites are likely to make between the inadequate performance of subordinates and a declared violation of norms is not the result of an overly touchy sense of honor. It originates rather in their understanding of the possible consequences of open defiance. Many forms of authority can tolerate a remarkably high level of practical nonconformity so long as it does not actually tear the public fabric of hegemony. The difference is captured nicely in Witwold Gombrowicz's account of what happens when the general indifference and foot-dragging that have typified students' attitude in a literature class were suddenly transformed when one student publicly declared precisely what all knew to be the case: that he felt none of the authorized feelings when reading the canon of authorized poets. At that moment, "the formidable shadow of general impotence . . . hovered over the class; and the master felt that he would succumb himself unless he took prompt counteraction by injecting a double dose of faith and confidence."[2] Once the lack of faith in the enterprise left the hidden transcript and became a public fact, it posed a threat to its legitimacy that offstage heresy alone could never pose.

On very rare occasions when what has been orchestrated as a mass public demonstration of domination and enthusiastic consent erupts into a public display of repudiation from below, the "formidable shadow of general impotence" becomes what can only be described as a symbolic rout. Millions of Rumanians witnessed just such an epoch-making moment during the televised rally staged by President Nicolae Ceausescu on December 21, 1989, in Bucharest to demonstrate that he was still in command after unprecedented demonstrations in the outlying city of Timisoara:

> The young people started to boo. They jeered as the President, who still appeared unaware that trouble was mounting, rattled along denouncing anti-communist forces. The booing grew louder and was briefly heard by the television audience before technicians took over and voiced-over a sound track of canned applause.
>
> It was a moment that made Rumanians realize that their all-powerful leader was, in fact, vulnerable. It unleashed an afternoon of demonstrations in the capital and a second night of bloodshed.[3]

The reproduction of hegemonic appearances, even under duress, is for

2. *Ferdydurke*, trans. Eric Mosbacher, 61.
3. "Ceausescu's Absolute Power Dies in Rumanian Popular Rage," *New York Times*, January 7, 1990, p. A15.

this reason vital to the exercise of domination. Institutions for which doctrine is central to identity are thus often less concerned with the genuineness of confessions of heresy and recantations than with the public show of unanimity they afford. Personal doubts and inward cynicism are one thing; public doubts and outward repudiations of the institution and what it stands for are something else.

The open refusal to comply with a hegemonic performance is, then, a particularly dangerous form of insubordination. In fact, the term *insubordination* is quite appropriate here because any particular refusal to comply is not merely a tiny breach in a symbolic wall; it necessarily calls into question all the other acts that this form of subordination entails. Why should a serf who refuses to bow before his lord continue to deliver grain and labor services? A single lapse in conformity can be repaired or excused with negligible consequences for the system of domination. A single act of successful public insubordination, however, pierces the smooth surface of apparent consent, which itself is a visible reminder of underlying power relations. Because acts of symbolic defiance have such ominous consequences for power relations, the Romans, as Veyne reminds us, dealt more harshly with *indocilité* than with mere infractions of the law.[4]

The question of whether a clear act of insubordination has occurred is not a simple matter, for the meaning of a given action is not given but is socially constructed. At the extremes, there is less interpretive freedom. When a slave strikes his master in front of other slaves, a reasonably clear public challenge has been made. When the thief or poacher moves surreptitiously at night it is reasonably certain that no public challenge to property relations has been issued. Between these extremes there is a great deal of interpretive freedom. When it suits them, the dominant may elect to ignore a symbolic challenge, pretend that they did not hear it or see it, or perhaps define the challenger as deranged, thus depriving his act of the significance it would otherwise have. Refusing to recognize a challenge may also be a strategy intended to afford the challenger an opportunity to reconsider his action (for example "I'll overlook this infraction providing . . ."). By the same token, the dominant may also choose to construe an ambiguous act as a direct symbolic challenge in order to make a public example of someone. Frederick Douglass noted how a master might, more or less arbitrarily, interpret the tone of an answer, a failure to answer, a facial expression, a nod of the head as an act of impudence and have the slave beaten for it.[5]

4. Veyne, *Le pain et le cirque,* 548.
5. *My Bondage and My Freedom,* 61.

How an act of this kind is construed is not merely a question of the mood, temper, and perceptiveness of the dominant; it is also very much a matter of politics. It is, for example, often in the interest of ruling elites to treat guerrillas or insurgents as bandits. By denying rebels the status in public discourse they seek, the authorities choose to assimilate their acts to a category that minimizes its political challenge to the state. This strategy meets its mirror image from below when peasants transform some bandits into mythical heroes, taking from the rich to give to the poor and dispensing rude justice on the order of Robin Hood. Some labels may be applied largely as a matter of habit or convention, but they are as likely to be part of a rhetorical strategy. Whether the definition propagated by elites prevails among a wider audience is another matter, but there is little doubt that it often serves elites to label revolutionaries as bandits, dissidents as mentally deranged, opponents as traitors, and so on. Thus the refusal to reproduce hegemonic appearances is not entirely straight-forward. The political struggle to impose a definition on an action and to make it stick is frequently at least as important as the action per se.

Breaking the Silence: Political Electricity

This official interpretation consequently merges with reality. A general and all-embracing lie begins to predominate; people begin adapting to it, and everyone in some part of their lives compromises with the lie or coexists with it. Under these conditions, to assert the truth, to behave authentically by breaking through the all-englobing web of lies—in spite of everything, including the risk that one might find oneself up against the whole world—is an act of extraordinary political importance.

—Czech playwright VÁCLAV HAVEL[6]

The reader may recall the electrifying impact of Mrs. Poyser's outburst to the squire. Here I want to concentrate on that particular political moment when the first public declaration of the hidden transcript is made. The most important thing to understand about this moment is the enormous impact it typically has on the person (or persons) who makes the declaration and, often, on the audience witnessing it. Conveying the subjective power of this moment requires listening to a number of firsthand accounts, summoning witnesses to give personal testimony.

Ricardo Lagos was one of dozens of cautious opposition politicians in Chile under General Augusto Pinochet's dictatorship. That all changed in June 1988, when the fifty-year-old economist broke the silence during a live,

6. Quoted in an interview in the *Times Literary Supplement*, January 23, 1987, p. 81. I should note that this epigraph was included in the manuscript nine months before Havel found steady, official, and safer work.

hour-long program on Chilean television. The drama of the moment is nicely captured by the news report:

> In the midst of the live hour-long interview program, he looked into the camera, pointed a finger and, with a strong oratorical voice directed his words to General Pinochet. He reminded him that after the plebiscite eight years ago he had said he did not intend to seek re-election this time. "And now," Mr. Lagos said, still seeming to speak directly to General Pinochet, "you promise the country eight more years with torture, assassination and the violation of human rights. To me, it seems inadmissible that a Chilean is so ambitious for power as to pretend to hold it for twenty-five years." . . . As the three interviewers tried repeatedly to interrupt, he brushed them aside, saying: "You'll have to excuse me. I speak for fifteen years of silence."[7]

The impact had, as the reporter emphasized, "the force of an earthquake." "It shocked some, thrilled some, and infuriated General Augusto Pinochet." "It also created a political star, a man generally viewed as the most capable of reviving socialism."[8] The political shock wave generated by Ricardo Lagos's outburst bears a family resemblance to the effect of Mrs. Poyser's speech. In each case, the political jolt of the speech is definitely not due to its novelty as information or sentiment to its hearers. One must imagine in the case of Chile that what Lagos said was, in fact, a rather restrained expression of views that had for long been shared among friends, workmates, and political intimates— from the Christian Democrats to the far left. Therefore, when Lagos says, "I speak for fifteen years of silence," what he clearly means is that he is now saying directly to Pinochet more or less what thousands of Chilean citizens had been thinking and saying in safer circumstances for fifteen years. The silence he breaks is the silence of defiance in the public transcript. Part of the political electricity, the high drama, of the moment is also the enormous personal danger Lagos courts when he breaks this silence. While Mrs. Poyser risked a tenancy in confronting the squire and speaking for much of the parish, Ricardo Lagos took his life into his hands when he defied the dictator and spoke for much of the Chilean population. The moment when the dissent of the hidden transcript crosses the threshold to open resistance is always a politically charged occasion.

7. Shirley Christian, "With a Thunderclap, Leftist Breaks Chile's Silence," *New York Times*, June 30, 1988, p. A4.
8. Ibid.

The sense of personal release, satisfaction, pride, and elation—despite the actual risks often run—is an unmistakable part of how this first open declaration is experienced. Although we have expressly avoided using the term *truth* to characterize the hidden transcript, it is all too apparent that the open declaration of the hidden transcript in the teeth of power is typically experienced, both by the speaker and by those who share his or her condition, as a moment in which truth is finally spoken in the place of equivocation and lies. If a postmodern sense of the tenuousness of any simple claim to truth keeps us from using the term, it must certainly not prevent us from recognizing, as Václav Havel does, that those who take this bold step experience it as a moment of truth and as a personal authentication.

What evidence we have from the slave narratives is unequivocal in this respect. It was common, for example, for slaves to be expected to wail at the death of their master or overseer and say publicly that he was "going home to heaven." Offstage it was evidently common for slaves to say among themselves that a hated master was going to hell "like a barrel full of nails." In the case of one particularly brutal and hated overseer, however, the joy at his death was so spontaneous and great that it spilled over into the public transcript. The slaves chanted, "Ole John Bell is de'd and gone; I hopes he's gone to hell." Another slave, reporting the scene said, "En dat was the onles' time I's ever seen dem niggers happy on dat plantation 'tel atter s'render."[9] The happiness, the account makes clear, arises not only from the death of an enemy but from the release experienced in the collective public expression of jubilation. Perhaps the best known instance of personal authentication through such defiance is Frederick Douglass's account of his physical fight with his master. Running the risk of death, Douglass not only spoke back to his master but would not allow himself to be beaten. Out of pride and anger, Douglass fought off his master while not going so far as to beat him in turn. The confrontation was a standoff and, miraculously, Douglass escaped punishment. What is crucial for our purposes, however, is the meaning of this experience for him: "I was *nothing* before; *I was a man now*. . . . After resisting him, I felt as I had never felt before. *It was a resurrection*. . . . I had reached the point where I was not afraid to die. This spirit made me a freeman in fact, while I remained a slave in form. When a slave cannot be flogged, he is more than half free."[10] For most

9. Raboteau, *Slave Religion*, 297.

10. *My Bondage and My Freedom*, 151–52. First emphasis in original, second added. Douglass and others write of slaves who have somehow survived physical confrontations and have convinced their masters that they may be shot but cannot be whipped. The master is then confronted with an all-or-nothing choice. The logic of machismo in societies without effective legal institutions is much the same; a credible willingness to risk death in avenging an insult makes one's

slaves, most of the time, the key to survival was to exercise a tight control over the impulse either to verbal or to physical defiance. On those exceptional occasions when the slave did defy the master, the act unleashed an exhilaration at his having finally acted authentically, mixed, one imagines, with a mortal fear of the consequences.

Even when the element of immediate physical danger is removed from the equation, there is a great sense of fulfillment and satisfaction at no longer having to feign deference to an often-despised master. Solomon Northrup, originally a freeman who was kidnapped into slavery for ten years before making good his escape, writes movingly of his demeanor in bondage: "Ten years I was compelled to address him with downcast eyes and uncovered head—in the attitude and language of a slave. . . . [Now that he is free] . . . I can raise my head once more among men. I can speak of the wrongs I suffered, and of those who inflicted them with upraised eyes."[11] We know from the rest of Solomon Northrup's narrative that he did, in fact, speak of the wrongs he suffered to other slaves while he was in bondage. The difference, then, is not that he had no domain in which he could raise his head and say what he felt, but that he can now speak directly, not only to other slaves offstage but directly to the dominant.

The intoxicating feeling that comes from the first public expression of a long-suppressed response to authorities is also typical in other forms of subordination. In her study of the links between the civil rights movement in the United States in the 1960s and the growth of feminist consciousness, Sara Evans recounts the experience of Darlene Stille. An educated woman trapped in a dead-end job and denied supervisory posts because of her sex, she finally mustered the courage to picket her employer together with other women. The process by which she managed to take that step is less important for our immediate purpose than the report of its psychological impact: "It was wonderful feeling that all this anger that had been backing up inside me now had a release, *that I could bark back somehow* . . . that I could find my voice in a larger community of women."[12] It is difficult to read self-descriptions of this kind without being struck by the strong sense of recaptured human dignity. Darlene Stille thus speaks of barking back as if she had been a dog and of finding her "voice" with others. Douglass writes of a "resurrection" and

---

opponents think very carefully before delivering such an insult. Deterrence theorists have examined this situation carefully but perhaps not so well as Joseph Conrad in his depiction of the touchy anarchist who walks around London with explosives strapped to his waist and to whom the police, consequently, give a wide berth. *The Secret Agent: A Simple Tale.*

11. In Osofsky, *Puttin' on Ole Massa*, 324.

12. Evans, *Personal Politics*, 299.

Northrup of looking up and speaking truly. The public declaration of the hidden transcript, because it supplies a part of a person's character that had earlier been kept safely out of sight, seems also to restore a sense of self-respect and personhood.

The courage to venture a part or all of a long-suppressed transcript is, in large part, a quite particular matter of individual temperament, anger, and bravado. There are, however, historical circumstances that suddenly lower the danger of speaking out enough so that the previously timid are encouraged. The *glasnost* campaign of Secretary General Mikhail Gorbachev in 1988 unleashed an unprecedented flurry of public declarations in the USSR. One fairly representative example was reported in which many of the citizens of the town of Yaroslav, incensed that a disrespected party hack had been selected as a local delegate to a party conference in Moscow, mobilized a large public meeting to demand his recall. Their success in the new atmosphere proved heady. Valentin Sheminov, a party member and teacher of party history at the local pedagogical institute, was so emboldened as to take the unheard of step of sending Gorbachev a telegram in his own name declaring that Gorbachev's idea of combining the leadership of local soviets with the party leadership was wrong. Again, it is not the substance of his complaint but the euphoria produced by writing critically in his own name that is notable:

> Hours after dispatching his thought to Moscow, Mr. Sheminov was still obviously energized by his "participation" in the party conference, his partaking of the still evolving freedom of *glasnost*. He withdrew from his pocket a carefully folded bill for the telegram and proudly displayed it. *"This is the first time I have ever done anything like this,"* he said, *"I feel as if a stone were removed from my soul."*[13]

Our analytical attention is focused less on the subjective experience of an isolated individual in openly declaring a previously hidden transcript than on the collective experience of groups that have shared a more or less common subjugation and, hence, a more or less shared hidden transcript. Before turning to the analytical importance of this collective experience, it will be helpful to describe briefly the social atmosphere generated when an entire category of people suddenly finds its public voice is no longer stifled. One of the best chronicled and most dramatic recent examples was the nationwide ferment in Poland in August 1980, when a strike at the Lenin Shipyard in Gdansk led to the formation of a nationwide labor movement known as

13. Esther B. Fein, "In a City of the Volga, Tears, Anger, Delight," *New York Times*, July 7, 1988, p. 7.

Solidarnosc and a vigorous new public life. The atmosphere was festive, if not carnivalesque. For example, the workers sent the director's limousine to bring back a popular crane worker, Anna Walentynowicz, whose most recent dismissal from work was related to a charge of theft; she had collected candle stubs from a nearby graveyard to make candles for the anniversary of strikers killed by the regime in 1970.[14] The entire situation was a ritual reversal. Here was a mobilized working class openly confronting the official proletarian party. As one statement put it, "The ruling party has been brought before a tribunal of the class from which it allegedly derives its pedigree and in whose name it pretends to govern."[15] The public declaration of the hidden transcript to powerholders was not just figurative. At the workers' insistence, the deputy prime minister was forced to come to the shipyard and negotiate with the workers; the proceedings were broadcast over loudspeakers directly to thousands of assembled shipworkers and delegates from other factories. The social impact of the public confrontation of the authorities with complaints and demands that were previously sequestered in the safety of the hidden transcript was tremendous. Lawrence Goodwyn has captured the significance of this moment:

> There is a necessary human rhythm here—they are at last able to speak and a Chief Censor is there, forced to listen. It is a fine moment in history, one that does not happen remotely enough in any society or in any unbalanced human relationship. A bit of excess seems always to be visible the first time; its presence verifies the humiliation and tragedy of the past and signals that some basic realignment is in the offing, or is possible, or is at least passionately longed for.[16]

Most commentators of this period emphasize the rush of popular volubility once open talk became possible. It was as if a dam impounding the hidden transcript had suddenly broken. The interpretation by Timothy Garton Ash places this popular enthusiasm in the context of three decades of public silence and is closely parallel to the analysis proposed earlier:

> To appreciate the quality of this "revolution of the soul" one must know that for thirty years most Poles had lived a double life. They grew up with two codes of behavior, two languages—the public and the private—two histories—the official and the unofficial. From their schooldays they learned not only to conceal in public their private opinions but also to

14. Timothy Garton Ash, *The Polish Revolution: Solidarity*, 38–39.
15. Ibid., 37.
16. "How to Make a Democratic Revolution," 31.

parrot another set of opinions prescribed by the ruling ideology. . . . *The end of this double life was a profound psychological gain* for countless individuals. Now at last they could speak their minds openly in the workplace as well as behind the closed doors of their homes. *No longer did they need to watch their words* for fear of the secret police. And now they discovered for certain that almost everyone around them actually felt the same way about the system as they did. This was a source of tremendous relief. The poet Stanislaw Baranczak compared it to coming up for air after living for years under water. *Being able to speak the truth in public was part of that sense of recovered dignity*—another key word—which even the casual visitor could hardly fail to notice in the faces and bearing of the strikers.[17]

Providing we recognize the active social sites in which the hidden transcript was elaborated and nurtured throughout this period as well as the public actions of Polish workers before 1980 (in 1956, 1970, and 1976), the description of nearly an entire people coming up for air is not wide of the mark. What was new in 1980 was the comparatively long-lived success of the popular movement, not its tone. The emotions of those who in 1970 had been in the crowd of workers who sacked the party headquarters in the Baltic city of Gdynia were broadly comparable. One explained that he experienced

> something that can't be written about. You have to have lived it in order to understand how in that band of people we felt our power. For the first time in our lives we had taken a stand against the state. Before it was a taboo, something absolutely unattainable. . . . I didn't feel I was protesting just the price rise, although that's what sparked it. It had to do with overthrowing at least in part everything we hated.[18]

Behind 1980, then, lay a long prehistory, one comprising songs, popular poetry, jokes, street wisdom, political satire, not to mention a popular memory of the heroes, martyrs, and villains of earlier popular protest.[19] Each failure lay down another sedimentary layer of popular memory that would nourish the movement of the 1980s.

17. *The Polish Revolution*, 281.

18. Roman Laba, "The Roots of Solidarity: A Political Sociology of Poland's Working Class Democratization," 45–46. A strikingly similar report described the mood at a large East Berlin protest meeting held in a church in mid-October 1989. "Such jokes are not new, nor is protest, particularly from the sanctuary of churches. But *their unvarnished directness*, the radical condemnation of the system and of the leaders' unwillingness to change it, and the *enthusiasm with which the public cheered were so new as to cause many to gasp and look at one another in disbelief*." Emphasis added. Henry Kamm, "In East Berlin, Satire Conquers Fear," *New York Times*, October 17, 1989, p. A12.

19. Ibid., 179.

Seeking Public Satisfaction

I want to tell you so to your face so that it carries more weight.

—PASCAL, *Pensées*

Both the psychological release and the social meaning of breaking the silence deserve emphasis. A variety of experimental data indicate that whenever subjects find themselves unjustly treated but unable, except at considerable cost, to respond in kind, they can be expected to show signs of aggressive behavior as soon as the opportunity presents itself. Thus children subjected to authoritarian leadership in which their hostility toward their leaders was inhibited would typically show a large amount of aggressive behavior when these repressive conditions were finally relaxed.[20]

The frustrations engendered by domination have a double aspect. The first aspect is, of course, the humiliations and coercion entailed by the exercise of power. The second is the frustration of having continually to rein in one's anger and aggression in order to prevent even worse consequences. This is perhaps why the evidence noting that aggression that is inhibited may be displaced on other objects rarely claims that such displaced aggression is an effective substitute for the direct confrontation of the frustrating agent. No matter how much displacement takes place, the dominated must, everyday, muzzle their anger before the dominant. When someone at last ventures a public act of defiance, the sense of satisfaction thus also has a double aspect. There is the release of resisting domination and, at the same time, the release of finally expressing the response one had previously choked back. Thus, the release of the tension generated by constant vigilance and self-censorship must itself be a source of great satisfaction.[21]

There is some evidence, in fact, of a systematic relationship between self-control and eventual levels of aggression. Philip Zimbardo describes that connection in the following way:

> The pattern that distinguishes the potentially assaultive overcontrolled person is outward conformity coupled with inner alienation. This pattern may arise from a socialization process that exaggerates conformity to the rules of the social system: to gain affection from their parents, such individuals have to deny or repress all hostility, however slight, . . . evidence

20. Berkowitz, *Aggression*, 87. In another series of experiments groups who were repeatedly given demeaning tasks to perform were then encouraged to complain and insist on better treatment; if they met with some success they became more aggressive, suggesting that previously inhibited hostility now had a safe outlet. Thibaut and Kelley, *The Social Psychology of Groups*, 183.

21. In a sense, one of the burdens of subordinate groups is that their desire for wholeness and authenticity is so often at odds with their instinct for safety—at least in the public transcript.

that such persons are *generally* unresponsive even to extreme provocation; but when they do finally aggress (clearly a necessary criterion to define them post hoc as overcontrolled), their actions tend to be extremely assaultive and in response to some minor provocation that just happened to be the last straw.[22]

The connections established here by Zimbardo are phrased entirely in the vocabulary of individual psychology and infant socialization. As such, they are not directly applicable to the social and cultural situation faced by subordinate groups. Something of the logic captured here may nevertheless hold lessons for the social psychology of domination. If we imagine an entire strata of subordinates for whom open deference and conformity with the wishes of the powerful were absolutely necessary survival skills, one might plausibly speak of "alienation," "overcontrol," and of assaultive tendencies that might be discerned in the hidden transcript. Compare, for example, the individual logic of Zimbardo with Zola's tendentious description of the French peasantry as a class:

> So, when his sufferings became unbearable, Jacques Bonhomme would rise in revolt. He had centuries of fear and submission behind him, his shoulders had become hardened to blows, his soul so crushed that he did not recognize his own degradation. You could beat him and starve him and rob him of everything, year in, year out, before he would abandon his caution and stupidity, his mind filled with all sorts of muddled ideas which he could not properly understand; and this went on until a culmination of injustice and suffering flung him at his master's throat like some infuriated domestic animal who had been subjected to too many thrashings.[23]

If Zimbardo's description of aggression is confined to the psychology of the individual personality, Zola's generic peasant is hardly a person at all, but rather a dumb brute whose viscera control his action. In each case, however, something like an excess of self-control finally fails to keep violent impulses in check. If we could substitute a social account of this process that could link these seemingly inexplicable explosions to the hidden transcript, to everyday forms of disguised practical and symbolic resistance, we might then contribute to a far less mystifying account of the politics of subordinate groups.

However satisfying the first act of refusal or defiance may be, we must never overlook the fact that its satisfaction depends on it being public. The deference, obsequiousness, and humiliations of subordination are extracted

22. *The Cognitive Control of Motivation*, 248.
23. *The Earth (La Terre)*, trans. Douglas Parmée, 90–91.

as part of a public transcript. To speak of a loss of dignity and status is necessarily to speak of a public loss. It follows, I think, that a public humiliation can be fully reciprocated only with a public revenge. To be publicly dishonored may lead to offstage discourses of dignity and secret rites of revenge, but these can hardly compare, in their capacity to restore one's status, to a public assertion of honor or a public turning of the tables, preferably before the same audience.

The importance of a public refusal to reproduce hegemonic appearances helps explain why the first open declaration of the hidden transcript so often takes the form of a public breaking of an established ritual of public subordination. Highly visible gestures such as, for example, the revolutionary exhumations and desecration of sacred remains from Spanish cathedrals in 1936 are intentional provocations. They did nothing in the way of improving the material situation of revolutionary crowds, but it would be difficult to imagine a more dramatic or inflammatory symbol of complete defiance of the church as an institution. The act accomplished at least three purposes. It was perhaps enormously satisfying to the anticlerical population that had not earlier dared to defy the powerful church; it conveyed that the crowds were not afraid of the spiritual or temporal powers of the church, which was in turn shown to be powerless to protect its most sacred precincts, and finally, it suggested to a large audience that anything was possible. The successful public breaking of a taboo imposed by the dominant—a refusal to salute, to bow one's head, to use respectful terms of address, and so on—is an extremely efficient means of encouraging a conflagration of defiance.[24]

The initial act that publicly breaks the surface of consent owes a part of its dramatic force to the fact that it is usually an irrevocable step. A subordinate who takes such a step has, symbolically speaking, burned his bridges. Once again, the public character of the step is a necessary part of its evocative power. An insult spoken behind the scenes or, for that matter, an insult that is thinly disguised is not irrevocable. But a direct, blatant insult delivered before an audience is, in effect, a dare. If it is not beaten back, it will fundamentally alter those relations. Even if it is beaten back and driven underground, something irrevocable has nonetheless occurred. It is now public knowledge that relations of subordination, however immovable in practice, are not entirely legitimate. In a curious way something that everyone knows at some level has only a

---

24. A taboo broken privately can be said in a certain sense to be a taboo that is not, in fact, infringed. In all those situations short of complete rupture, the open declaration of a hidden transcript is likely to be more measured than its offstage variant. So long as the subordinate presumes that the relationship of subordination will persist in some form afterward, even a bold expression of dissent will often make some concessions to the view of the dominant.

shadowy existence until that moment when it steps boldly onto the stage.[25]
Slaves or servants, for example, can and often do negate their subordination
offstage and in oblique public acts. Masters, at the same time, may suspect or
perhaps even overhear some of what is said behind their backs. This mutual
knowledge, however, assumes a fundamentally different form when it finally
punctures the public pretense of domination. To take a concrete historical
example, it is one thing for most of the Polish people, their leaders, and
Russian officials to know that Soviet forces were responsible for the Katyn
Forest Massacre. It is another thing for this known fact to be declared openly.
The breaking of the public fiction that all parties know to be untrue makes a
claim for public truth that represents a direct challenge. It was perhaps the
rush of such claims at the onset of the French Revolution that explains why
one newspaper was called *Réalités bonnes à dire* (Truths that are good to speak).
The perpetrators of certain acts of defiance may be repressed, but their
speech and actions cannot be retracted from the popular memory.[26]

The precise form an open declaration of defiance takes will naturally
depend on the severity of indignities and oppression of the form of domination
it is intended to challenge. It is possible, however, to say something about the
circumstances that are most likely to produce an outburst that a Zola might
wish to describe as blind fury. Borrowing the terms of Lévi-Strauss, we might
distinguish between public declarations of defiance that are relatively "raw"
and those that are relatively "cooked."[27] Cooked declarations are more likely
to be nuanced and elaborate because they arise under circumstances in which
there is a good deal of offstage freedom among subordinate groups, allowing
them to share a rich and deep hidden transcript. In a sense, the hidden
transcript of such subordinate groups is already a product of mutual communication that already has a quasi-public existence. Raw declarations, in turn,
are most likely to come from subordinate groups who are not only subjected to
indignities to which they cannot respond but who, in addition, are relatively

25. Much of routine social life may depend on keeping such mutual knowledge out of the
public transcript. Everyone may know the boss is an alcoholic but until it is publicly declared,
things can continue as if it were not the case. Or assume two marriages in which the facts of the
relationship are identical; but one is marked by the outward appearances of harmony and the
other by public arguments and brawls. The *public* marking of the "failure" of the latter creates its
own crisis above and beyond what is the case offstage.

26. One might say this of Gorbachev's era of *glasnost:* The facts, books, and revelations made
known in this period cannot easily be effaced or unlearned even though the period of *glasnost* itself
may be terminated.

27. The term *relatively* is absolutely essential here since there is, strictly speaking, no such
thing as an "unsocialized," purely individual, "raw" hidden transcript any more than there is an
abstract individual agent who is not the product of a particular culture and history.

atomized by the process of domination. Whether due to heavy surveillance, geographical separation, linguistic differences, or fear, the effect of atomization is to impede the growth of an elaborate, shared hidden transcript. One result is that the explosive realm of public defiance is nearly the only social site where communication among subordinates is possible. Another result is that although regimes which systematically atomize the dominated, thereby depriving them of much of the social space in which a dissident subculture can be elaborated, may minimize the possibility of large-scale acts of defiance, they paradoxically raise the likelihood that, when and if such defiance does occur, it will take the form of relatively unstructured acts of vengeance. Subordinates who have never even been afforded the opportunity to build a collective culture offstage have little choice but to improvise when they do take the stage, and this improvisation will have a large component of unassociated, suppressed longing.[28] The most repressive regimes are, then, the most liable to the most violent expressions of anger from below if only because they have so successfully eliminated any other form of expression.

Timing: Voluntarism and Structure

Who will be the first to make an open declaration of the hidden transcript and exactly how and when it will be made are matters largely beyond the scope of social science techniques. Once all the structural factors that might shed some light on this matter have been considered, there will be a large and irreducible element of voluntarism left. The vagaries of temperament, personal circumstances, and individual socialization ensure that, under the same circumstances, one can anticipate a wide variety of responses to systematic subordination. In one respect, however, the open declaration of the hidden transcript can be considered a constant rather than a variable. Thus there have always been insolent serfs, "baaad niggers," insubordinate untouchables, and cheeky servants. The reason they may not seem particularly significant, I imagine, is because, under the usual circumstances, they are severely and quickly punished with chilling effect on other subordinates and that is the end of the matter.

We will never be able to predict why one employee quits when insulted

28. For a parallel distinction between what Lawrence Goodwyn would call the "anarchic" crowd and the "democratic" crowd, see "How to Make a Democratic Revolution," 74. It has, on the other hand, always struck me that "popular violence," even of a revolutionary kind, is relatively short-lived in the absence of enemies who are a palpable threat. Postrevolutionary bloodbaths, when they occur, seem more often to be the work of state bureaucratic apparatuses than of popular movements.

while another doesn't, why one slave suffers a beating in silence while another strikes back, why one servant returns an insult and another turns away. What are we to make, for example, of Simone Weil's account of political "guts" at the moment of the Popular Front in 1936: "After having always suffered everything, taken it all in silence for months and years, it is a matter of finally having the guts to stand up. To take one's turn to speak. To feel like men, for a few days."[29] How can we explain the sudden acquisition of guts? Weil's statement could be read as akin to Zola's description: that it was simply a question of the accumulation of injuries and insults until it became too much. This account implies a steadily rising anger that finally overcomes one's caution and inhibitions. While a description of this kind may accord well with subjective experience, it is of little use unless we also assume, against all the evidence, that the capacity to absorb indignities or to suppress anger is the same for all. Even at the level of subjective experience it may convey a far too deliberative tone to the decision finally to stand up. Outbursts of this kind are perhaps more often experienced as a loss of temper, a rush of anger that overwhelms one's deliberative self rather than an act of calculated anger. We may wish to classify such acts under the heading of voluntarism, but we must never forget that the acts we are describing are frequently experienced as essentially involuntary. And if the actors cannot supply a rational account of their actions, this poses additional difficulties for the outside analyst.

There is, however, a role for social analysis in understanding this phenomenon. A public health physician may not be able to predict whether a particular individual will fall ill, but he or she may be able to say something useful about the conditions that may promote an epidemic. Epidemics of political courage, of public declarations of the hidden transcript do occur, and part of the explanation for them is entirely structural. Thus, in his discussion of the values and actions of agricultural laborers in Andalusia, Juan Martinez-Alier notes that virtually all the workers believe in the justice of *reparto*: the redistribution of land to those who work it.[30] For the most part, this belief was not publicly voiced under Franco for the obvious reason that the consequence of speaking out in this manner might well be jail as well as dismissal from employment and blacklisting. In public, workers conducted themselves as if they accepted the existing land tenure system. And yet, we know that under the Republic prior to Franco and again after Franco, when the danger of publicly embracing this view was much reduced, it was openly voiced. Other-

29. L. Bodin and J. Touchard, *Front Populaire*, 112, quoted in Zolberg, "Moments of Madness," 183.

30. *Labourers and Landowners*, 202–06, 314–15.

wise it remained sequestered in the hidden transcript among workers. Thus one can discern an understandable variation in the open declaration of claims from below whenever the state or elites seemed less implacably hostile to such claims. Here there is no question of variations in the level of political courage or bravado, but rather the level of perceived danger in speaking out. A comparable epidemic of open defiance, in this case by slaves, was apparently experienced in the U.S. South during the last months of the Civil War, when the signs of a military defeat for the Confederacy became increasingly obvious. In addition to the shirking and flight encouraged by the approach of victorious Northern troops, instances of insolence, vituperation, and attacks by slaves on masters multiplied. White slave owners were particularly surprised at the desertion and assertiveness of house-slaves who, on earlier appearances, had been devoted and faithful. As one wrote, "On my arrival was surprised to hear that our negroes stampeded to the Yankees last night or rather a portion of them. . . . Eliza and her family are certain to go. She does not conceal her thoughts but plainly manifests her opinions by her conduct—insolent and insulting."[31] Such brief saturnalias of power are hardly surprising when the tables were turned. Those who, in fact, remained to take employment with their erstwhile masters and mistresses must have now comported themselves differently, knowing that the possibility of leaving was now open.

If we return to an earlier metaphor of water pressure against a dam, events that weaken the power of dominant groups are analogous to a weakening of the dam wall, thereby permitting more of the hidden transcript to leak through and increasing the probabilities of a complete rupture. By the same token any number of events might also raise the water pressure behind a dam to a point that threatens its (unchanged) retaining capacity. Thus, economic or political changes that result in an increase in the indignities and appropriations to which subordinate groups are subjected will, other things equal, increase the probability that more acts of open defiance—both symbolic and material—will occur.[32]

31. Genovese, *Roll, Jordan, Roll*, 109 and 97–112 more generally. See also Armstead L. Robinson, *Bitter Fruit of Bondage: Slavery's Demise and the Collapse of the Confederacy*, chap. 6.

32. *Indignities* in this context must be understood to include collective insults. Thus, for example, Judith Rollin's study of domestic servants (mostly black) in the Boston area reports an instance in which it seems that the massacre of mostly black prisoners during the takeover of the prison at Attica, New York, was the occasion for one housekeeper losing her normal reserve. As her employer reported, "I didn't know what she was so angry about. But it became apparent during Attica. She couldn't hold herself in. She poured out what white people did to black people. . . . She was really furious." In this case it was apparently the woman's anger *on behalf of* her people that provoked the outburst. *Between Women*, 126.

There are at least two problems with this hydraulic structuralism. The first is its crudeness: it amounts to saying that more acts of defiance will occur if the danger they entail is reduced or if the anger and indignation that impel them are increased. This may be true enough, but it is not very interesting. The second problem is that this structuralism implies that these variables are objective facts when, of course, they are social facts. So long as we take them to be only objective facts, objectively apprehended, we miss much of the social logic by which open declarations of the hidden transcript operate. A purely objectivist view, for example, would never allow us to understand the provocation and excitement generated by the first act of defiance. In and of itself, such an act is something of an incitement to others in the same situation to repeat the act or to associate themselves with its sentiments. An objectivist view would also have us assume that the determination of the power of the dominant is a straightforward matter, rather like reading an accurate pressure gauge. We have seen, however, that estimating the intentions and power of the dominant is a social process of interpretation highly infused with desires and fears. How else can we explain the numerous instances in which the smallest shards of evidence—a speech, a rumor, a natural sign, a hint of reform—have been taken by slaves, untouchables, serfs, and peasants as a sign that their emancipation is at hand or that their adversaries are ready to capitulate? I do not mean to assert that subordinate groups simply believe whatever they wish to believe about power relations but only that the evidence is never entirely unambiguous and that the subjectivity of subordinate groups is not irrelevant to its reading. If this were not the case, if the evidence were unambiguous and always accurately apprehended, all acts of defiance and rebellion would succeed. And if any failed, we would be obliged to write them off either as acts of madness or self-conscious "gestures" taken in full knowledge of their futility.[33]

Perhaps the central issue here is what Barrington Moore calls "the conquest of inevitability."[34] So long as a structure of domination is viewed as inevitable and irreversible, then all "rational" opposition will take the form of infrapolitics: resistance that avoids any open declaration of its intentions. Open defiance will be confined entirely to those who have lost their temper or else have an inexplicable taste for gestures. We have already noted that no social order is likely to be seen as entirely inevitable and immovable. What we have yet to explain is how an initial act of defiance that may originate in bravado, anger, or gestures can occasionally bring on an avalanche of defiance.

33. Such acts of defiance for the record do, in fact occur: the Warsaw ghetto uprising is an obvious and moving case in point. But they are an exceptionally rare form of collective action.
34. *Injustice*, 8off.

Charisma and the Structure of the Hidden Transcript

How is it possible that so many people immediately understood what to do and that none of them needed any advice or instructions?

—VÁCLAV HAVEL, president of the Czechoslovak Republic, New Year's Day 1990

The injury that a crime inflicts upon the social body is the disorder that it introduces into it, the scandal that it gives rise to, the example that it gives, the incitement to repeat it if it is not punished, and the possibility of becoming widespread that it bears within it.

—MICHEL FOUCAULT, *Discipline and Punish*

If the essentials of our argument to this point are correct, they may help to demystify many important forms of charisma and crowd action. Let us return to Mrs. Poyser one last time to explain the connection.

How is the electricity clearly generated by Mrs. Poyser's speech to the squire actually produced? Although she is a forceful woman, there is no indication that she enjoyed any particularly exalted status among cottagers and tenants before her outburst. Nor is it exactly the speech as words and sentiments alone that produced the effect since, as Eliot has pointed out, those kinds of things were said behind the back of the squire throughout the parish. What Mrs. Poyser adds to "the text" is her personal courage in having spoken that text in the face of power. When the encounter is immediately told and retold around the parish with glee, the emphasis is on "what she said to the squire," with the text and its addressee both being essential for the electricity of the moment. Putting the matter more generally, we may say fairly that if Mrs. Poyser becomes a charismatic heroine to the parish it is because she was the first person who publicly confronted power with the hidden transcript.

Charisma, as it is normally understood, has a suspect air of manipulation about it. In ordinary usage, it suggests that someone possesses a personal quality or aura that touches a secret nerve that makes others surrender their will and follow. The term *personal magnetism* is frequently used, as if charismatic figures had a force that aligned followers like so many iron filings caught in their field of force. I would not want to deny that instances of charisma along these lines exist, but the complete surrender of personal will to a figure of power is, I believe, a comparatively rare and marginal phenomenon.

The moment we insist on the importance of the hidden transcript to the social production of charisma, it seems to me that we restore the reciprocity that is at the center of this concept. As sociologists are fond of pointing out, the relational character of charisma means that one "has charisma" only to the extent that others confer it upon one; it is their attribution of charisma that establishes the relationship. We know, as well, that such relationships are often highly specific and relational. What is charismatic for one audience is not compelling for another; what works in one culture falls flat in another.

From this perspective, it is the cultural and social expectations of followers that exercise a controlling or at least limiting influence over the would-be charismatic figure. Mrs. Poyser, as we noted much earlier, had her basic speech written for her in the realm of the hidden transcript. The role of heroine in this case is to a large extent scripted in advance offstage by all members of the subordinate group, and the individual who fills that role is that one who somehow—through anger, courage, a sense of responsibility, or indignation—summons the wherewithal to speak on behalf of others to power. The degree of shock provided by such a speech as the one given by Mrs. Poyser depends to a great extent on how successfully it expresses the hidden transcript that all share. Her courage and particular eloquence, of course, matter; had she said it badly its impact would have suffered. But the main point is that Mrs. Poyser's status as a heroine depends centrally on having spoken *on behalf of,* in a quite literal sense, all the tenants of the squire. They did not appoint her to the post of spokesperson, but they defined the role.

Those who then sing Mrs. Poyser's praises are far from being the simple objects of manipulation. *They quite genuinely recognize themselves in her speech; she quite genuinely speaks for them.* A relationship that has historically been seen as a relationship of power, manipulation, and submission becomes, on this view, a social bond of genuine mutuality. Mrs. Poyser, to invoke Jean-Jacques Rousseau, "wills the general will." The powerful emotional valence of the charismatic speech or act for subordinate groups—their sense of elation, joy release—depends, I think, on it finding this resonance within the hidden transcript.

The highly charged atmosphere created by the open declaration of the hidden transcript may produce social effects that bear the marks of collective madness. If the first act of defiance succeeds and is spontaneously imitated by large numbers of others, an observer might well conclude that a herd of cattle with no individual wills or values had been stampeded inadvertently or by design. The same pattern of action can, however, be produced when a subordinate group learns from a breakthrough event that they may now, more safely, venture open defiance. Nearly any member of the subordinate group could substitute for Mrs. Poyser, inasmuch as the collectivity of tenants resembles what Sartre called "the un-alienated group in fusion": "For instance, if someone were to shout a *mot d'ordre* it would be effective . . . each senses himself and everyone else as possible leaders, but no one assumes sovereignty over others. Each is capable of expressing the sense of the group in the midst of action as an aid to the group's purpose."[35] The bond described here is not some mystical link of human solidarity. It is the shared discourse of the hidden transcript created and ripened in the nooks and crannies of the social order, where subordinate groups can speak more freely. If there seems to be an instantaneous mutuality and commonness of purpose, they are surely derived from the hidden transcript. Such mutuality may not be a pretty sight; for example, it might take the form of a previously muffled popular anti-Semitism, as appears to be the case in the post-*glasnost* Soviet Union.

The first public unveiling of the hidden transcript frequently sets in motion a crystallization of public action that is astonishingly rapid. This too, I believe, can be put in less than mythical perspective by relating it to the circumstances under which the hidden transcript was developed. For most subordinate groups, the social locations in which one can speak with real safety are narrowly restricted. Generally speaking, the smaller and more intimate the group, the safer the possibilities for free expression. The more effective dominant groups are in preventing subordinates from assembling in substantial numbers free of surveillance, the smaller the social scope of the hidden transcript. Thus, for example, the effective social reach of the hidden transcript under normal circumstances might not extend much beyond, say, one plantation, one hamlet of untouchables, the neighborhood pub, or perhaps merely the family. *It is only when this hidden transcript is openly declared that subordinates can fully recognize the full extent to which their claims, their dreams, their anger is shared by other subordinates with whom they have not been in direct touch.* It is, of course, a touch of poetic justice that while elites who successfully atomize much of their subordinate population set themselves up for a rapid crystallization of defiance once it does occur. The mutual recognition that public action permits is captured in this fashion by Zolberg: "as the 'torrent of words' involves a sort of intensive learning experience whereby new ideas, formulated initially by coteries, sects, etc. emerge as widely shared beliefs among much larger publics."[36] This formulation is useful providing the phrase "intensive learning experience" is understood very broadly: providing we understand how much prior "learning," however socially confined, has already taken place offstage. The process, then, is more one of recognizing close relatives of one's hidden transcript rather than of filling essentially empty heads with novel ideas.

The social reach of a particular charismatic act or speech becomes, on this view, something of an empirical question. To the degree that the conditions of

35. *The Critique of Dialectical Reason*, trans. Alan Sheridan-Smith, 379. I have benefited from a fine paper by Andrzej Tymowski on Sartre's book that established the connection for me.

36. "Moments of Madness," 206.

subordination have been relatively uniform for large numbers of people, I assume there will be a comparable family resemblance in their hidden transcript. Assuming they define themselves as acting within some larger frame of reference (for example, nationality, mother tongue, religion, and so on) they are likely to be susceptible to the same kinds of public acts, the same forms of symbolic assertion and refusal, the same moral claims. If we return to the question of the social electricity generated by the first public declaration of the hidden transcript, we can metaphorically think of those with comparable hidden transcripts in a society as forming part of a single power grid. Small differences in hidden transcript within a grid might be considered analogous to electrical resistance causing losses of current. This is not to say that every declaration of the hidden transcript will ramify through the entire grid, only that the grid itself, as defined by the hidden transcript, delimits the maximum possible symbolic reach of such acts, the population for whom such acts carry comparable meaning.[37]

Breaking the Charm

Now the domestic servants would raise their heads. Below stairs gossip had already begun. Now the vulgar, demoralized and made more insolent by . . . [the slapping of a gentleman by a servant], were beginning to mock their masters, plebeian criticism was rising like a tide.

—WITWOLD GOMBROWICZ, *Ferdydurke*

Social scientists, not to mention ruling elites, are often taken by surprise by the rapidity with which an apparently deferential, quiescent, and loyal subordinate group is catapulted into mass defiance. That ruling elites should be taken unaware by social eruptions of this kind is due, in part, to the fact that they have been lulled into a false sense of security by the normal posing of the powerless. Neither social scientists nor ruling elites, moreover, are likely to fully appreciate the incitement a successful act of defiance may represent for a subordinate group, precisely because they are unlikely to be much aware of the hidden transcript from which it derives much of its energy. It is somewhat more surprising to recognize how frequently revolutionary elites and parties have been astounded by the radicalism of their erstwhile following.

In the carnival at Romans examined by Le Roy Ladurie, elites on both sides of the eventual revolt are taken aback by the zeal of both urban plebeians

37. One might imagine, on this basis, an analysis that would seek to explain why so many real interests never see the light of day as organized movements. Aside from the effects of repression and atomization that impede their elaboration and expression, many real interests are not sufficiently cohesive or widespread to create the latent power grid on which charismatic mobilization depends.

and the peasantry. A small act of symbolic defiance, seemingly trivial but giving evidence of an enlarged political space, touches off a flurry of bold assertions and claims. As the eventual leader of the rebels wrote, "So encouraged were the villagers that they did things they would not have dared to think of at the outset."[38] When a tax protest in Romans was partly successful and when urban notables, fearing for their safety, left for other towns where they would be safer, much of the populace took this as a sign they might be winning. It had the look of a breakthrough. The sign itself was enough to provoke increasingly audacious acts of insolence and defiance. A prominent opponent of the plebeians reported, "Verbal, or more than verbal abuse against the nobility and even against the extant system of landholding was swiftly spreading around Romans: in the said town and surrounding villages *the meanest lout thought himself as great a lord as his own seigneur.*"[39] In these accounts of the events in Romans it is hard to avoid the impression of an entire discourse of equality, justice, and revenge, held in abeyance under normal circumstances, but unleashed once it appears that power relations have changed. The acts of daring and haughtiness that so struck the authorities were perhaps improvised on the public stage, but they had been long and amply prepared in the hidden transcript of folk culture and practice.

Much the same might be said of the radical popular movements during the English Civil War. It is simply impossible to understand the explosion of enthusiasm and activity that characterized these movements without examining the previous offstage culture and resistance of the lower classes. As Christopher Hill so compellingly demonstrates, each facet of the popular revolution unleashed, and then crushed, by Cromwell had its counterpart in low-profile popular culture and practice long predating its public manifestation.[40] Thus the Diggers and the Levellers staked an open claim to a fundamentally different version of property rights than the one publicly prevailing at the time. Their popularity and the force of their moral claim derived from an offstage popular culture that had never accepted the enclosures as just and that found expression in practices of poaching, tearing down new fences, and so forth. With the onset of the Civil War and the revolutionary promise it seemed to hold, this hidden transcript could, as it were, openly declare itself and act on its fondest dreams of justice and revenge. Winstanley, the ideological spokesman of the Diggers, accomplished what might be seen as simply a more elaborate and sustained version of what Mrs. Poyser accomplished. He

---

38. Ladurie, *Carnival in Romans*, 99.
39. Ibid., 130, emphasis added.
40. *The World Turned Upside Down*, chap. 7.

did not say anything novel when he proposed to make the buying and selling of land a capital crime. He merely tapped the popular energy implicit in a set of beliefs and practices hitherto denied full expression. The power generated by his appeal depended on the grid of the hidden transcript.

The simultaneous outburst of heterodox religious practices among the Seekers, Ranters, and early Quakers was also the open expression of beliefs and practices that had a subterranean existence earlier.[41] They could be discerned in the evasive practice of Lollardy, in a popular antinomianism that Hill calls the "alter-ego" of Calvinism, in the popular skepticism of the clergy and formal religious law expressed at alehouses and taverns, in a popular avoidance of formal church ritual, and a host of popular heresies. Owing to surveillance by the established religious authorities (and later of Calvinism), folk religion had had a fugitive existence at the margins of public life. The Civil War parted the curtains and allowed folk heterodoxy finally to develop to new levels as an outspoken and tumultuous competitor of official doctrine and practices.[42]

Whenever, at the beginning of a social movement, a particular slogan seems to be on everyone's lips and to capture the mood, its power is likely to come from the fact that it condenses some of the most deeply felt sentiments of the hidden transcript. In the working-class riots and demonstrations in the Baltic cities of Poland in 1970, "Down with the Red Bourgeoisie" was such a slogan. Quite apart from the rhetorical force of the adjective *red* modifying the noun *bourgeoisie*, one imagines that this slogan captured the essence of thousands upon thousands of bitter jokes, resentments, and outrage accumulated around kitchen tables, in small groups of workers, in beer halls, and among close companions.[43] The soft life of the representatives of the proletariat—their special shops, their vacation spas and hunting lodges, their party hospitals, their privileged housing and consumer durables, the educational advantages of their children, their arrogance and social distance, their appropriation of the state budget, their corruption—must have fueled a discourse, in safe places, of enormous moral anger and power. It was this social reservoir created

41. Ibid., chaps. 8, 9. Quote in following sentence is from 130.

42. In a more literate society one might want to make some of the same connections between the importance of a written text in the popular imagination and the extent to which it embodies the hidden transcript of the public to whom it appeals. Thus Christopher Hill writes that the enormous appeal in England of Thomas Paine's work is explained by the fact that "the tramp of their feet [craftsmen and uprooted countrymen] and the muttering of their illegal discourses is the essential background to Paine's writings." *Puritanism and Revolution: The English Revolution of the Seventeenth Century,* 102.

43. Goodwyn, *How to Make a Democratic Revolution,* chap. 3, suggests as much.

offstage well before 1970 that explains the force behind a seemingly simplistic phrase.

The first public declaration of the hidden transcript, then, has a prehistory that explains its capacity to produce political breakthroughs. If, of course, the first act of defiance meets with a decisive defeat it is unlikely to be emulated by others. The courage of those who fail, however, is likely to be noted, admired, and even mythologized in stories of bravery, social banditry, and noble sacrifice. They become themselves part of the hidden transcript.

When the first declaration of the hidden transcript succeeds, its mobilizing capacity as a symbolic act is potentially awesome. At the level of tactics and strategy, it is a powerful straw in the wind. It portends a possible turning of the tables. Key symbolic acts are, as one sociologist puts it, "tests of whether or not the whole system of mutual fear will hold up."[44] At the level of political beliefs, anger, and dreams it is a social explosion. That first declaration speaks for countless others, it shouts what has historically had to be whispered, controlled, choked back, stifled, and suppressed. If the results seem like moments of madness, if the politics they engender is tumultuous, frenetic, delirious, and occasionally violent, that is perhaps because the powerless are so rarely on the public stage and have so much to say and do when they finally arrive.

44. Collins, *Conflict Sociology*, 367.

Bibliography

Abbiateci, André. 1970. "Arsonists in Eighteenth-Century France: An Essay in the Typology of Crime." Translated by Elborg Forster and reprinted in *Deviants and the Abandoned in French Society: Selections from the Annales*, edited by Robert Forster and Orest Ranum. Baltimore: Johns Hopkins University Press.

Abbot, Jack Henry. 1982. *In the Belly of the Beast*. New York: Vintage.

Abercrombie, Nicholas, Stephen Hill, and Bryan S. Turner. 1980. *The Dominant Ideology Thesis*. London: Allen and Unwin.

Abu-Lughod, Lila. 1986. *Veiled Sentiments: Honor and Poetry in a Bedouin Society*. Berkeley: University of California Press.

Adas, Michael. 1979. *Prophets of Rebellion: Millenarian Protest against European Colonial Order*. Chapel Hill: University of North Carolina Press.

Adriani, N., and Albert C. Kruyt. 1951. *De barée sprekende torajas van Midden-Celebes*. Amsterdam: Nord: Hollandische Vitgevers Maatschappig.

Agulhon, Maurice. 1970. *La république au village: Les populations du Var de la révolution à la seconde république*. Paris: Plon.

Alcoff, Lind. 1988. "Cultural Feminism versus Post-structuralism: The Identity Crisis in Feminist Theory." *Signs: Journal of Women in Culture and Society* 13 (3): 405–36.

Allport, Gordon W., and Leo Postman. 1947. *The Psychology of Rumor*. New York: Russell and Russell.

Althusser, Louis. 1970. *Reading Capital*. London: New Left Books.

Ardener, Shirley, ed. 1977. *Perceiving Women*. London: J. M. Dent and Sons.

Ash, Timothy Garton. 1983. *The Polish Revolution: Solidarity*. New York: Charles Scribner's Sons.

Atkinson, Jane Mannig. 1984. "Wrapped Words: Poetry and Politics among the Wana of Central Sulawesi, Indonesia." In *Dangerous Words: Language and Politics in the Pacific*, edited by Donald Lawrence Brenneis and Fred B. Myers. New York: New York University Press.

Babcock, Barbara, ed. 1978. *The Reversible World: Symbolic Inversion in Art and Society.* Ithaca: Cornell University Press.

Bachrach, Peter, and Morton S. Baratz. 1970. *Power and Poverty: Theory and Practice.* New York: Oxford University Press.

Bakhtin, Mikhail. 1984. *Rabelais and His World.* Translated by Helene Iswolsky. Bloomington: Indiana University Press.

Balzac, Honoré de. 1949. *Les paysans.* Paris: Pleiades.

––––––. 1970. *A Harlot High and Low [Splendeurs et misères des courtisanes].* Translated by Reyner Happenstall. Harmondsworth: Penguin.

Bauman, Zygmunt. 1976. *Socialism, the Active Utopia.* New York: Holmes and Meier.

Belenky, Mary, et al. 1986. *Womens' Ways of Knowing: The Development of Self, Voice, and Mind.* New York: Basic Books.

Bell, Colin, and Howard Newby. 1973. "The Sources of Agricultural Workers' Images of Society." *Sociological Review* 21 (2): 229–53.

Benveniste, Émile. 1974. *Problèmes de linguistique générale,* vol. 2. Paris: Gallimard.

Berée, Yves-Marie. 1976. *Fêtes et révolte: Des mentalités populaires du XVIᵉ au XVIIIᵉ siècle.* Paris: Hachette.

Berkowitz, Leonard. 1962. *Aggression: A Social Psychological Analysis.* New York: McGraw Hill.

Bernstein, Basil. 1971. *Class, Codes, and Control.* London: Routledge and Kegan Paul.

Berreman, Gerald D. 1959. "Caste in Cross Cultural Perspective." In *Japan's Invisible Race: Caste in Culture and Personality,* edited by George DeVos and Hiroshi Wagatsuma. Berkeley: University of California Press.

Bloch, Marc. 1970. *French Rural History: An Essay on Its Basic Character.* Translated by Janet Sondheimer. Berkeley: University of California Press.

Bodin, L., and J. Touchard. 1961. *Front Populaire.* Paris: Armand Colin. In "Moments of Madness," by Aristide R. Zolberg. *Politics and Society* 2 (2): 183–207.

Boulle, Pierre. 1985. "In Defense of Slavery: Eighteenth-Century Opposition to Abolition and the Origins of a Racist Ideology in France." In *History from Below: Studies in Popular Protest and Popular Ideology in Honour of George Rudé,* edited by Frederick Krantz. Montreal: Concordia University.

Bourdieu, Pierre. 1977. *Outline of a Theory of Practice.* Translated by Richard Nice. Cambridge: Cambridge University Press.

––––––. 1984. *Distinction: A Social Critique of the Judgement of Taste.* Translated by Richard Nice. Cambridge: Harvard University Press.

Brehm, Sharon S., and Jack W. Brehm. 1981. *Psychological Reactance. A Theory of Freedom and Control.* New York: Academic Press.

Brenneis, Donald. 1980. "Fighting Words." In *Not Work Alone: A Cross-cultural View of Activities Superfluous to Survival,* edited by Jeremy Cherfas and Roger Lewin. Beverly Hills: Sage.

Brown, R., and A. Gilman. 1972. "The Pronouns of Power and Solidarity." In *Language and Social Context,* edited by Pier Paolo Giglioli. Harmondsworth: Penguin.

Brun, Viggo. 1987. "The Trickster in Thai Folktales." In *Rural Transformation in Southeast Asia,* edited by C. Gunnarsson et al. Lund: Nordic Association of Southeast Asian Studies.

Burke, Peter. 1978. *Popular Culture in Early Modern Europe.* New York: Harper and Row.

———. 1982. "Mediterranean Europe, 1500–1800." In *Religion and Rural Revolt: Papers Presented to the Fourth Interdisciplinary Workshop on Peasant Studies,* University of British Columbia, edited by Janos M. Bak and Gerhard Benecke. Manchester: Manchester University Press.

Campbell, Colin. 1971. *Toward a Sociology of Religion.* London: Macmillan.

Chakrabarty, Dipesh. 1983. "On Deifying and Defying Authority: Managers and Workers in the Jute Mills of Bengal circa 1900–1940." *Past and Present* 100: 124–46.

Chanana, Dev Raj. 1960. *Slavery in Ancient India.* New Delhi: People's Publishing House.

Chesnut, Mary. 1949. *A Diary from Dixie.* Boston: Houghton Mifflin.

Christian Shirley. 1988. "With a Thunderclap, Leftist Breaks Chile's Silence." *New York Times.* June 30.

Cobb, R. C. 1970. *The Police and the People: French Popular Protest, 1789–1820.* London: Oxford University Press.

Cocks, Joan Elizabeth. 1989. *The Oppositional Imagination: Adventures in the Sexual Domain.* London: Routledge.

Cohen, Abner. 1974. *Two-Dimensional Man: An Essay on the Anthropology of Power and Symbolism in Complex Society.* Berkeley: University of California Press.

Cohen, Robin. 1980. "Resistance and Hidden Forms of Consciousness among African Workers." *Review of African Political Economy* 19: 8–22.

Cohn, Bernard. 1959. "Changing Traditions of a Low Caste." In *Traditional India: Structure and Change,* edited by Milton Singer. Philadelphia: American Folklore Society.

Cohn, Norman. 1957. *The Pursuit of the Millennium.* London: Secker and Warburg.

Collins, Randall. 1975. *Conflict Sociology: Toward an Explanatory Science.* New York: Academic Press.

Comaroff, Jean. 1985. *Body of Power, Spirit of Resistance: The Culture and History of a South African People.* Chicago: University of Chicago Press.

Conrad, Joseph. 1953. *The Secret Agent: A Simple Tale.* Garden City, N.Y., Doubleday.

Coser, Lewis. 1974. *Greedy Institutions: Patterns of Undivided Commitment.* New York: Free Press.

Crapanzano, Vincent. 1985. *Waiting: The Whites of South Africa.* New York: Vintage.

Craton, Michael. 1982. *Testing the Chains.* Ithaca: Cornell University Press.

Dahl, Robert A. 1961. *Who Governs? Democracy and Power in an American City.* New Haven: Yale University Press.

Dance, D. C., ed. 1978. *Shuckin' and Jivin': Folklore from Contemporary Black Americans.* Bloomington: University of Indiana Press.

Davis, Natalie Zemon. 1978. "Women on Top: Symbolic Sexual Inversion and Political Disorder in Early Modern Europe." In *The Reversible World: Symbolic Inversion in Art and Society,* edited by Barbara A. Babcock. Ithaca: Cornell University Press.

Detienne, Marcel, and Jean-Pierre Vernant. 1978. *Cunning Intelligence in Greek Culture and Society.* Translated by Janet Lloyd. Atlantic Highlands, N.J.: Humanities Press.

Djilas, Milovan. 1957. *The New Class.* New York: Praeger.

Douglass, Frederick. 1987. *My Bondage and My Freedom.* Edited and with an introduction by William L. Andrews. Urbana: University of Illinois Press.

Dournes, Jacques. 1973. "Sous couvert des maîtres." *Archives Européennes de Sociologie* 14: 185–209.

Du Bois, W. E. B. 1969. "On the Faith of the Fathers." In *The Souls of Black Folks* by W. E. B. Du Bois. New York: New American Library.

Eagleton, Terry. 1981. *Walter Benjamin: Towards a Revolutionary Criticism.* London: Verso. Quoted in *Politics and Poetics of Transgression* by Peter Stallybrass and Allon White. Ithaca: Cornell University Press, 1986.

Edelman, Murray. 1974. "The Political Language of the 'Helping Professions.'" *Politics and Society* 4 (3): 295–310.

Elias, Norbert. 1982. *Power and Civility.* Vol. 2 of *The Civilizing Process.* Translated by Edmund Jephcott. New York: Pantheon.

Eliot, George. 1981. *Adam Bede.* Harmondsworth: Penguin.

Elliot, J. H. 1985. "Power and Propaganda in the Spain of Philip IV." In *The Rites of Power: Symbolism, Ritual, and Politics since the Middle Ages,* edited by Sean Wilentz. Philadelphia: University of Pennsylvania Press.

Ellison, Ralph. 1952. *Invisible Man.* New York: New American Library.

Evans, Sara. 1980. *Personal Politics: The Roots of Women's Liberation in the Civil Rights Movement and the New Left.* New York: Vintage Books.

Fein, Esther B. 1988. "In a City of the Volga, Tears, Anger, Delight." *New York Times.* July 7.

Fick, Carolyn. 1985. "Black Peasants and Soldiers in the St. Domingue Revolution: Initial Reactions to Freedom in the South Province." In *History from Below: Studies in Popular Protest and Popular Ideology in Honour of George Rudé,* edited by Frederick Krantz. Montreal: Concordia University.

Field, Daniel. 1976. *Rebels in the Name of the Tsar.* Boston: Houghton Mifflin.

Figes, Orlando. 1989. *Peasant Revolution, Civil War: The Volga Countryside in Revolution*. Oxford: Clarendon Press.

Finlay, M. I. 1968. "Slavery." In *International Encyclopedia of the Social Sciences*, vol. 14, edited by D. Sills. New York: Macmillan.

Foucault, Michel. 1979. *Discipline and Punish: The Birth of the Prison*. Translated by Alan Sheridan. New York: Vintage Books.

———. 1979. *Michel Foucault: Power, Truth, Strategy*. Edited by Meaghan Morris and Paul Patton. Sydney: Feral Publications.

———. 1980. *The History of Sexuality. An Introduction*. Vol. 1. Translated by R. Hurley. New York: Vintage Books.

Freeman, James M. 1979. *Untouchable: An Indian Life History*. Stanford: Stanford University Press.

Friedman, Susan. 1989. "The Return of the Repressed in Women's Narrative." *The Journal of Narrative Technique* 19: 141–56.

Friedman, Thomas. 1988. "For Israeli Soldiers, 'War of Eyes' in West Bank." *New York Times*. January 5.

Gaventa, John. 1980. *Power and Powerlessness: Quiescence and Rebellion in an Appalachian Valley*. Urbana: University of Illinois Press.

Geisey, Ralph E. 1985. "Models of Rulership in French Royal Ceremonial." In *The Rites of Power: Symbolism, Ritual, and Politics since the Middle Ages*, edited by Sean Wilentz. Philadelphia: University of Pennsylvania Press.

Genovese, Eugene. 1974. *Roll, Jordan, Roll: The World the Slaves Made*. New York: Pantheon.

Giap, Nguyen Hong. 1971. *La condition des paysans au Viet-Nam à travers les chansons populaires*. Paris, thèse 3ème cycle, Sorbonne.

Giddens, Anthony. 1975. *The Class Structure of Advanced Societies*. New York: Harper.

———. 1979. *Central Problems in Social Theory: Action, Structure, and Contradiction in Social Analysis*. Berkeley: University of California Press.

Gilman, Sander. 1968. *Jewish Self-Hatred: Anti-Semitism and the Hidden Language of the Jews*. Baltimore: Johns Hopkins University Press.

Gilmore, Al-Tony. 1975. *Bad Nigger!: The National Impact of Jack Johnson*. Port Washington, N.J.: Kennikat Press.

Gilmore, David. 1987. *Aggression and Community: Paradoxes of Andalusian Culture*. New Haven: Yale University Press.

Glass, James M. 1985. *Delusion: Internal Dimensions of Political Life*. Chicago: University of Chicago Press.

Gluckman, Max. 1954. *Rituals of Rebellion in South-East Africa*. Manchester: University of Manchester Press.

———. 1970. *Order and Rebellion in Tribal Africa*. London: Allen Lane.

Goffman, Erving. 1956. "The Nature of Deference and Demeanor." *American Anthropologist* 58 (June).

————. 1971. *Relations in Public: Microstudies of the Public Order.* New York: Basic Books.

Gombrowicz, Witwold. 1966. *Ferdydurke.* Translated by Eric Mosbacher. New York: Harcourt, Brace, and World.

Goodwin, Lawrence. "How to Make a Democratic Revolution: The Rise of Solidarnosc in Poland." Book manuscript.

Goody, Jack. 1968. *Literacy in Traditional Societies.* Cambridge: Cambridge University Press.

Gramsci, Antonio. 1971. *Selections from the Prison Notebooks.* Edited and translated by Quinten Hoare and Geoffrey Nowell Smith. London: Wishart.

Graves, Robert. n.d. *Lars Porsena, or the Future of Swearing and Improper Language.* London: Kegan Paul, Trench, Trubner and Co.

Greene, Graham. 1966. *The Comedians.* New York: Viking Press.

Guha, Ranajit. 1983. *Elementary Aspects of Peasant Insurgency.* Delhi: Oxford University Press.

Guillaumin, Emile. 1983. *The Life of a Simple Man.* Edited by Eugen Weber, revised and translated by Margaret Crosland. Hanover, N.H.: University Press of New England.

Habermas, Jürgen. 1975. *Legitimation Crisis.* Boston: Beacon Press.

————. 1984. *The Theory of Communicative Action.* Vol. 1 of *Reason and the Rationalization of Society.* Translated by Thomas McCarthy. Boston: Beacon Press.

Hall, Stuart, and Tony Jefferson. 1976. *Resistance Through Rituals: Youth Subcultures in Post-war Britain.* London: Hutchinson.

Halliday, M. A. K. 1978. *Language as Social Semiotic.* London: Edward Arnold.

Harper, Edward B. 1968. "Social Consequences of an Unsuccessful Low Caste Movement." In *Social Mobility in the Caste System in India: An Interdisciplinary Symposium, Comparative Studies in Society and History,* Supplement #3, edited by James Silverberg. The Hague: Mouton.

Havel, Václav. 1987. In *Times Literary Supplement.* January 23.

Hearn, Frank. 1978. *The Incorporation of the 19th-Century English Working Class. Contributions in Labor History,* no. 3. Westport, Conn.: Greenwood Press.

Hebdige, Dick. 1976. "Reggae, Rastas, and Rudies." In *Resistance Through Rituals: Youth Subcultures in Post-war Britain.* London: Hutchinson.

Heusch, Luc de. 1964. "Mythe et société féodale: Le culte de Kubandwa dans le Rwanda traditional." *Archives de Sociologie des Religions* 18: 133–46.

Hill, Christopher. 1958. *Puritanism and Revolution: The English Revolution of the Seventeenth Century.* New York: Schocken.

————. 1972. *The World Turned Upside Down.* New York: Viking.

————. 1982. "From Lollardy to Levellers." In *Religion and Rural Revolt: Papers Presented to the Fourth Interdisciplinary Workshop on Peasant Studies,* University of British Columbia, edited by Janos M. Bak and Gerhard Benecke. Manchester: Manchester University Press.

————. 1985. "The Poor and the People in Seventeenth-Century England." In

History from Below: Studies in Popular Protest and Popular Ideology in Honour of George Rudé, edited by Frederick Krantz. Montreal: Concordia University.

Hirschman, Albert O. 1970. *Exit, Voice, and Loyalty: Responses to Decline in Firms, Organizations, and States*. Cambridge: Harvard University Press.

Hobsbawn, Eric. 1965. *Primitive Rebels: Studies in Archaic Forms of Social Movement in the 19th and 20th Centuries*. New York: Norton.

————, and George Rudé. 1968. *Captain Swing*. New York: Pantheon.

————. 1973. "Peasants and Politics." *Journal of Peasant Studies* I (1): 13.

Hochschild, Arlie Russell. 1983. *The Managed Heart: The Commercialization of Human Feeling*. Berkeley: University of California Press.

Hoggart, Richard. 1954. *The Uses of Literacy: Aspects of Working Class Life*. London: Chatto and Windus.

Huang, Ray. 1981. *1571: A Year of No Significance*. New Haven: Yale University Press.

Hurston, Zora Neale. 1973. "High John de Conquer." In *Mother Wit*, edited by Alan Dundes. Englewood Cliffs: Prentice Hall.

Ileto, Reynaldo Clemeña. 1975. "Pasyon and the Interpretation of Change in Tagalog Society." Ph.D. dissertation, Cornell University.

Isaac, Rhys. 1985. "Communication and Control: Authority Metaphors and Power Contests on Colonel Landon Carter's Virginia Plantation, 1752–1778." In *The Rites of Power: Symbolism, Ritual, and Politics since the Middle Ages*, edited by Sean Wilentz. Philadelphia: University of Pennsylvania Press.

Jayawardena, Chandra. 1968. "Ideology and Conflict in Lower Class Communities." *Comparative Studies in Society and History* 10 (4): 413–46.

Jones, Charles C. 1842. *The Religious Institution of the Negroes in the United States*. Savannah.

Jones, Edward. 1964. *Ingratiation: A Social Psychological Analysis*. New York: Appleton-Century-Crofts.

Joyner, Charles. 1984. *Down by the Riverside*. Urbana: University of Illinois Press.

Jürgensmeyer, Mark. 1980. "What if Untouchables Don't Believe in Untouchability?" *Bulletin of Concerned Asian Scholars* 12 (1): 23–30.

————. 1982. *Religion as Social Vision: The Movement against Untouchability in 20th Century Punjab*. Berkeley: University of California Press.

Kamm, Henry. 1989. "In East Berlin, Satire Conquers Fear." In *New York Times*, October 17.

Kanter, Rosabeth Moss. 1972. *Commitment and Community: Communes and Utopias in Sociological Perspective*. Cambridge; Harvard University Press.

Kardiner, Abram, and Lionel Ovesey. 1962. *The Mark of Oppression: Explorations in the Personality of the American Negro*. Cleveland: Meridian Books.

Kerr, Clark, and Abraham Siegel. 1954. "The Inter-Industry Propensity to Strike: An International Comparison." In *Industrial Conflict*, edited by Arthur Kornhauser et al. New York: McGraw-Hill.

Khare, R. S. 1984. *The Untouchable as Himself: Ideology, Identity, and Pragmatism among the Lucknow Chamars.* Cambridge Studies in Cultural Systems, #8. Cambridge: Cambridge University Press.

Khawam, René B., trans. 1980. *The Subtle Ruse: The Book of Arabic Wisdom and Guile.* London: East-West Press.

Klausner, William J. 1987. "Siang Miang: Folk Hero." In *Reflections on Thai Culture.* Bangkok: The Siam Society.

Kolchin, Peter. 1987. *Unfree Labor: American Slavery and Russian Serfdom.* Cambridge: Harvard University Press.

Kundera, Milan. 1983. *The Joke.* Translated by Michael Henry Heim. Harmondsworth: Penguin.

Kunzle, David. 1978. "World Upside Down: The Iconography of a European Broadsheet Type." In *The Reversible World: Symbolic Inversion in Art and Society,* edited by Barbara A. Babcock. Ithaca: Cornell University Press.

Laba, Roman. Forthcoming. "The Roots of Solidarity: A Political Sociology of Poland's Working Class Democratization." Princeton: Princeton University Press.

Ladurie, Emmanuel Le Roy. 1979. *Carnival in Romans.* Translated by Mary Feeney. New York: George Braziller.

Lakoff, Robin. 1975. *Language and Women's Place.* New York: Harper Colophon.

LeBon, Gustav. 1895. *La psychologie des foules.* Paris: Alcan.

Lefebvre, Georges. 1973. *The Great Fear of 1789: Rural Panic in Revolutionary France.* Translated by Joan White. New York: Pantheon.

Levine, Lawrence W. 1977. *Black Culture and Black Consciousness.* New York: Oxford University Press.

Lewis, I. M. 1971. *Ecstatic Religion: An Anthropological Study of Spirit Possession and Shamanism.* Harmondsworth: Penguin.

Lichtenstein, Alex. 1988. "That Disposition to Theft, with which they have been Branded: Moral Economy, Slave Management, and the Law." *Journal of Social History* (Spring).

Lincoln, Bruce. 1985. "Revolutionary Exhumations in Spain, July 1936." *Comparative Studies in Society and History* 27 (2): 241–60.

Linebaugh, Peter. 1976. "Karl Marx, the Theft of Wood, and Working-class Composition: A Contribution to the Current Debate." *Crime and Social Justice* (Fall-Winter), 5–16.

Livermore, Mary. 1889. *My Story of the War.* Hartford, Conn. In Albert J. Raboteau. 1978. *Slave Religion: The "Invisible Institution" of the Antebellum South.* New York: Oxford University Press.

Lockwood, P. 1966. "Sources of Variation in Working-Class Images of Society." *Sociological Review* 14 (3): 249–67.

Lukes, Steven. 1974. *Power: A Radical View.* London: Macmillan.

McCarthy, John D., and William L. Yancey. 1970. "Uncle Tom and Mr. Charlie: Metaphysical Pathos in the Study of Racism and Personality Disorganization." *American Journal of Sociology* 76: 648–72.

McCarthy, Thomas. 1989. *The Critical Theory of Jürgen Habermas.* London: Hutchinson.

McKay, Ian. 1981. "Historians, Anthropology, and the Concept of Culture." *Labour/Travailleur,* vols. 8–9: 185–241.

Malcolmson, R. W. 1973. *Popular Recreations in English Society 1700–1850.* Cambridge: Cambridge University Press.

Marriott, McKim. 1955. "Little Communities in an Indigenous Civilization." In *Village India,* edited by McKim Marriott. Chicago: University of Chicago Press.

Martinez-Alier, Juan. 1971. *Labourers and Landowners in Southern Spain.* St. Anthony's College Oxford Publications, no. 4. London: Allen and Unwin.

Mathiesen, Thomas. 1965. *The Defenses of the Weak: A Sociological Study of a Norwegian Correctional Institution.* London: Tavistock.

Melville, Herman. 1968. "Benito Cereno." In *Billy Budd and Other Stories.* New York: Penguin.

Milgram, Stanley. 1974. *Obedience to Authority: An Experimental View.* New York: Harper and Row.

Miliband, Ralph. 1969. *The State in Capitalist Society.* London: Weidenfeld and Nicholson.

Moffat, Michael. 1979. *An Untouchable Community in South India: Structure and Consensus.* Princeton: Princeton University Press.

Moore, Barrington, Jr. 1987. *Injustice: The Social Bases of Obedience and Revolt.* White Plains, N.Y.: M. E. Sharpe.

Mullin, Gerard W. 1972. *Flight and Rebellion: Slave Resistance in 18th Century Virginia.* New York: Oxford University Press.

Najita, Tetsuo, and Irwin Scheiner. 1978. *Japanese Thought in the Tokugawa Period, 1600–1868: Methods and Metaphors.* Chicago: University of Chicago Press.

Newby, Howard. 1975. "The Deferential Dialectic." *Comparative Studies in Society and History* 17 (2): 139–64.

Nietzsche, Friedrich. 1969. *On the Genealogy of Morals.* Translated by Walter Kaufman and F. J. Hollingsdale. New York: Vintage.

Nicholls, David. 1984. "Religion and Peasant Movements during the French Religious Wars." In *Religion and Rural Revolt: Papers Presented to the Fourth Interdisciplinary Workshop on Peasant Studies,* University of British Columbia, edited by Janos M. Bak and Gerhard Benecke. Manchester: Manchester University Press.

Nonini, Donald, and Arlene Teroka. Forthcoming. "Class Struggle in the Squared Circle: Professional Wrestling as Working-Class Sport." In *Dialectical Anthropology: The Ethnology of Stanley Diamond,* edited by Christine W. Gailey and Stephen Gregory. Gainesville: University of Florida Press.

O'Donnell, Guillermo. 1986. "On the Fruitful Convergences of Hirschman's *Exit, Voice, and Loyalty* and *Shifting Involvements:* Reflections from Recent Argentine Experience." In *Development, Democracy and the Art of Trespassing: Essays in Honor of Albert Hirschman,* edited by Alejandro Foxley et al. Notre Dame: Notre Dame University Press.

Orwell, George. 1962. *Inside the Whale and Other Essays.* Harmondsworth: Penguin.

Osofsky, Gilbert, ed. 1969. *Puttin' on Ole Massa: The Slave Narratives of Henry Bibb, William Wells, and Solomon Northrup.* New York: Harper and Row.

Owen, Robert. 1920. *The Life of Robert Owen.* New York: Alfred Knopf.

Parkin, Frank. 1971. *Class, Inequality and the Political Order.* New York: Praeger.

Patterson, Orlando. 1982. *Slavery and Social Death: A Comparative Study.* Cambridge: Harvard University Press.

Piven, Frances Fox, and Richard Cloward. 1977. *Poor People's Movements: Why They Succeed, How They Fail.* New York: Vintage.

Poulantzas, Nicos. 1978. *State, Power, Socialism.* London: New Left Books.

Polsby, Nelson. 1963. *Community Power and Political Theory.* New Haven: Yale University Press.

Pred, A. 1989. "The Locally Spoken Word and Local Struggles." *Environment and Planning D: Society and Space* 7: 211–33.

———. 1989. *Lost Words and Lost Worlds: Modernity and the Language of Everyday Life in Late Nineteenth-Century Stockholm.* Cambridge: Cambridge University Press.

Raboteau, Albert. 1978. *Slave Religion: The "Invisible Institution" of the Antebellum South.* New York: Oxford University Press.

Reddy, William M. 1977. "The Textile Trade and the Language of the Crowd at Rouen, 1752–1871." *Past and Present* 74: 62–89.

Reeves, Marjorie E. 1972. "Some Popular Prophesies from the 14th to 17th Centuries." In *Popular Belief and Practice: Papers Read at the 9th Summer Meeting and 10th Winter Meeting of the Ecclesiastical History Society,* edited by G. J. Cuming and Derek Baker. Cambridge: Cambridge University Press.

Rhys, Jean. 1974. *After Leaving Mr. McKenzie.* New York: Vintage.

Rickford, John R. 1983. "Carrying the New Wave into Syntax: The Case of Black English BIN." In *Variation in the Form and Use of Language,* edited by Robert W. Fasold. Washington: Georgetown University Press.

Robinson, Armstead L. Forthcoming. *Bitter Fruit of Bondage: Slavery's Demise and the Collapse of the Confederacy.* New Haven: Yale University Press.

Rogers, Susan Carol. 1975. "Female Forms of Power and the Myth of Male Dominance: A Model of Female/Male Interaction in Peasant Society." *American Ethnologist* 2 (4): 727–56.

Rollins, Judith. 1985. *Between Women: Domestics and Their Employers.* Philadelphia: Temple University Press.

Rosengarten, Theodore. 1974. *All God's Dangers: The Life of Nate Shaw.* New York: Knopf.

Rothkrug, Lionel. 1984. "Icon and Ideology in Religion and Rebellion, 1300–1600: Bayernfreiheit and Réligion Royale." In *Religion and Rural Revolt: Papers*

Presented to the Fourth Interdisciplinary Workshop on Peasant Studies, University of British Columbia. Manchester: Manchester University Press.

Rudé, George. 1959. *The Crowd in the French Revolution.* Oxford: Clarendon Press.

————. 1964. *The Crowd in History: A Survey of Popular Disturbances in France and England, 1730–1848.* New York: Wiley.

Rudwin, Maximillian J. 1920. *The Origin of the German Carnival Comedy.* New York: G. E. Stechert.

Sabean, David Warren. 1984. *Power in the Blood: Popular Culture and Village Discourse in Early Modern Europe.* Cambridge: Cambridge University Press.

Sales, Roger. 1983. *English Literature in History, 1780–1830: Pastoral and Politics.* London: Hutchinson.

Sartre, Jean-Paul. 1976. *The Critique of Dialectical Reason.* Translated by Alan Sheridan-Smith. London: New Left Books.

Scheler, Max. 1961. *Ressentiment.* Translated by William W. Holdheim and edited by Lewis A. Coser. Glencoe, Ill.: Free Press.

Schopenhauer, Arthur. 1891. *Selected Essays of Arthur Schopenhauer.* Translated by Ernest Belfort Bax. London: George Bell. In Sander Gilman, *Jewish Self-Hatred: Anti-Semitism and the Hidden Language of the Jews.* 1968. Baltimore: Johns Hopkins University Press.

Scott, James C. 1977. "Protest and Profanation: Agrarian Revolt and the Little Tradition." *Theory and Society* 4 (1): 1–38, and 4 (2): 211–46.

————. 1985. *Weapons of the Weak: Everyday Forms of Peasant Resistance.* New Haven: Yale University Press.

————. 1987. "Resistance Without Protest and Without Organization: Peasant Opposition to the Islamic *Zakat* and the Christian Tithe." *Comparative Studies in Society and History* 29 (3).

Searles, Harold F. 1965. *Collected Papers on Schizophrenia and Related Subjects.* New York: International Universities Press.

Sennett, Richard, and Jonathan Cobb. 1972. *The Hidden Injuries of Class.* New York: Knopf.

————. 1977. *The Fall of Public Man.* New York: Knopf.

Sharpe, Gene. 1973. *The Politics of Nonviolent Action,* part I of *Power and Struggle.* Boston: Porter Sargent.

Skinner, G. William. 1975. *Marketing and Social Structure in Rural China.* Tucson: Association of Asian Studies.

Slamet, Ina E. 1982. *Cultural Strategies for Survival: The Plight of the Javanese.* Comparative Asian Studies Program, monograph #5. Rotterdam: Erasmus University.

Stallybrass, Peter, and Allon White. 1986. *The Politics and Poetics of Transgression.* Ithaca: Cornell University Press.

Stinchcombe, Arthur. 1970. "Organized Dependency Relations and Social Stratification." In *The Logic of Social Hierarchies,* edited by Edward O. Laumann et al. Chicago: Chicago University Press.

Strauss, Leo. 1973. *Persecution and the Art of Writing*. Westport, Conn.: Greenwood Press.

Taal, J. F. 1963. "Sanskrit and Sanskritization." *Journal of Asian Studies* 22 (3).

Thibaut, John, and Harold Kelley. 1959. *The Social Psychology of Groups*. New York: Wiley.

Thompson, E. P. 1966. *The Making of the English Working Class*. New York: Vintage.

――――. 1974. "Patrician Society, Plebeian Culture." *Journal of Social History* 7 (4).

――――. 1975. *Whigs and Hunters: The Origin of the Black Act*. New York: Pantheon.

Trudgill, Peter. 1974. *Sociolinguistics: An Introduction to Language and Society*. Harmondsworth: Penguin.

Turner, Victor. 1969. *The Ritual Process: Structure and Anti-Structure*. Chicago: Aldine.

Veyne, Paul. 1976. *Le pain et le cirque*. Paris: Editions de Seuil.

Viola, Lynne. 1986. "Babí bunty and Peasant Women's Protest during Collectivization." *The Russian Review* 45: 23–42.

Walker, Alice. 1982. "Nuclear Exorcism." *Mother Jones*, Sept.–Oct.

Walker, Jack E. 1966. "A Critique of the Elitist Theory of Democracy." *American Political Science Review* 60: 285–95.

Walthall, Anne. 1983. "Narratives of Peasant Uprisings in Japan." *Journal of Asian Studies* 43 (3): 571–87.

――――. 1986. "Japanese *Gimin*: Peasant Martyrs in Popular Memory." *American Historical Review* 91 (5): 1076–102.

Weber, Max. 1963. *The Sociology of Religion*. Boston: Beacon Press.

Weiner, Annette B. 1984. "From Words to Objects to Magic: 'Hard Words' and the Boundaries of Social Interaction." In *Dangerous Words: Language and Politics in the Pacific*, edited by Donald Lawrence Brenneis and Fred R. Myers. New York: New York University Press.

Weininger, Otto. 1906. *Sex and Character*. London: William Heinemann. In Sander Gilman, *Jewish Self-Hatred: Anti-Semitism and the Hidden Language of the Jews*. 1968. Baltimore: Johns Hopkins University Press.

Weller, Robert. 1987. "The Politics of Ritual Disguise: Repression and Response in Taiwanese Popular Religion." *Modern China* 13 (1): 17–39.

Wertheim, W. F. 1973. *Evolution or Revolution*. London: Pelican Books.

Wilentz, Sean, editor. 1985. *The Rites of Power: Symbolism, Ritual, and Politics since the Middle Ages*. Philadelphia: University of Pennsylvania Press.

Willis, Paul. 1977. *Learning to Labour*. Westmead: Saxon House.

Winn, Denise. 1983. *The Manipulated Mind: Brainwashing, Conditioning, and Indoctrination*. London: Octogon Press.

Wofford, Susanne. Forthcoming. "The Politics of Carnival in *Henry IV*." In *Theatrical Power: The Politics of Representation on the Shakespearean Stage*, edited by Helen Tartar. Stanford University Press.

Wortmann, Richard. 1985. "Moscow and Petersburg: The Problem of the Political Center in Tsarist Russia, 1881–1914." In *The Rites of Power: Symbolism, Ritual, and Politics since the Middle Ages,* edited by Sean Wilentz. Philadelphia: University of Pennsylvania Press.

Wright, G. O. 1954. "Projection and Displacement: A Cross-cultural Study of Folk-tale Aggression." *Journal of Abnormal Psychology* 49: 523–28.

Wright, Richard. 1937. *Black Boy: A Record of Childhood and Youth.* New York: Harper and Brothers.

Yetman, Norman. 1970. *Voices from Slavery.* New York: Holt, Rinehart.

Zimbardo, Philip G. 1969. *The Cognitive Control of Motivation: The Consequences of Choice and Dissonance.* Glencoe, Ill.: Scott, Foresman.

Zola, Emile. 1980. *The Earth (La Terre).* Translated by Douglas Parmée. Harmondsworth: Penguin.

Zolberg, Aristide R. 1972. "Moments of Madness." *Politics and Society* 2 (2): 183–207.

Index

Abbiateci, André, 154
Abbot, Jack Henry, 34*n*28
Abu-Lughod, Lila, 166*n*69
Abuses of domination, 37
Acting, power and, 28–36
Adam Bede (George Eliot), 6–10
Address, terms of, 31–32
Afrikaans, second person pronoun in, 32
Aggression: control of, 40–41; displaced, 213; magical, 143–44; reactance theory, 109–10; self-control and, 213–14
Agulhon, Maurice, 189
Alexander I, czar of Russia, 56
Algeria, 50
American Civil War: use of euphemism in folk songs, 153; slaves in, 117*n*16, 219
Andalusia: carnival in, 174–75; power relations among farmworkers, 27; *reparto*, farmworkers' belief in, 218–19
Anger, control of, 40–41
Anonymity, 140–52, 160–61
Anonymous letters, 149
Anticolonial rebellion in Burma, 15–16
Apologies, public, 57–58
Appeals: to hegemonic values, 92–96; *lettres de cachet* in France, 93; peasant petitions in Japan, 95. *See also* Petitioning
Appropriation, domination and, 188
Arbitrariness, naturalization of, 75–76
Argentina, Plaza de Mayo protests in, 166*n*70
Ash, Timothy Garton, 211–12

Audience for performance, 66–69
Authorized gatherings, unauthorized gatherings and, 61
Autonomous slave religion, 115–17
Autonomy, dignity and, xi

Bakhtin, Mikhail, 122–23, 175–76, 179
Ball, Charles, 116–17
Ball, John, 167
Balzac, Honoré de, 13
Baranczak, Stanislaw, 212
Bedouin poetry by women, 166*n*69
Beliefs, utopian, 80–82
Bengal, 103*n*67
Bentham, Jeremy, 83
Berlin, East. *See* East Berlin
Black Acts, 194
Blacks in Southern U.S. under slavery. *See* Slavery
Blacks in U.S., double-consciousness of, 44
Blasphemy, euphemisms in, 152
Bloch, Marc, 78–79
Bodin, Jean, 180
Boheim, 125
Bolshevik revolution, 77
Bonifacio, Andreas, 102*n*65
Books of character, 47
Bourdieu, Pierre, 47–48, 75, 76, 133
Brer Rabbit tales, 19, 163–66
British colonial officials, 12–13, 14–16
British working class, use of deference by, 34–35

Burke, Peter, 101, 121–22, 181
Burma: anticolonial rebellion in, 15–16; British colonial officials in, 14–15

Cahiers de doléances, 77, 146
Calvinism, 226
Capitalism, unemployment under, 53–54
Caribbean, Tamil plantation labor force in, 131–32
Carnival, 123; in Andalusia, 174–75; church as object of mockery in, 174; disguise in, 149; in France, 60*n*29, 179, 179–81, 224–25; as mechanism of social control, 178–79; revolt and, 181–82; in Russia, 181; safety-valve theory and, 177–79; Spanish Civil War and, 179; symbolic subordination of, 177–78; uninhibited speech in, 175–76
Carriers of hidden transcript, 123–24
Caste relations: discursive negation of, 104. *See also* Untouchables
Catechism for "Colored Persons," 116, 165
Catherine II, 98
Catholicism: folk form of, 68; public declaration of hidden transcript and, 203–04
Ceausescu, Nicolae, 204
Censoriousness, 94
Ceremonies: May Day parade in Red Square, 46; parades, 58–61
Chakrabarty, Dipesh, 103*n*67
Character assassination, 143
Charisma, hidden transcript and, 221–22
Charismatic acts, 20
Cheatam, Henry, 120
Chile, 206–07
China, literacy in, 158
Christianity: in antebellum U.S. South, 115–17, 158; Calvinism, 226; Catholic hierarchy, public declaration of hidden transcript and, 203–04; passion play in Philippines, 159–60
Church, as object of mockery in carnival, 174
Church and King riots, 101
Church ritual, passion play and, 159–60
Circus, 187, 187*n*7
Civil rights movement, women and, 148*n*31
Classroom, teacher's presence in, 25
Club-rooms, 122–23
Coffeehouses, 122–23
Cohesion of hidden transcript, 134–35

Collective hidden transcript, 8–9
Collective insults, 219*n*32
Collective madness, 222–23
Collectivization of agriculture, 60; peasant women's protests and, 150
Colonial officials, British, 12–13, 14–15
Comaroff, Jean, 65, 138
Command performances, 29
Commodity fetishism, 72*n*3
Community power literature, 71–72
Compliance: forced, 108–10; hegemonic performance and, 203–06; practical failure to comply, 203–04; public refusal to comply, 203–04
Compulsion, 109–10
Concealment, 50–52
Conflict, social, 78–82
Conforming behavior, 70–76
Conformity: as manipulation, 33–35; slavery and, 24; working class and, 24–25
Consciousness, dominated, 90–91
Control: of anger, 40–41; of oral culture, 161–62. *See also* Self-control; Social control of hidden transcript
Coser, Lewis, 127–28
Court cultures, language codes in, 31
Craton, Michael, 147
Critiques within hegemony, 105–07
Crowd action, anonymity of, 150–52
Cultural barriers: in Laos, 132; in South Africa, 133
Culture: dualism in, 51; elite, 133; gender and, 52; official, 157–58; oral, 160–62. *See also* Popular culture
Cunning, 164*n*63
Curse, 42–43
Czar, myth of, 97–101
Czechoslovakia, self-indictment in, 57*n*27

Defection, among elites, 67*n*42
Deference, 23–25; acts of, 28–29; British working class's use of, 34–35; linguistic, 30–32; manipulation of, 33–36; public transcript of, 25; speech patterns and, 36
Democracy, liberal. *See* Liberal democracies
Deprivation, spirit possession and, 141
Dialect use, in England, 129
Diggers, 225
Dignity, 7; autonomy and, xi; public injury and, 113–15; slavery and, 114
Dirty dozens, self-control in, 136–37

Discursive affirmation from below, 57–58
Discursive negation of power, 104
Discursive sites under slavery, 26–28
Disguise: anonymity, 140–52; in carnival,
    149; elementary forms of, 138–40; in
    folktales, 162–66; political, 173; in popu-
    lar culture, 156–90; symbolic inversion,
    166–72; in trickster tales, 162–66; in
    women's narrative, 138*n*6; world-upside-
    down prints, 166–72
Disguised resistance, public resistance and,
    198–201
Displaced aggression, 184–87, 213
Display of domination, 46–47; as substitute
    for use of force, 48–49
Dissimulation of resistance, 2–3, 86, 88–89
Divide and rule principle, 85*n*38
Djilas, Milovan, 12, 192
Dolet, Etienne, 179
Dominant group, public transcript and, 4
Dominant ideology, 71–72
Dominated consciousness, 90–91
Domination: abuses of, 37; appropriation
    and, 188; display of, 46–47; forms of, x–
    xi, 21–22; gender-based, 22; haughtiness
    and, 11; impersonal, 21*n*3; self-dramatiza-
    tion of, 67–69
Double-consciousness of blacks in U.S., 44
Douglass, Frederick, 116, 185–86, 205, 208
Dozens, self-control in, 136–37
Dramatization of power relations, 66–67
Du Bois, W. E. B., 44
Duel, challenge to, 37

Eagleton, Terry, 177
East Berlin, protest meeting in, 212*n*18
Eastern Europe, exaggerated compliance in,
    139–40
Election, as symbolic affirmation, 46*n*1
Electric shock experiment, 110*n*4
Eliot, George, 1, 6–10, 221
Elite culture, 133
Elites: defection among, 67*n*42; seclusion of,
    12–13
Ellison, Ralph, 133
England: Black Acts, 194; Church and King
    riots, 101; dialect use in, 129; poaching in,
    189–91, 193–94; working class in, 24–25,
    74. *See also* Colonial officials, British
English Civil War, 88, 169, 171–72, 225–26
English Peasants' Revolt of *1381*, 81, 167

English Revolution, 61
Etiquette, 1, 47–48
Eunuchs, 127–28
Euphemisms, 52–55, 152–54
Europe, forest crimes in, 189–91
Evans, Sara, 65*n*37, 148*n*31, 209
Exhumations, revolutionary, 197, 215
Exploitation, negation of pattern of, 80–82

False consciousness theory, 72, 73–74
Familists, 88
Fantasy: hidden transcript and, 37–39; re-
    versals, 41–42; *schadenfreude*, 41–42
Feast of Fools, 177–78
Field, Daniel, 96–101
Figes, Orlando, 196*n*29
Flight attendants: concealed aggression by,
    155*n*46; imagined acts of retaliation by,
    38*n*37
Folk Catholicism, 68
Folk culture. *See* Popular culture
Folk religion, 226
Folktales, 162–66
Folk utopias, 80–82
Forced compliance, consequences of, 108–
    10
Forced labor camps, in USSR, 51
Forest crimes: in Europe, 189–91; in Ger-
    many, 194–95
Foucault, Michel, 20, 21*n*3, 55, 62*n*31, 83,
    93, 111*n*5
France: *cahiers de doléances*, 77, 146; carnival
    in, 60*n*29, 179, 224–25; use of euphe-
    misms by arsonists, 154; gender relations
    in, 52; *lettres de cachet*, 93; Parisian magis-
    trates, 13; peasant petitions, 96; rites of
    monarchy in, 69; second person pronoun,
    forms of, 31–32; tithe collection in, 195–
    96; working-class gatherings in, 64; Zola's
    description of peasantry, 214
Freedom, interpretive, 205
French Revolution: use of euphemism in,
    153–54; rituals of reversal in, 172; role of
    rumor in, 145–47
French royal court, power and acting in, 29
Friedman, Susan, 138*n*6

Gaventa, John, 73
Gender: culture and, 52; subordination and,
    36
Gender-based domination, 22

Genet, Jean, 50
German Peasants' War, 125, 171
Germany, forest crimes in, 194–95
Giddens, Anthony, 75
Gilmore, David, 143, 174–75
Glasnost campaign, 210
Gluckman, Max, 185
Goffman, Erving, 57, 155
Gombrowicz, Witwold, 204
Goodwyn, Lawrence, 123, 211
Gorbachev, Mikhail, 210
Gossip, 142–43
Gramsci, Antonio, 19, 90–91
Graves, Robert, 160
Greece, cunning in, 164n63
Grumbling, 154–56
Guerrilla warfare, 192–93
Guha, Ranajit, 144–45, 185, 196

Habermas, Jürgen, 38n36, 115n12, 176
Hatred: hidden transcript and, 40; idealiza-
    tion and, 39–40
Haughtiness, domination and, 11
Havel, Václav, 208
Hegel, Georg Wilhelm Friedrich, 37, 185
Hegemonic appearances, reproduction of,
    204–05, 215
Hegemonic ideology, 71–72
Hegemonic incorporation, 19–20
Hegemonic performance, refusal to comply
    with, 203–06
Hegemonic values, appeals to, 92–96
Hegemony: critiques within, 105–07; natu-
    ralization and, 78–80; social conflict and,
    78–82; use value of, 90–96
Hidden transcript, xii–xiii; in *Adam Bede*
    (George Eliot), 6–10; carriers of, 123–24;
    characteristics of, 14; charisma and, 221–
    22; cohesion of, 134–35; collective, 8–9;
    as condition of practical resistance, 191–
    92; control of anger and, 40–41; defense
    of, 128–34; fantasy and, 37–39; first pub-
    lic declaration of, 206–12; hatred and, 40;
    hidden transcript within, 27n13; imaginary
    speech and, 8–9; open statement of, 7–8;
    of parents, 12n19; personal, 8–9; as pos-
    ing, 184–87; as practice, 187–92; preven-
    tion of, 124–28; public declaration of,
    202–03; public transcript and, 4–5; in
    slave narratives, 5–6; social control of,

124–28; wish-fulfillment component of,
    38–39
Hill, Christopher, 87–88, 121, 225–26
Hinduism, untouchables and, 117
Hirschman, Albert, 137n3
Hitler, Adolf, 49
Hobsbawm, Eric, 133
Hochschild, Arlie Russell, 28–29, 38n37,
    155n46
Hoggart, Richard, 34–35, 74
Holidays, in plantation system, 64
Holland, world-upside-down prints in, 168
Horizontal linkages between subordinate
    groups, 62
Hurston, Zora Neale, 43, 153
Hutu of Rwanda, 50–51
Hydraulic structuralism, 219–20

Idealization, hatred and, 39–40
Ideal speech situation, 38n36, 115n12, 176
Ideological incorporation, 86
Ideological negation, 115–18
Ideology, dominant, 71–72
Ileto, Reynaldo, 159
Imaginary speech, hidden transcript and, 8–
    9
Impersonal domination, 21n3
India: manipulation of deference in, 35; spir-
    it possession in, 141
Indirect aggression, 184–87
Indonesia, Torajans of, 50
Infrapolitics of subordinate groups, 19, 183–
    84, 199–201
Ingratiation, 89–90
Injury, public, 113–15
Insubordination, interpretive freedom and,
    205
Insult: collective, 219n32; rituals of, 136–37
Interpretive freedom, insubordination and,
    205
Intoxication, anger control and, 41
Inversions. *See* World-upside-down prints
Involuntary subordination, 82–85
Ireland, power relations among rural work-
    ers, 27
Islamic tithe, 54, 89

Jamaican slaves, 3
Japan: cult of Sakura, 158–59; *namazu*
    prints, 171n79; petitioning, in 63, 95

Jayawardena, Chandra, 131–32
Jeffries, Jim, 41
Jews, manipulation of deference by, 36
Joachim of Fiore, 170–71
Johnson, Jack, 41
Jones, Charles, 116
Jürgensmeyer, Mark, 147

Kant, Immanuel, 118
Kardiner, Abram, 39–40
Karma, 75n13
Katyn Forest Massacre, 216
Keil, Hans, 125–26
Korean War: forced compliance by American prisoners in, 110; prisoner-of-war camps in, 83–84
Kundera, Milan, 57n27, 139–40
Kunzle, David, 170

Ladurie, Emmanuel Le Roy, 60n29, 96, 167, 179–81, 195, 224–25
Lagos, Ricardo, 206–07
Lakoff, Robin, 30–31
Language: deference and, 36; euphemism in, 53; power and, 30–32
Language codes: in court cultures, 31; in Malaysia, 31; women's speech, 36
Laos, bogus officials in hill villages, 132
Laotian Communist party, anniversary celebration by, 58–61
Leadership, patron-client structure of, 61–62
Lefebvre, Georges, 145–47
Lenin, Vladimir Il'ich, 97
Lettres de cachet, 93
Levellers, 88, 225
Levine, Lawrence, 137
Lévi-Strauss, Claude, 216
Lewis, I. M., 141–42
Liberal democracies, working-class values in, 112
Limit testing in resistance, 192–97
Linguistic deference, 30–32
Linguistic marks of subordination, 30–31
Literacy, in China, 158
Livermore, Mary, 5
Lollards, 88, 226
Long Qing, Chinese emperor, 12
Lower-class dialect, recording of, 32
Lying, women and, 36

Madness, collective, 222–23
Magical aggression, 143–44
Malaysia, language codes in, 31
Malaysian village: cultural meaning of poverty in, 113; power relations among tenant farmers in, 27; public discourse monopoly in, 54; tithe system in, 54, 89
Manipulation of deference, 33–36
Manumission, 83n34
Markets, 122–23
Martinez-Alier, Juan, 130, 218–19
Marx, Karl, 66, 72n3, 195
Mass action, anonymity of, 150–52
Mathiesen, Thomas, 94–95
May Day parade in Red Square, 46
Metaphor, theatrical, 11
Milgram, Stanley, 84, 110n4
Militancy of working class, 134–35
Military, subordination in, 82n33
Misrepresentation, in public transcript, 2–3
Mob riots, anonymity of, 150–52
Monarchism, naive, 96–103
Monarchy rites in France, 69
Moore, Barrington, 76, 91–92, 185, 220
Münzer, Thomas, 171
Mutuality, 118–19

Naive monarchism, 96–103
Namazu prints, 171n79
Naturalization, hegemony and, 78–80
Negation, 111–15; ideological, 115–18
Nietzsche, Friedrich, 38n38, 76n20
Niklashausen, drummer of, 125, 169
Norman English, 31
Northrup, Solomon, 209
Norwegian prison, 94–95

Official culture, 157–58; unofficial culture and, 51
Open statement of hidden transcript, 7–8
Oral culture: control of, 161–62; disguise in, 160–62
Order-serving effects, rituals of reversal of, 185–86
Orwell, George, 10–11, 14–15, 49, 67, 172
Ovesey, Lionel, 39–40
Owen, Robert, 46–47

Paine, Thomas, 226n42
Palestinian teenagers, stares by, 155

Parades, 58–61

Parents, hidden transcript of, 12*n*19

Pariah-intelligentsia, 124

Parisian magistrates, 13

Passion play, church ritual and, 159–60

Pathet Lao, anniversary celebration by, 58–61

Patron-client structure of leadership, 61–62

Patterson, Orlando, 24

Peasant petitions, 95, 96–101

Persecution, 183

Personal hidden transcript, 8–9

Personal magnetism. *See* Charisma

Personal names: in Punjab, 32; in Southern Rhodesia, 32

Petitioning, 63, 95, 96–101

Pilfering, 118

Pinochet, Augusto, 206–07

Plantation system, holidays in, 64

Poaching, in England, 189–91, 193–94

Poland: Lenin Shipyard strike in Gdansk, 210–11; popular volubility, 211–12; social sites of hidden transcript, 123; *Solidarnosc*'s forms of protest, 140; working-class riots, 226–27

Politeness, 1, 47–48

Political discourse, among subordinate groups, 18–19

Political disguise, carnival as, 173

Political environment of subject classes, 199

Popular culture: anonymity in, 160–61; disguise in, 156–90; English Civil War and, 225–26; use of euphemism in, 153

Possession, cults of, 141–42

Poverty, in Malaysian village, 113

Power: acting and, 28–36; discursive negation of, 104; language and, 30–32

Power relations: among subordinates, 26–27; dramatization of, 66–67; levels of, 73; public transcript and, 3–4

Prevention of hidden transcript, 124–28

Prints: *namazu* prints in Japan, 171*n*79; world-upside-down prints, 166–72

Prisoner-of-war camps, 83–84

Prison inmates, 26, 94–95, 152

Protective ingratiation, 89–90

Proverbs of slavery, 3

Psychological consequences of racial domination, 39–40

Psychological impact of public defiance, 208–10

Public apologies, 57–58

Public declaration of hidden transcript, 202–03, 206–12, 216–17; social sites for, 223; timing of, 217–20

Public injury, dignity and, 113–15

Public resistance, disguised resistance and, 198–201

Public ritual, in Yugoslavia, 12

Public transcript, 13–14; of deference, 25; dominant group and, 4; euphemisms in, 52–55; hidden transcript and, 4–5; misrepresentation in, 2–3; parades as, 58–61; power relations and, 3–4; social action and, 45–46; as social fact, 87–90; stigmatization in, 55; trickster tales as part of, 164–65; unanimity in, 55–58

Pugachev, Stepan, 98

Punjab: mass meetings in, 65; personal names in, 32

Purges and show trials in USSR, 57

Quiescence, 70–76

Rabelais, François, 175, 179

Racial domination, psychological consequences of, 39–40

Reactance theory, 109–10

Rebellion: anticolonial, 15–16; initiation of, 193*n*21; slavery and, 79. *See also* Revolt

Reddy, William, 150

Reeves, Marjorie, 170

Reincarnation, 75*n*13

Religion: autonomous slave religion, 115–17; folk, 226; Hindu doctrines among untouchables, 117; passion play in Philippines, 159–60

Religious ideology, 68

Religious order, subordination in, 82*n*33

Reparto, 218–19

Reputation in subordinate groups, 131

Resistance: disguised, 198–201; dissimulation of, 86, 88–89; forest crimes as, 189–91; guerrilla warfare as, 192–93; hidden transcript as condition of, 191–92; limit testing, 192–97; pilfering as, 188–89; public retribution and, 197; retribution and, 197; safe forms of, 139–40; theft as, 188–89; to tithe collection, 195–96

"Ressentiment," 38*n*38

Retribution, resistance and, 197

Reversal, rituals of, 41–42, 172–82; order-serving effects of, 185–86. *See also* World-upside-down prints

Revolt: carnival and, 181–82; English Peasants' Revolt of *1381*, 81, 167. *See also* Rebellion

Revolutionary exhumations, in Spain, 197, 215

Revolutionary vacuum, Russian peasantry and, 196*n*29

Rhodesia, personal names of black miners in, 32

Rhys, Jean, 29*n*15

Riots, anonymity of, 150–52

Ritualized aggression, 184–87

Robin Hood, 206

Rogers, Susan, 52

Rollin, Judith, 219*n*32

Rothkrug, Lionel, 125

Rousseau, Jean-Jacques, 222

Rudwin, Maximillian, 179

Rumania: public display of repudiation from below, 204; rumors after Ceausescu's fall, 145*n*21

Rumor, 144–48

Russia: carnival in, 181; naive monarchism in, 96–101; world-upside-down prints in, 168. *See also* USSR

Russian peasantry, revolutionary vacuum and, 196*n*29

Rwanda, 50–51

Sabean, David, 125–26

Safe expression of aggression, 184–87

Safety-valve theory, 177–79, 186

Sakura, cult of, 158–59

Sales, Roger, 177

Sartre, Jean-Paul, 222

Saxon English, 31

Sayings, slave, 163

Schadenfreude, 41–42

Scheler, Max, 38*n*38

Schopenhauer, Arthur, 36

Seclusion of elites, 12–13

Second-person pronoun, forms of, 31–32

Self-control, 136–37; aggression and, 213–14

Self-dramatization of domination, 67–69

Self-esteem, 7

Sennett, Richard, 112

Shakers, 128

Shaw, Nate, 34

Sheminov, Valentin, 210

Show trials in USSR, 57

Silent monitor, 46–47

Slavery: autonomous slave religion, 115–17; conformity and, 24, 33–34; dignity and, 114; discursive sites in, 26–28; dissimulation in, 2–3; gatherings in, 63–64; hidden transcript in, 5–6; humbling oneself in, 57; pilfering in, 188–89; plurality of transcripts in, 25–28; proverbs of, 3; public defiance in, 208–09; rebellion and, 79; theft in, 188–89

Social action, public transcript and, 45–46

Social conflict, hegemony and, 78–82

Social control of hidden transcript: from above, 124–28; from below, 128–34; carnival and, 178–79

Social criticism, 91–92

Social sanctions in subordinate groups, 129–30; in South Africa, 131

Social sites of hidden transcript, 118, 120–23; in antebellum U.S. South, 120–21; club-rooms, 122–23; coffeehouses, 122–23; markets, 122–23; taverns, 122–23

Social subordination, 2

Solidarity in subordinate groups, 131–32

Solidarnosc, forms of protest by, 140, 211

South Africa, 65; cultural barriers in, 133; social sanctions in subordinate groups, 131

Southern Rhodesia, personal names of black miners in, 32

Spain: conformity among agricultural workers, 130; revolutionary exhumations in, 197, 215

Spanish Civil War, carnival and, 179

Speech patterns, deference and, 36

Spirit possession, 141–42; deprivation and, 141

St. Domingue, rumors in, 147

Stalinist purges and show trials, 57

Stallybrass, Peter, 122

Stammering, 30

Stares by Palestinian teenagers, 155

Status, paying respect to, 28–29

Stigmatization, 55

Stille, Darlene, 209

Strauss, Leo, 183

Students for a Democratic Society, 65*n*37

Subordinate groups: anonymity in, 140–52; euphemisms in, 152–54; grumbling in,

Subordinate groups (*continued*)
154–56; horizontal linkages between, 62; infrapolitics of, 19; as observers of the powerful, 33*n*25; political discourse among, 18–19; power relations among, 26–27; reputation, 131; social sanctions in, 129–30; solidarity in, 131–32

Subordination, 2; forms of, 22–23; gender and, 36; involuntary, 82–85; kinds of, 82*n*33; linguistic marks of, 30–31

Surveillance, 64, 109–10

Symbolic defiance, 196–97

Symbolic dissent, 196–97

Symbolic inversion, 166–72

Symbolic subordination, in carnival, 177–78

Taborites, 81

Taverns, 122–23

Tell, William, 169

Theatrical metaphor, 11

Thibaut, John W., 29*n*16

Thompson, E. P., 121, 138, 148–49, 150, 189, 193–94

Threat, euphemism as, 154

Titanic, sinking of, 42

Tithe collection: Islamic, 54, 89; resistance to, 195–96

Torajans of Indonesia, 50

Trelawny, Bishop, 190

Trickster tales, 19, 162–66

Trotsky, Leon, 185

Tswana of South Africa, 65

Turner, Victor, 185

Tutsi of Rwanda, 50–51

Ukraine, 99

Unanimity, in public transcript, 55–58

Unauthorized gatherings: authorized gatherings and, 61; public gatherings as, 63–66

Uncle Tom behavior, 35

Unemployment under capitalism, 53–54

Uninhibited speech, in carnival, 175–76

Unofficial culture, official culture and, 51

Untouchables: within caste systems, 75; conformity in, 33; Hindu doctrines and, 117; mass meetings of, 65; role of rumor among, 147

U.S. South, antebellum: Brer Rabbit tales, 163–66; catechism for "Colored Persons," 116, 165; Christianity in, 115–17, 158; control of social sites of hidden transcript, 126–27; open defiance in, 219; social sites of hidden transcript in, 120–21. *See also* Slavery

Use value of hegemony, 90–96

USSR: collectivization program, 150; forced labor camps, 51; *glasnost* campaign, 210; Katyn Forest Massacre, 216; May Day parade in Red Square, 46; Stalinist purges and show trials, 57. *See also* Russia

Utopian beliefs, 80–82

Utopian communities, 127–28

Utopias, folk. *See* Folk utopias

Veyne, Paul, 205

Vietnamese folksong, utopia in, 80

Viola, Lynn, 150

Voice under domination, 137

Voinovich, Vladimir, 106

Voluntarism, 218–19

Walker, Alice, 43*n*49

Weber, Max, 68, 124, 157

Weil, Simone, 218

Weininger, Otto, 36

West Indies, 126–27; holidays in, 64

White, Allon, 122

Willis, Paul, 75, 78, 106–07

Wish-fulfillment component of hidden transcript, 38–39

Witchcraft, 143–44

Women: Bedouin poetry, 166*n*69; civil rights movement and, 148*n*31; lying and, 36; Plaza de Mayo protests in Argentina, 166*n*70; protests of collectivization in USSR, 150; public defiance by, 208–10. *See also* Gender-based domination

Women's narrative, disguise in, 138*n*6

Women's speech, 30–31, 36

Working class: cohesion in, 134–35; conformity and, 24–25; use of deference by, 34–35; militancy of, 134–35; surveillance of gatherings, 64

Working-class culture, 22–23, 129

Working-class values, in liberal democracies, 112

World-upside-down prints, 166–72
Wright, Richard, 38–39

Yugoslavia, public ritual in, 12

Zakat, 54, 89
Zimbardo, Philip, 213–14
Zola, Emile, 214, 218
Zolberg, Aristide R., 223

Also by James C. Scott and available from —Yale University Press—

SEEING LIKE A STATE
How Certain Schemes to Improve the Human Condition Have Failed

"One of the most profound and illuminating studies of this century to have been published in recent decades. . . . A fascinating interpretation of the growth of the modern state. . . . Scott presents a formidable argument against using the power of the state in an attempt to reshape the whole of society."
—John Gray, *New York Times Book Review*

WEAPONS OF THE WEAK
Everyday Forms of Peasant Resistance

"A highly readable, contextually sensitive, theoretically astute ethnography of a moral system in change. . . . *Weapons of the Weak* is a brilliant book, combining a sure feel for the subjective side of struggle with a deft handling of economic and political trends."
—John R. Bowen, *Journal of Peasant Studies*

THE MORAL ECONOMY OF THE PEASANT
Rebellion and Subsistence in Southeast Asia

"This book will last. No one interested in peasant societies in Southeast Asia, or for that matter elsewhere, can afford to ignore it. . . . It is as well written as it is sophisticated and enlightening. It should be assigned . . . to undergraduates . . . , recommended as a matter of course to graduate students working on social change, and mentioned always to anyone puzzled by the intricacies of economic, social, and political structure in countries with large peasant populations."
—Daniel S. Lev, *Journal of Politics*

For other books on these subjects, visit our Web site at
http://www.yale.edu/yup/